A DIVIDED UNION

A Divided Union delves deep into ten pressing political challenges central to the dysfunction in Congress and the country today. The core of the book is an original analysis by experts on key topics such as geographic challenges, demographic change, a polarized media, gerrymandering, the role of money in politics, and the structure of primary elections. Contributors include former federal elected officials, political science professors, members of the press, and scholars immersed in their fields of study. *A Divided Union* is appropriate for all political science students as well as the general public frustrated and alarmed by political deadlock.

Dario Moreno is an Associate Professor in the Department of Politics & International Relations at Florida International University.

Eduardo Gamarra is a Professor in the Department of Politics & International Relations at Florida International University.

Rep. Patrick E. Murphy represented Florida's 18th district, covering the Treasure Coast and northern Palm Beach County, from 2013 until 2017. He is now Executive Vice President of Coastal Construction Group and a Senior Fellow at Florida International University's Steven J. Green School of International and Public Affairs.

Rep. David Jolly represented Florida's 13th Congressional District, including the communities of St. Petersburg, Clearwater, and surrounding beaches, from 2014 until 2017. He is now Executive Vice President of Shumaker Advisors Florida and a political analyst for the networks and media platforms of NBC Universal.

A DIVIDED UNION

Structural Challenges to Bipartisanship in America

Edited by Dario Moreno, Eduardo Gamarra, Rep. Patrick E. Murphy, and Rep. David Jolly

With Anthony Kusich

Routledge
Taylor & Francis Group

NEW YORK AND LONDON

First published 2021
by Routledge
605 Third Avenue, New York, NY 10158

and by Routledge
2 Park Square, Milton Park, Abingdon, Oxon, OX14 4RN

Routledge is an imprint of the Taylor & Francis Group, an informa business

Library of Congress Cataloging-in-Publication Data
A catalog record for this title has been requested

ISBN: 978-0-367-56540-4 (hbk)
ISBN: 978-0-367-56537-4 (pbk)
ISBN: 978-1-003-09826-3 (ebk)

Typeset in Bembo
by Deanta Global Publishing Services, Chennai, India

CONTENTS

List of editors   vii
List of contributors   ix
Preface   xiii
Acknowledgments   xvii

Introduction   1
Rep. Patrick E. Murphy and Rep. David Jolly

1 The Geography of Polarization   6
   Patrick J. Villalonga and Dario Moreno

2 Demographic Change   24
   Susan A. MacManus and Anthony A. Cilluffo

3 The Polarization of the Media   50
   Sara Gorman

4 Gerrymandering   64
   Brian Amos

5 Money in Politics   83
   Sean D. Foreman

6 The Structure of Primaries 102
Steve Vancore, Glenn Burhans, Dario Moreno, Anthony Kusich,
and Patrick J. Villalonga

7 No "Regular Order" 112
Nicol C. Rae

8 Cameras and Legislative Committees 129
Kathryn DePalo-Gould

9 The Demise of Relationships in Washington, D.C. 151
Thomas B. Langhorne

10 The Disappearance of Bipartisan Representation 170
Todd Makse

Conclusion 187
Rep. Patrick E. Murphy, Rep. David Jolly, Dario Moreno,
Eduardo Gamarra, and Anthony Kusich

Index *193*

EDITORS

Dario Moreno holds a Ph.D. from the University of Southern California. He conducts research on Miami politics, Florida politics, and Cuban-American politics. He has published over 50 scholarly articles and book chapters, and two books. Dr. Moreno is a nationally recognized expert on Florida and Miami Politics and is often quoted in both the national and local media. He has been a Pew Scholar at the Kennedy School of Government at Harvard University, and a Fulbright scholar in Costa Rica. He teaches a variety of classes in the Department of Politics and International Relations at FIU, including Miami politics, Cuban politics, Florida politics, and election and political parties. Since 2008 he has been co-teaching courses on American and International politics with Senator Marco Rubio.

Eduardo Gamarra is Professor in the Department of Politics and International Relations at Florida International University. Dr. Gamarra holds a Ph.D. in political science from the University of Pittsburgh. His areas of expertise include Latin American politics, democratization, and neo-populism. Between 1994 and 2007, he served as director of Florida International University's Latin American and Caribbean Center. At LACC he also cofounded and edited *Hemisphere*, a magazine on Latin American and Caribbean affairs. In February 2016 he was appointed founding director of the Latino Public Opinion Forum at the Steven J. Green School of International and Public Affairs. Dr. Gamarra is the author, coauthor, and editor of twelve books, including *Culture and National Security in the Americas*, (co-edited with Brian Fonseca) (2017); *Centro América 2020: Un nuevo modelo de desarrollo regional* (2002); *Democracy Markets and Structural Reform in Latin America: Argentina, Bolivia, Brazil, Chile, and Mexico* (1995); *Latin American Political Economy in the Age of Neoliberal Reform* (1994); *Entre la droga y la democracia* (1994); three volumes of the *Latin America and Caribbean Contemporary Record* (1988–89); and

Revolution and Reaction: Bolivia, 1964–1985 (1988). He is also the author of nearly one hundred articles on Latin America and the Caribbean.

Rep. Patrick E. Murphy represented Florida's 18th district, covering the Treasure Coast and northern Palm Beach County, from 2013 until 2017. A CPA and businessman who grew frustrated with the dysfunction in Washington, Murphy defeated Tea Party firebrand Allen West in 2012 in one of the closest and most expensive U.S. House races in history, and was re-elected by a 20-point margin two years later. Murphy's key accomplishments in office include helping secure nearly $2 billion in Everglades restoration funding, introducing the SAVE Act to eliminate billions in wasteful government spending, and passing legislation to reform the national flood insurance market. In his role as one of the first Millenials elected to Congress, Murphy formed the bipartisan United Solutions Caucus, bringing members of both parties together to explore ways to get the nation's fiscal house in order, and had one of the most independent voting records among all members during his two terms. He was named 2014's Champion of the Everglades by Audubon Florida for his strong environmental advocacy. After leaving office in 2017, Murphy was named chair of the Future Forum Foundation, a nonprofit group working to address economic issues facing Millenials. He was selected to be one of six Visiting Fellows at the prestigious Georgetown Institute of Politics and Public Service for the fall 2017 semester, and in 2018 became a Senior Fellow at Florida International University's Steven J. Green School of International and Public Affairs.

Rep. David Jolly served in the U.S. House of Representatives from 2014 until 2017, representing Florida's 13th Congressional District, including the communities of St. Petersburg, Clearwater, and the surrounding beaches. A student of the institution, Jolly has held virtually every position in Congress, from intern to member, and has worked outside Congress as an attorney and political consultant, as well as in specialty finance. Today, Jolly serves as Executive Vice President of Shumaker Advisors Florida, and as a Political Analyst for the networks and media platforms of NBC Universal. Known for his fierce independent streak and bipartisan approach, Jolly was first elected in a nationally watched special election in Florida as a Republican winning a Democratic-leaning district. It was his first run for elective office and became one of the most expensive Congressional races in U.S. history at the time. It made Jolly a fierce campaign finance reform advocate, and his resulting legislative effort to prohibit members of Congress from directly soliciting campaign contributions was ultimately featured on CBS's *60 Minutes*. Jolly's work has been published in *Time*, *USA Today*, *Roll Call*, the *Washington Post*, *CNN.com*, *NBCNews.com*, *NewsMax*, the *Washington Times*, and the *Tampa Bay Times*. Jolly received his Bachelor of Arts from Emory University in 1994, and his Juris Doctor Cum Laude from George Mason University in 2001.

CONTRIBUTORS

Brian Amos is an Assistant Professor of Political Science at Wichita State University whose research explores the cross-section of geography and elections, with a focus on partisan gerrymandering. He has also done work on election administration and political methodology, and served as a consulting expert for challengers in *Benisek v. Lamone* and the Florida gerrymandering cases. As one of the lead members of the Florida Election Science Team, he is also helping collect, collate, and distribute election geography and results for use in tools to allow average citizens the chance to participate in the redistricting process after the 2020 Census.

Glenn Burhans is a lawyer with Stearns Weaver where he represents clients in complex civil and government-related matters across the country. He focuses on class actions, governmental investigations, election and political activity law, and administrative proceedings. Glenn also consults on drafting proposed legislation and ballot initiatives, conducts internal investigations, and handles appeals in various federal and state jurisdictions. Glenn also represents cannabis investors, medical marijuana cultivators, processors, and dispensaries, as well as applicants for medical marijuana treatment center licensing. Glenn's intellectual property experience includes trademark and copyright registration and litigation.

Anthony A. Cilluffo is a student in the Master in Public Affairs program in the Woodrow Wilson School of Public and International Affairs at Princeton University. He is focusing on economics and public policy, with interests in public economics and fiscal policy. Prior to attending Princeton, Anthony worked at Pew Research Center on the Social and Demographic Trends team. He focused on income and wealth inequality, education and student loans, and demographics.

He was also a research assistant to University of South Florida Distinguished Professor Susan MacManus, co-authoring chapters on the economic and demographic trends that reshaped the U.S. South since 1970 in *The South and the Transformation of U.S. Politics* (Oxford University Press, 2019) and the conclusion to Larry Sabato's *Trumped: The 2016 Election That Broke All the Rules* (Rowman & Littlefield, 2017). He graduated from the University of South Florida with degrees in Economics and Political Science and attended the London School of Economics.

Kathryn DePalo-Gould received her Ph.D. in Political Science from Florida International University in 2006. Her book *The Failure of Term Limits in Florida* was published in 2015 from the University Press of Florida and examines the effects of term limits on Florida's state legislature. She also holds a Master of Arts degree in Political Science from Florida Atlantic University and a B.A. in Communications from the University of Connecticut. Dr. DePalo has extensive experience in state and local government processes and elections both in Connecticut and Florida. She has managed several campaigns, including a successful countywide judicial campaign in Broward County, Florida. Her teaching focus is American politics, including judicial process, gender and politics, and state and local government. Dr. DePalo's primary research interest is in Florida politics, and she has published on topics such as state judicial selection, the effects of gender in state legislative politics, and career paths of term-limited legislators. Dr. DePalo is the Director of PLATO, Pre-Law Advising and Training Office. She is the past president of the Florida Political Science Association. Dr. DePalo has been quoted in numerous local, national, and international media outlets and is a featured columnist for the Sayfie Review. Dr. DePalo has been a full-time faculty member in the Department of Politics and International Relations at Florida International University since 2006.

Sara Gorman, Ph.D, MPH is a public health and mental health expert and author based in New York. She is currently Director of High School Programming at The Jed Foundation (JED), an emotional health and suicide prevention organization focusing on adolescents and young adults. Her primary focus at JED is a new program called Set to Go, a national program that works to emotionally prepare high school students for the transition to college. She has written extensively about psychology, behavioral science, mental health, and global health, among other topics. Her work has appeared or been reviewed in *TIME*, *The New Yorker*, *Science*, *Scientific American*, *Psychology Today*, *The Atlantic*, *New York Magazine*, *Daily Kos*, and NPR, among others. Sara's book *Denying to the Grave: Why We Ignore the Facts That Will Save Us* was published by Oxford University Press in September 2016. The book examines the psychology of healthcare decision making and theorizes about public perception of risk.

Sean D. Foreman, Ph.D. chairs the Department of History and Political Science at Barry University. He earned a B.A. in Political Science from Clarion University of Pennsylvania and received his M.A. in International Studies from Florida International University (FIU) with a graduate certificate from the Latin American and Caribbean Center. In 2003, Foreman earned his doctoral degree in Political Science from FIU. Dr. Foreman has taught American Government, State and Local Government, Public Policy and Administration, American Political Parties and Elections, Congress, Presidency, American Political Institutions, Political Theory, Religion in American Politics, and Leadership in Public Purpose Organizations at Barry. He is the advisor to the College Democrats, College Republicans, and Model United Nations student clubs. Dr. Foreman is quoted in publications around the world and has been interviewed on numerous radio and television stations. He is a regular panelist and occasional host on WPBT-TV's "Issues" and often on local news stations including WIOD News Radio 610, where he was the 2016 Presidential Election Analyst, and WFTL 850 AM as well as nationally through NBC News Radio (formerly 24/7 News service).

Anthony Kusich is a political strategist who served as Deputy Chief of Staff to Florida Congressman Rep. Patrick E. Murphy, overseeing his D.C. office and serving as a senior adviser during his 2016 U.S. Senate bid. He previously managed both of Mr. Murphy's successful U.S. House campaigns, including the recount-decided 2012 race that remains one of the most expensive in congressional history. Prior to that, Anthony spent nearly ten years in politics and campaigns across the country, serving as Communications Director for Silicon Valley Congressman Mike Honda, a Legislative Aide in the Virginia legislature, and a grassroots field lead for the Iowa presidential caucus and U.S. Senate races in Montana, Colorado, and Connecticut. Anthony has a background in media, earning a degree from the UCLA School of Theater, Film, and Television with a concentration in Documentary Film. He is currently a Senior Associate at the public affairs firm Dewey Square Group.

Thomas B. Langhorne is reporter at the Evansville (Ind.) *Courier & Press*. He has been a print journalist for 25 years, working at papers in Virginia and both Carolinas before coming to the *Courier & Press* in 2005. He has covered sports, American history, politics, and fitness.

Susan A. MacManus is a Distinguished Professor in the Department of Government and International Affairs at the University of South Florida. The leading expert on politics in Florida, MacManus is nationally known for her expert and incisive commentary on public opinion and intergenerational politics. She routinely designs and analyzes surveys of public opinion on a wide range of issues for various local governments, think tanks, and the media. MacManus has authored and co-authored numerous political books, including co-authoring *Politics in States and Communities*, the nation's leading textbook on state and local politics, with mentor Thomas R. Dye.

Todd Makse is an associate professor in the Department of Politics and International Relations at Florida International University. He is co-author of *Politics on Display: Yard Signs and the Politicization of Social Spaces*. His research interests include state politics, legislative politics, redistricting, political behavior, and policy diffusion.

Nicol C. Rae serves as the Dean of the College of Letters and Science and is a professor of political science at Montana State University. Before coming to MSU in 2013, Dr. Rae served as the senior associate dean in the College of Arts and Sciences at Florida International University. At Florida International University, Dr. Rae led associate deans, assistant deans, directors and department chairs in his role since 2008. His professional administrative experience includes serving as the chair of the Department of Political Science, co-director of the Miami European Union Center, and director of European Studies. He began his career at Florida International University in 1988 and was chair of the Department of Political Science from 1999 to 2005. His scholarship is often cited, and his research interests focus on American national political institutions, comparative political parties and party systems, European government and politics, and conservative politics. He is the author of five books on American politics. Dr. Rae holds a doctorate in politics from Oxford University and an undergraduate degree in politics from Edinburgh University.

Steve Vancore is a political consultant and researcher. He is the founding partner at VancoreJones Communications, a political consulting firm that works on legislative communications, public relations, and political campaigns from local races to statewide races. He is also the president of Clearview Research, which focuses on polling and focus group research, and teaches in the Masters of Applied American Politics and Policy program at Florida State University.

Patrick J. Villalonga is a Ph.D. student in Political Science at Florida International University. His research focuses on political behavior, political geography, political psychology and theories of personality, social capital, and democratic theory. In his forthcoming dissertation, he investigates how more walkable urban spaces promote a greater sense of community, social interaction, and thus higher levels of democratic participation.

PREFACE

Eduardo Gamarra and Dario Moreno

Intense partisanship has become the central reality of contemporary American politics. Public opinion surveys over the last few decades chronicle a growing division among voters, politicians, and media outlets along partisan lines. This era of hyper-partisanship presents political institutions with the challenge of debating, analyzing, and making public policy in a political landscape dominated by the political vitriol of the so-called "culture wars." Our national institutions have become suffused in this increasingly bitter ideological and cultural debate, creating stress which threatens their proper functioning and longtime legitimacy. Congress has become one of the forums where the bitter partisan divisions of the last 30 years have been played out, frequently paralyzing Congress, and undermining its proper constitutional role.

Our concern centers on the United States; however, a similar pattern is affecting polities all over the world. Culture wars are now an ever-present reality across Europe, Latin America, and elsewhere. Party systems are collapsing, citizens have lost trust in democratic political institutions, and societies are becoming increasingly polarized. The consequences of this situation are already evident as representative democracies are under great stress and some may even fail. Our concern with intense partisanship in the United States is informed by these global trends.

The widening partisan divide was clearly visible in the 2016 Presidential election. The Pew Research Center found that the campaign unfolded "against a backdrop of intense partisan division and animosity" (Doherty et al., 2016). Today this level of partisan division and animosity, including negative sentiments toward members of the opposing party, has only deepened. Emory political scientists Alan Abramowitz and Steven Webster explain the current hyper-partisanship by introducing the concept of *negative partisanship* (Abramowitz and Webster, 2018). That is to say, voters now form strong loyalties based more on a dislike for the opposing party than the older kind of tribal loyalty that used to bind someone to their party. Furthermore, the party system has split decisively along racial, cultural, and religious lines, creating a new kind of partisanship where each party's supporters regard the other side with incomprehension and loathing.

Evidence for the concept of negative partisanship appeared in *The 2018 American Institutional Confidence Poll*, done by the Knight Foundation and Georgetown. The study found that "large majorities of both parties think that the opposing party rarely or never has the best interests of the country at heart and that it constitutes at least a somewhat serious threat to the country and its people" (Ladd et al., 2018). Specifically, 65 percent of the Democrats thought that Republicans were either a very serious or somewhat serious threat to the country. Conversely, 62 percent of the Republicans thought that Democrats were either a very serious or somewhat serious threat to the country. Similarly, 83 percent of the Democrats and 81 percent of the Republicans thought that the opposing party rarely or never has the best interests of the country at heart.

The Pew Research Center found additional evidence for negative partisanship in both its 2016 and 2019 surveys. These studies report that both Republicans and Democrats express negative views about several traits and characteristics of those in the opposing party and that these opinions have grown more negative since 2016. In 2019, "55 percent of Republicans say Democrats are 'more immoral' when compared with other Americans; 47 percent of Democrats say the same about Republicans" (Pew Research Center, 2019). This pattern can be compared to 2016 when 47 percent of Republicans and 35 percent of Democrats said members of the other party were less moral than other people.

Our concern is then compounded by statistics which show that negative partisanship extends beyond politics. In the 2019 Pew Survey, "fewer than half of Democrats (45 percent) and just 38 percent of Republicans say that they share many of their *other* values and goals. Majorities in both parties say those in the opposing party do not share their nonpolitical values and goals" (Pew Research Center, 2019).

In 2016, Lynn Vavreck – a political science professor at the University of California–Los Angeles – resurrected a Gallup survey question last posed in 1958. It asked, "if you had a daughter of marriageable age, would you prefer she marry a Democrat or a Republican, all other things being equal?" The 1958 results were predictable – only 18 percent said they would want their daughter to marry a Democrat and 10 percent a Republican, while an overwhelming 72 percent said they would not care. When Vavreck reused the question, she included the words "son" as well as "daughter." Her results confirm the growing partisan division not only in politics but across society:

> In 2016, 28 percent of respondents said they wanted their son or daughter to marry a Democrat and 27 percent a republican, leaving only 45 percent to say they did not care. People who identified with a party had even more

intense feelings. In 1958, 33 percent of Democrats wanted their daughters to marry a Democrat, and 25 percent of Republicans wanted their daughters to marry a Republican. However, by 2016, 60 percent of Democrats and 63 percent of Republicans felt that way.

(Vavreck, 2017)

Hyper-partisanship has also severely affected public confidence in U.S. political institutions. The annual Gallup survey on confidence in U.S. institutions shows a steady decline in public trust with the notable exception of the military and the police. Venerable institutions such as the Supreme Court, newspapers, universities, and the presidency have all seen a significant erosion of public trust. Congress, however, is clearly in the basement, ranking the lowest of any American political institution. In its 2019 survey, Gallup reported that only 11 percent of the public had a "great deal" or "a lot" of confidence in Congress, compared to 42 percent in 1973 (Gallup, 2019).

Many observers argue that hyper-partisanship has contributed to Congressional gridlock. In turn, Congress's inability to take action on critical issues has created a crisis of public confidence in the institution. Of course, this is not the first time factions have split our legislature. The First Congress was highly polarized, as were the Congressional sessions of the 1850s when the significant issue of slavery stirred deep passions and even bloodshed in Congress. Nevertheless, even then, bipartisanship and compromise were much more the rule than the exception.

It should be noted that the Senate did not elect party leaders until 1920 for Democrats and 1925 for Republicans. Even in the 1990s, it was common for members of both parties to work across the aisles. We might be seeing the end of such cooperation.

Our co-editors, two former U.S. Congressmen from Florida (Reps. Patrick E. Murphy and David Jolly), clearly blame partisan gridlock for the public lack of trust in Congress. Both gentlemen from Florida – one a Republican, the other a Democrat – witnessed Congressional inaction during their tenure in the House of Representatives, where partisan bickering was "preventing most things of consequence from getting done." As they mention in their introduction, both were frustrated by the "blind partisanship… preventing action on healthcare, entitlement spending, climate change, immigration, infrastructure, and a host of other issues" (see Introduction).

The two Congressmen both lost elections in the extremely divisive 2016 cycle and are now out of office, but they remain strong advocates for structural reform of Congress. They have developed a series of proposals that they hope will alleviate the extreme partisan paralysis that has gripped the legislative branch. The two of us were invited to join this project in the hopes of combining their political and policy perspective with a more academic perspective. Our hope that this book will offer an analysis of the pathologies that plague the body politic, but also prescribe some possible solutions.

Both of us are uniquely qualified to be part of this endeavor. Both of us have been advisors to candidates, elected officials, and decision-makers while at the same time being professors at Florida International University. Moreover, like our co-editors, we have very different political views. Eduardo, a progressive Democrat from Key Biscayne, is an expert on Latin American Politics and has been involved in elections and policymaking in South America, Central America, and the Caribbean. Dario, a conservative Republican from Coral Gables, is an expert on Miami and Florida politics and has been involved in elections and policymaking in Florida.

This book evaluates the structural reforms put forward by the two Congressmen through both an academic and a policy lens. We readily concede that many of the fundamental cultural, demographic, economic, and technological advances that have contributed to polarization are deep-seated and resistant to change. The reforms proposed here are not a panacea for the deep partisan division in American politics, but instead the first step to reduce passions and build consensus. On the eve of the 2020 elections, we seek to start a constructive conversation and put aside the vitriol, even if just for a little while.

References

Abramowitz, A.I. and Webster, S.W., 2018. Negative Partisanship: Why Americans Dislike Parties but Behave Like Rabid Partisans. *Political Psychology, 39*, pp. 119–135.

Doherty, C., Kiley, J. and Jameson, B., 2016. Partisanship and Political Animosity in 2016. *Pew Research Center, 75.*

Gallup, 2019. Confidence in Institutions. *Gallup.* https://news.gallup.com/poll/1597/confidence -institutions.aspx.

Ladd, J.M., Tucker, J.A. and Kates, S., 2018. *2018 American Institutional Confidence Poll.* Georgetown University Baker Center McCourt School of Public Policy. http://aicpoll.com.

Pew Research Center, 2019. Partisan Antipathy: More Intense, More Personal. *Pew Research Center for the People and the Press,* 10 October. https://www.people-press.org/2019 /10/10/ partisan-antipathy-more-intense-more-personal/.

Vavreck, L., 2017. A Measure of Identity: Are You Married to Your Party? *The New York Times,* 31 January. https://www.nytimes.com/2017/01/31/upshot/are-you-married-to-your-party. html.

ACKNOWLEDGMENTS

Dario Moreno and Eduardo Gamarra

This book was shaped by a simple question: *how do we find ourselves in one of the most polarized eras in our country's history?* To answer that question, we brought together four editors and thirteen authors with diverse political views, from different backgrounds, spanning the academic and policy world. The purpose of this book was not just to analyze the problem, but to prescribe workable solutions to the twin problems of polarization and policy gridlock. The scope of this project required the contribution and hard work of many talented and dedicated individuals.

First and foremost, we want to thank all the authors who contributed to this book. Without their efforts, there would be no book. We would like to especially thank Anthony Kusich who not only contributed to the writing of the book, but also kept the four editors on task and focused. Anthony's leadership was essential for the successful completion of this project. We were also fortunate to have the best doctoral student assistant you can ask for in Patrick Villalonga. He not only contributed to the book, but also worked conscientiously and diligently throughout the editing process.

The editors are incredibly grateful to the founding dean of Florida International University's Steven J. Green School of International and Public Affairs, John F. Stack. Dean Stack was the intellectual godfather of this project. He helped bring together the editors and offered his support. Many of the contributors have a close association with the Green School. Also at FIU, we would like to thank Brian Fonseca of the Jack D. Gordan Institute of Public Policy for his support and encouragement.

Rep. Patrick E. Murphy

I would like to thank my loving parents, Tom and Leslie, my good friend Ibrahim al-Rashid, and my terrific political and legislative teams.

Rep. David Jolly

With thanks to the voters who allowed me to serve and to learn, and to all those who believe the work of our republic is yet unfinished.

Anthony Kusich

I would like to thank my loving wife Bethany, my parents, Liz and Glenn, for their never-ending encouragement, and all the friends who've supported me over the years.

INTRODUCTION

Rep. Patrick E. Murphy and Rep. David Jolly

As sure as the sun setting in the west, the gridlock between Democrats and Republicans is a permanent fixture of the Washington landscape – as stiff and resilient as the monument which bears our first President's name. Our politics have become tribal, and our tribes are further apart than they have been in a generation. What may be most alarming is that the causes of our current political stalemate are so deep-rooted – so ingrained in our ways of life – that it is going to require major reconstructive action to correct them. Partisanship bleeds out of our radios, televisions, family dinners, football stadiums, sneaker stores, churches, schools, smart phones, music concerts, and street corners. It is now as much a part of our identity as religion or astrological signs.

Policy positions may change with the times, but these days the desire to see your side "win" supersedes most other political considerations. How did we find ourselves in one of the most polarized eras in our country's history?

America is at a crossroads. It is a time when trust in our federal representatives is at its lowest, when the truth about objective events is questioned or dismissed, and when the ideals our nation was founded on are too easily rejected. It would be easy to point the finger at specific elected officials or media personalities for engendering this toxic climate. And no doubt there is plenty of blame to go around – from President Trump on down to Congressional leaders of both parties, and to the hosts on Fox News and MSNBC. But the true causes lie much deeper and have been festering in our political discourse for far too long for us to clumsily place blame on a few scapegoats so easily.

What we have witnessed over the past several decades is a gradual fraying of political norms and customs that had held together for a remarkable period of time – through multiple wars, several Presidential scandals, and enormous social change. There is no longer one set of agreed-upon facts or any sort of unifying framework that can bring people of different belief systems together. America witnessed a brief return to mass unity in the aftermath of 9/11, but that quickly dissipated once we invaded Iraq.

Our modes of communication have fundamentally changed. Twitter feeds are now the main supplier of breaking news. The days of three networks delivering the same nightly stories is a relic of the past; there is now a news channel that speaks directly to the preferences you already hold. Computer programs are now sophisticated enough to slice and dice legislative districts with pinpoint accuracy so that lawmakers will never have to worry about another competitive general election. Voters can be sure that no matter what block they live on, the representative they have shares the same political views as all of their neighbors. The increased abundance of money in politics concurrent with the loosening of campaign finance laws has turned members of Congress into call machines, dialing for dollars during every free minute they have in Washington. The never-ending cycle of elections has forced the political class into permanent campaign mode. Lawmakers are now forced to eschew relationships with their colleagues in Washington – which used to grease the wheels of compromise and negotiation in eras past – in favor of fundraising and campaign events back home.

The combination of these factors has simply ground Washington to a halt, preventing most things of consequence from getting done. The success of the American experiment in democracy has, for many years, masked these flaws. Blind partisanship now weighs us down in numerous ways, preventing action on healthcare, entitlement spending, climate change, immigration, infrastructure, nuclear disarmament, and a host of other issues that we have a moral imperative to tackle immediately, but which face political roadblocks as imposing and monumental as, well, the aforementioned Washington Monument.

What was uncertain upon the ratification of the Constitution in 1788 was that political parties would soon form in our infant nation, and some two centuries later would dominate every facet of government: which side's Supreme Court nominees receive a vote in the U.S. Senate, whether a federal budget is passed, which types of voters get drawn into legislative districts. Indeed, political parties go unmentioned in our founding document and were scorned by George Washington, who agonized over the increasing influence of partisanship in public affairs.

Is his farewell address, President Washington lamented that although political parties "may now and then answer popular ends, they are likely in the course of time and things, to become potent engines, by which cunning, ambitious, and unprincipled men will be enabled to subvert the power of the people and to usurp for themselves the reins of government, destroying afterwards the very engines which have lifted them to unjust dominion" (Washington, 1796).

Years later, in a letter to his close aide John Trumbull concerning the French influence on American life, Washington again excoriated partisan politicians who he believed "regard neither truth nor decency; attacking every character, without respect to persons — public or private — who happen to differ from themselves in politics" (Washington, 1799). Washington's grim words could not better foreshadow our current political culture, where working with someone on the other side of the aisle has been vilified to the point of impossibility.

Among his many critical accomplishments, Washington's decision to step aside after two terms as President was an acknowledgment that the authority of this nation — and its limitations — come from the American people, not any one individual, political party, or ideology (Murphy, 2018). That was the power of his restraint and wisdom. It remains the guiding principle of our Republic and should give each of us hope that if enough Americans reject a philosophy that dictates "my way or the highway," we may indeed reach consensus on the many issues at hand.

So where does that leave us today? The 2016 U.S. Senate elections offer an instructive lesson. That year in Florida, the two of us were opposing candidates for a period of time. Patrick, who represented northern Palm Beach County in Congress, was the Democratic nominee, while David, who represented St. Petersburg on the Gulf Coast, ran for the Republican nomination as Marco Rubio briefly exited the stage to wage an unsuccessful bid for President. When his higher aspirations faltered, Rubio ultimately decided to run for re-election to the Senate; he triumphed over Patrick after an expensive and hard-fought campaign while Trump was simultaneously eking out a narrow 1.2% victory in the state. In the interim, court-ordered redistricting significantly altered the boundaries of David's Congressional district, and he too lost election that November.

More notably, it was the first time since the passage of the 17th Amendment — mandating the direct election of U.S. Senators — that the winning party of every Senate race was identical to the party which had won the state's Presidential race, with not one exception. That is an amazing statistic. Thirty-four Senate races took place that day, and the party affiliation of all 34 winners matched exactly whichever Presidential candidate, Hillary Clinton or Donald Trump, won their state's electoral votes.

After the dust settled in Florida, both of us were out of Congress and Washington had lost two of the few remaining moderates from either party who were willing to reach across the aisle in a Capitol that more closely resembles a parliament as each year passes. Beyond the partisan outcome of the Senate race — or the Presidential race, for that matter — was the growing frustration that the system is simply stacked against any sort of change that could alter the political establishment. A rigged system favors those already in power. There's no place for independents and soft partisans to have their voices heard; there's no fundraising avenue for those who don't toe the party line; there's no way to introduce a distinct political message if the powers that be in Washington want to have it silenced.

Rather than just shake our fists in the air in frustration, we decided it was time to speak up and hopefully influence the voters who have the least tenuous connection to the ossified political class. We both realized it was vital to share just how toxic the halls of Congress have become and what it will take to correct the troublesome course our democracy is on. We first spoke at a handful of universities in Florida, then at schools up and down the East Coast, and eventually across the country. Despite belonging to different parties, the two of us shared many of the same priorities in Congress, from addressing climate change, to enacting campaign finance reform, to making our electoral process more inclusive.

Instead of speculating about the cultural or geo-political drivers of extremism in America and around the world, our analysis focused on specific structural issues that have contributed to the gridlock. In order to address income inequality, automation, and large-scale displacement – all factors helping to fuel this divide – we believe we must first have a functioning system that fosters healthy debate on these issues and the vast array of others.

The structural causes of this extreme partisan paralysis are tremendous, but definable. Excessive gerrymandering has forced lawmakers to run for office in districts that are becoming increasingly one-sided. Our media landscape has become an echo chamber filled with the views you already hold. And thanks to divisive court rulings in campaign finance law, outside groups with no accountability to voters can spend tens of millions of dollars to influence elections. In other words, the system favors those already in power.

The extreme partisans who President Washington once observed "regard neither truth nor decency" will always be with us, but it is up to the voters in our home state of Florida and across the nation to make sure their voices are heard even louder. In this volume, we hope to outline some of the biggest challenges facing our democracy, with experts from each respective field weighing in on how we got here – and how to get us out. But it is ultimately up to the voters themselves to not only show up, but to vote for those they believe can help fix the system.

In the following chapters, authors will dissect many of the ways in which the electoral process itself is responsible for gridlock and stagnation in the nation's capital. These include the aforementioned drawing of Congressional districts to favor one party in perpetuity, which contributes to one-party rule in states and communities across the country; how the vast sums of money in politics – increasingly steered toward unaccountable Super PACs – have warped outcomes and priorities for elected officials; how the structure of primary elections caters only to the partisan extremes, leaving out the vast middle; and how voters are increasingly sorting themselves into communities where similar political opinions are shared and dissenting views are scarce.

At the same time, various factors outside of the electoral process are contributing to divisions in our country, chief among them the polarization of the media, which ultimately guides how millions of Americans digest, interpret, and internalize public policy. Finally, authors will discuss how the lack of personal relationships among members of Congress has contributed to the fraying of bipartisanship, as has the structure of Congressional committees and a breakdown in the lawmaking process itself.

References

Murphy, P., 2018. "Extreme Partisanship Strangling Democracy." *Tallahassee Democrat*. https ://www.tallahassee.com/story/opinion/2018/02/09/partisanship-same-ever/3187 78002/.

Washington, G., 1796. *Washington's Farewell Address*. U.S. Senate. https://www.senate.gov/ artandhistory/history/resources/pdf/Washingtons_Farewell_ Address.pdf.

Washington, G., 1799. *From George Washington to Jonathan Trumbull, Jr. 21 July 1799*. National Archives. https://founders.archives.gov/documents/Washington/ 06-04-02-0165.

1

THE GEOGRAPHY OF POLARIZATION

Patrick J. Villalonga and Dario Moreno

Rep. David Jolly: We are a diverse nation. But we are also a divided nation – geographically, politically, and far too often culturally and racially. There is a richness in our diversity and there is richness in celebrating our many cultures. It is fundamentally who we should be as a nation. But throughout history diversity has also been susceptible to political exploitation, using our differences against each other.

It is sadly too easy to recall dark chapters of America's exploitation of communities of color, of immigrant communities, of communities of gender and sexual diversity. Such times have been rooted in raw prejudice from the early days of our republic. But there is today a growing challenge caused by geography itself. As our coastal and urban corridors become increasingly diverse both culturally and racially and our suburban and rural communities, particularly within the part of the country sometimes referred to as "flyover" states, remain largely white and predominately Christian by influence, our two major political parties have each found electoral success in representing and at times fueling this polarization.

Basic trend analysis would suggest that without a significant shift in our demographics or our politics, this geographic polarization will worsen. And the tendency of our major political parties will be to chase the trend, not lead us toward a healing of the trend. Republicans know that national elections can be won by running up the score among their existing flyover constituencies, as the Electoral College affirmed for the GOP in the elections of 2000 and 2016. Democrats likewise know they can grow their national vote numbers by strengthening their performance among its natural constituencies.

But the missed opportunity each party has in front of them is crystal clear. The party that can create a governing agenda that bridges this natural geographical divide, that embraces our geographical differences, that reflects the full diversity of the nation, is the party that will create a governing majority for decades to come.

Rep. Patrick E. Murphy: After running in two successful U.S. House campaigns and one unsuccessful U.S. Senate campaign in Florida, I have little doubt that political segregation is increasing polarization. As the authors point out, framing is important in this discussion, and a single congressional district can reflect numerous beliefs and ideologies. Based on where you travel in Florida's 18th district, which I represented for two terms, you might hear priorities ranging from lowering taxes and Israel policy (the suburbs and retiree communities of Palm Beach County) to citrus farming and water quality (the more working-class towns and rural farmland of Martin and St. Lucie counties). Driving 20 minutes in any direction one would not hear of the previous issue.

I believe that with increased geographical segregation and the ever-increasing effects of social media and targeted advertising, we have more single-issue voters than previous decades. I also believe that with the increase in unaccountable fundraising and Super PACs, there are more organizations formed, funded, and supported to take advantage of the cultural differences outlined above and drive an even deeper wedge between the parties all for a political advantage in the next election. As technology and voter targeting become more advanced – and political and geographic segregation increases – it is alarming to consider how few states and districts will matter for political control of our democracy. Politicians and parties can focus their resources in under 10% of states to win a presidential election or under 10% of districts to win control of Congress. As discussed later in this book, money, media, and gerrymandering work together to increase this polarization, but there is no escaping the fact that we are segregating our democracy between urban and rural voters.

We would wager that even the most unenthusiastic American voters are aware of California's liberal lean and Alabama's staunch conservatism. The stereotypes are typically well known: New York and Oregon vote Democratic, whereas the Bible Belt goes for the GOP. These states are so dominated that voting Republican in California is considered futile – more a sign of solidarity and defiance than anything else. One could drive around upstate New York a month before the 2016 election and find rural New Yorkers proudly boasting their Trump yard signs and MAGA hats, fully aware their vote would ultimately be pointless, yet resolute in their conviction to show the country where they stood on the matter.

It is funny to recall that scholars once complained about the similarity between the two parties, believing that the distinction between Democrats and Republicans was merely nominal. When the parties' ideologies differed very little, it was easier for a Republican to usurp a Democratic incumbent, or vice versa.

For better or worse, times have certainly changed. Now that the parties have become significantly different, a Republican in California has no hope of catching moderate or independent voters because so few exist. In some states and locales, a party's domination may be so overwhelming that the minority party often finds it impossible to present viable candidates in local and state elections, allowing the dominant party to run unopposed. U.S. House elections have become significantly less competitive in the past 50 years according to one analysis. Between 1980 and 2002 alone, the number of competitive districts fell by around 35 percent (Abramowitz et al., 2006). This phenomenon on its own is not necessarily a problem; people should be free to choose as they please, regardless of how overwhelming that choice may be. But the ideological divergence of the two parties produces other consequences that are not so benign. Further up the federal ladder, congressional gridlock has become more rigid than ever. Since 1950, two-thirds of American presidents have presided over Congresses controlled by the opposing party (what is called a "divided government"), requiring them to form a consensus between members of their own party and those of the opposing party in order to pass legislation. This was not so difficult when the two parties were closer to the center and their ideologies overlapped. Today, however, the task appears almost impossible as their ideologies have become increasingly dissimilar (Rodden, 2015).

The public's perception of this shift is also dire. The chasm between the two parties has grown so wide that 26 percent of the country no longer believes the two parties can collaborate. Twenty percent of moderates and 32 percent of the "politically disengaged" believe the same (Yudkin, 2019). Some might not find these figures so alarming. They might feel secure so long as the majority of the country is not hopeless. They may also argue that public perception of Congressional collaboration is not an accurate picture of how the parties are actually getting along. But consider what this statistic implies: a quarter of the country believes that we have passed the point of no return. How many more Americans might be acutely aware of the growing divide between liberals and conservatives, perhaps not yet completely disillusioned, but slowly reaching that point? How many more Americans might feel a growing sense of anxiety, fueled by mounting ideological tension? Might this increasing anxiety drive them to adopt extreme views as some form of political adaptation, or cause them to check out of the political game altogether because our political future seems so hopeless?

We could speculate about these questions, but it is difficult to offer any concrete, empirical answers in one fell swoop. Several studies clearly indicate that polarization is on the rise, that much is certain. The distance between the median Democrat and median Republican has widened, and the number of people identifying as consistent liberals and conservatives has grown. Meanwhile, the number of centrists has decreased (Pew Research Center, 2014).

It is not often discussed, but geography is a crucial factor in our democratic republic, mainly in the form of our federal system, which divides power among various geographic units (local, state, national, etc.) Our presidential elections, which appoint a national political figure, are driven by state and local procedures. The geographic diversity of the United States also means that presidential candidates must alter their strategies to gain votes in each state, because different geographies produce different socio-political and economic preferences. Voters' political identities are often place-based; one fascinating study reports how rural voters often desire small government solely because they believe political power is concentrated in the cities, for the cities, which is expressed in the form of big government – this despite the fact that they could stand to benefit economically from supposed big government policies (Walsh, 2012).

If people's political identities are so intimately tied to their neighborhood, or county, or state, we might wonder if a county with a 70–30 liberal advantage would breed extreme leftist opinions? Does white nationalism fester in areas dominated by conservatism, or can it breed even in the most balanced communities? Would a country without swing states, where each region is decidedly either conservative or liberal, be a fast track to political gridlock? This chapter explores these questions indirectly by looking at the concept underlying our concerns: political segregation.

From Segregation to Polarization

Scholars use the word "sorting" to denote the process by which individuals come to identify with a political party. "Polarization," on the other hand, is the process by which one's political opinions become more extreme or dissimilar from the opinions of one's political opponents. "Political segregation" is a spatial phenomenon, although potentially related to sorting and polarization. It is the concentration of people with similar political preferences, or copartisans, in a geographic space. A county with a 50–50 split of liberals and conservatives would be considered perfectly not segregated, or perfectly heterogenous. A space with a 100–0 advantage to a political party would be perfectly segregated, or perfectly homogenous.

The general assumption is that in a county with a 70–30 conservative advantage, moderates or people without any preference would be more likely to eventually sort into conservatives. Polarization in this county might also be more likely; it is plausible that center–right voters would become consistently conservative over time, and consistent conservatives would be more likely to adopt far-right beliefs. By contrast, moderates or inactive voters in a county with more heterogeneity, say a 55–45 split, could be equally likely to sort liberal or conservative. And amongst the voters already sorted, there ought to be a smaller likelihood of polarization because there is enough ideological diversity to challenge extreme political opinions.

The key difference between our two hypothetical counties is the varying concentration of partisans – to put it in our technical term, varying degrees of political segregation. This is where we begin our investigation. We first have to ask if political segregation exists and whether it is increasing. Are partisans living in spaces with higher concentrations of copartisans than they have before? Is the proportion of liberal voters in New York increasing? Is the proportion of conservative voters in Texas decreasing? Are the so-called swing states we hear so much about disappearing?

The short answer is: yes. The general intuition seems to be that people are indeed segregating themselves based on their political values, although the story of this trend is not a straightforward one. Research on this topic has become more sophisticated in the past 15 years, allowing us to overcome methodological issues which once hindered nuanced analysis. Psychology and the science of personality traits may explain why liberals and conservatives are indeed segregating themselves.

But how about polarization? Are voters in these highly segregated areas also developing more extreme political opinions? Conservative pundits claim leftist havens in New York, California, and Oregon are breeding elements of the far-left, and similar suspicions abound among progressives about conservative enclaves being hotbeds for white nationalism. But is this the full picture, or just fallacious cherry-picking meant to cook up headline news?

Although plenty of evidence shows that polarization is occurring nationwide, it is still debatable whether geography and segregation are contributing factors. In fact, we will see some evidence to the contrary, indicating that spaces with more political heterogeneity may be the centers of polarization.

At the core of our argument is a fundamental belief about political identity – which we think is substantiated by the evidence to come – that at the bottom of our political preferences sit our socio-cultural identities and our personality traits, both of which are intimately tied to the spaces we inhabit. Culture is fundamentally what motivates political ideology, and as culture is tied to space, we should not be surprised to find political trends play out geographically.

The Big Sort

Bill Bishop's *The Big Sort* (2009) is the most recent popular harbinger of political segregation and became the center of considerable academic debate upon publication. Bishop argued that the number of landslide counties – one in which a party won by at least a 60–40 margin – increased from 38 to 60 percent between 1976 and 2004. The proportion of the population living in these counties went from 27 percent to 48 percent in the same time period (Bishop, 2009).

Bishop's theory for this phenomenon was just as interesting. He explained that this rapid segregation was not the result of a conscious process. People were increasingly segregating themselves into politically homogenous communities not because they consciously sought politically friendly neighborhoods, but rather as a consequence of conscious lifestyle choices that also happened to be associated with their political preferences. As one researcher puts it, "this de facto segregation might emerge as people strive to satisfy basic psychological needs," particularly the sense of harmony we feel from belonging to a group that shares our interests and values (Motyl et al., 2014). Our lifestyle choices correlate so well with our political preferences, that political segregation is an inevitable byproduct of choosing our ideal residence.

Bishop was definitely touching a nerve. As it turns out, three-quarters of consistent conservatives prefer to live in areas where "the houses are larger and farther apart, but schools, stores, and restaurants are several miles away." Similarly, three-quarters of consistent liberals prefer neighborhoods where "the houses are smaller and closer to each other, but schools, stores, and restaurants are within walking distance" (Pew Research Center, 2014). Differences in socio-cultural preferences extend to things like racial diversity, which liberals desire in their neighborhoods. Conservatives on the other hand prefer living in a community that shares their religious views. In fact, religion, and not income, is a better predictor of voting Republican; going to church a few times per year means one would vote Republican 43 percent of the time, but going to church once a week means you would vote Republican 75 percent of the time (Glaeser and Ward, 2006). Living near an art museum is important for three-quarters of liberals, but only for one-quarter of conservatives. In short, space matters (Pew Research Center, 2014). There is nothing explicitly political about an art museum, but such choices have political consequences because our personal interests are also tied to our political interests.

What really drives this theory home is that the political composition of a neighborhood is nearly irrelevant when people are deciding where they would like to reside. One paper remarks straightforwardly that neighborhood safety, quietness, and affordability are the top three criteria regardless of party affiliation (Gimpel and Hui, 2015). Proximity to one's social network, one's workspace, and amenities are the next priorities, still well above political composition which can be found at the bottom of the list. But what if two properties meet one's primary criteria – both equidistant to work, both close to one's social network, both relatively safe and under budget? All else equal, would the political context of the two houses influence how people choose where to live? The research we have suggests it would. People will devalue their appraisal of a property once they are told the neighborhood is dominated by partisans from the opposing political party, meaning that, all other things equal, people want to avoid living in unfriendly political environments in favor of an area more hospitable to their political preferences (Hui 2013; Gimpel and Hui, 2015).

Perhaps more important though is the idea that people are capable of making judgments about a neighborhood's political climate based on non-political information. Realtors do not gather and offer information about a neighborhood's political makeup, but individuals can still use socio-cultural information like demographic makeup, racial diversity, and distance to the city center to make inferences about an area's political composition that end up influencing their housing decisions (Gimpel and Hui, 2015). This again emphasizes the correlation between our lifestyle choices and political preferences. Politics may not consciously be an important feature of our home search, but our housing decisions may still have political consequences.

Migration and Social Networks

But can migration really be so influential in causing political segregation? There would have to be significant mobility within and across states, which is not common. Although nearly 40–50 million Americans move each year, it is not clear how many people have the financial flexibility to be overly selective about where they set down roots (Florida, 2019). People certainly have preferences about where to settle down, but they do not often have the resources to find a location which meets all of their criteria (Nall and Mummolo, 2013).

Another possible explanation for segregation is called social network theory. It works just how it sounds. People are more likely to identify with a political party if one's family, friends, and acquaintances tend to identify with that same party. Under this view, communities are becoming more politically segregated because individuals are being converted by the predominant political ideology in that space, thanks to the influence of the people in their social networks. The longer a liberal resides in Alabama, the more likely they are to develop a social network consisting mainly of conservatives. The longer they maintain this social network, the more likely they are to begin adopting conservative ideas and voting for conservative candidates.

Then consider the influence of political campaigns. During any given election, the Republican Party will focus its campaign efforts in counties or districts where its chances of success are good. They will go into a county in Alabama and message their base consistently. A liberal living in this county will not only be exposed to the GOP's messaging, but the liberal's social network will also receive the messaging. Altogether, the messaging from the GOP and the social pressure from one's network are likely to change the liberal's political preferences over time.

Also important to note is that these campaigns work within an institutional framework. The rules of political campaigning are not open-ended, and neither is the geographic chess board on which they play the political game. Districts are drawn up by elected officials (mostly) to determine what groups of people will be represented together by a single individual. The lewd version of this practice we call gerrymandering, where politicians strive to create districts which concentrate friendly voters to maximize party dominance, or to minimize the strength of a voting bloc. As Dr. Brian Amos discusses in Chapter 4, redistricting, whether it is done in good faith or not, significantly influences the workings of our political system, political segregation included.

In measuring a competitive district as a 45–55 outcome or a 48–52 outcome, redistricting led to fewer competitive congressional districts from 1980 to 2012. There were 169 districts with a 45–55 margin, but this number decreased to 100, while districts with a 48–52 margin went from 69 to 30 (Altman and McDonald,

2015). Other scholars question the influence of redistricting, pointing instead to sweeping demographic changes and ideological realignment as additional causes for less competitive districts, but also the inability for challengers to compete financially (Abramowitz et al., 2006). Some have argued that while redistricting does increase polarization, this is by no means the only cause of a polarized polity or legislature (Carson et al., 2007; McCarty et al., 2009). Segregation and polarization are also explained by changes to the socio-economic makeup of these districts and parallel deviations in party strategies made to appeal to the voters experiencing these changes.

This does not however detract from the simple fact that more representatives are emerging from uncompetitive districts, which ought to have consequences for congressional productivity. A representative from an uncompetitive Democratic district, for example, has little electoral incentive to cooperate with Republican members of Congress. Crossing party lines may actually cost the member reelection if the strongly leftist constituency discovers collusion with the opposition.

Are Americans Segregating?

Both theories discussed so far regarding social networks and migration offer viable accounts of political segregation, and of course there is no reason to believe they occur exclusively. People's residential choices are driven by lifestyle choices and the search for social belonging that inevitably bring liberals together with other liberals, and conservatives with other conservatives. At the same time, as a segment of the population relocates to politically compatible neighborhoods, the social networks people create in these spaces drive sorting – moderates become leaners, leaners become consistent partisans, and consistent partisans become ideologues. The interaction between migration and the sorting caused by social networks both increase segregation simultaneously. Politically segregated areas essentially become spatial echo chambers which inevitably breed political polarization, or so the story goes. It certainly seems intuitively correct – these theories appear to explain what is driving our citizens to the ideological fringes. However, not all scholars are convinced political segregation is happening at all.

Those scholars challenge our story, citing methodological concerns. As they explain it, measuring segregation through voter turnout is inaccurate because it is an unreliable measure of political identity. Simply voting for the Republican presidential candidate does not make one a conservative. The personalities and political beliefs of our candidates influence turnout in ways that might exaggerate or underrepresent individuals' true political identities (Abrams and Fiorina, 2012).[21] Take for example two centrist congressional candidates who are hardly distinguishable. An election between them might result in a 51–49 outcome, even if the majority of the voters are strongly Republican or strongly Democratic. Given the choice between two nearly identical candidates, a strong partisan is theoretically just as likely to vote for either.

A subsequent election in the same district between two ideologically oppo-site candidates may then surprisingly result in a 75–25 margin, not because the voters in that area suddenly became more ideological – they always were. The 75–25 margin was caused by voters siding with a distinct candidate who aligns directly with their political preferences in opposition to another candidate who very clearly does not. This aspect of candidate identity makes it difficult to tell how much of the population is truly liberal or conservative over time.

Then consider that an individual might vote for the Democratic presidential candidate, but also turn out for a Republican governor or Republican senator of their state. Should we assume that this voter is more Democratic than Republican, or more Republican than Democratic? It is not clear which selection best repre-sents the voter's ideology or political preferences.

In light of these issues, some researchers prefer measuring political identity using party registration. If measured this way, then Bishop's results are contra-dicted. From 1976 to 2004, the proportion of the population residing in landslide counties fell from 50 to 15 percent while the percentage of people registering as independents increased, indicating that people live in more heterogenous coun-ties, not more segregated ones (Abrams and Fiorina, 2012). The apex of political segregation actually occurred in the 1920s, when most Republican voters lived in a county where 70 percent of voters were also Republican. In 2004, that number was only at 53.4 percent, indicating near perfect parity between liberals and con-servatives (Glaeser and Ward, 2006). This again contradicts Bishop's warning call.

Then there is the problem of context. Even if we should measure segregation based on voter turnout (and not party registration), our current levels of segrega-tion are relatively mild when compared to the long span of American political history. Segregation has by some measures increased since the 1970s; however, Americans are currently not as segregated as they were during the Civil War, or during the 1920s. In their study, Glaser and Ward concede that the percent-age of voters in landslide counties *has increased* from 36 to 44 percent between 2000 and 2004 alone. In fact, the number of landslide counties has increased 30 percent since the early 1990s – the exact trend Bishop was concerned about. But at 44 percent, this is not yet the 60 percent observed during the 1920s or 1960s (Glaeser and Ward, 2006). In this light, Bishop's warning exaggerates the danger of contemporary political segregation. This does not negate that segregation is happening, but it calls into question the extent to which it might be occurring. We have to question whether Bishop's analysis was reasonably alarmist, or merely a piece of sensational journalism.

Does Segregation Even Matter?

But in some ways, the most scathing critique of Bishop's work might be that provided by Abrams and Fiorina who argue that even if segregation is occur-ring at an alarming rate, it simply does not matter; segregation is benign and not responsible for the political polarization we are experiencing today. As already mentioned, we can imagine that as a community becomes more Republican, or more Democratic, a spatial echo chamber is formed in which citizens discuss political events and ideas with other like-minded people. Their ideas go unchallenged and therefore become more extreme over time

As Abrams and Fiorina point out though, this narrative rests on two very important assumptions about American communities: 1) that people are interacting with their neighbors or other citizens residing in their broader community and 2) this interaction is political. Both premises are highly questionable. Only 65 percent of Americans know the name of even one-fourth of their neighbors, which doesn't bode well for the first premise. If people do interact with their neighbors, 54 percent report never talking politics, while another 29 percent report rarely talking politics. If Americans aren't talking politics with their neighbors, then there is no local echo chamber, and segregation isn't all that important (Abrams and Fiorina, 2012).

Abrams and Fiorina's critique seems decisive at first, but we think they make too much of neighborhood interactions, or the lack thereof. Failure to cultivate relationships with one's neighbors does not imply that people lack social networks in general. It may simply be that people's social networks are much broader than the immediate neighborhood, for whatever reason. An individual's social network may span the city or county they live in and include people whom they can trust to discuss politics. That our neighbors are no longer parts of our social networks may be concerning, but this concern ignores the political influence of the social networks we maintain with people in the cities and counties we live in.

The Frame Problem

Abrams and Fiorina's (2012) critique offers a good segue into what scholars call the "frame problem." This issue applies to any analysis that focuses on space as ours does. It poses the question: at what scale should we measure what we are trying to understand? As we could see from their analysis, Abrams and Fiorina were evaluating social interaction at the neighborhood level, but there is no reason why that should be the only level at which social interaction is measured. Social exchanges at the city and county level may also be influential to people's political opinions.

As another example, let's say we want to measure segregation by tallying how many votes were cast for candidates in a presidential election; it is not immediately obvious if we should tally those votes at the precinct, county, state, or regional level. Different levels may present certain analytical advantages and disadvantages. We may find heterogeneity at the state level, but homogeneity in the counties or precincts. Measurements at different levels may even yield results that appear paradoxical.

Take for example the correlation between income and being a Republican. If we compare how many people vote Republican in each state and the average or median income of each state, a clear relationship emerges: as the average income of a state increases, there is a greater likelihood of that state going Republican. Look a little closer at a smaller unit of analysis, and this result falls apart. When we compare an individual's income with their voting preferences, income has no relationship to voting Republican. Actually, attending church is a better predictor of voting Republican at the individual level (Glaeser and Ward, 2006). The reasons behind this incongruence are beyond the scope of the chapter, but we mention it to point out the complexities that emerge when relationships are analyzed at different levels of aggregation (i.e. individual, neighborhood, city, county, state, nation, etc.)

So then at which level should we focus our analysis of political segregation? Presumably every level, from the broadest to the narrowest if we could. This would give us the most comprehensive picture of what is happening. The question then becomes, just how broad and just how narrow? The broadest we could go is the regional level; this is the largest territorial division through which we could measure change and make comparisons between spatial units (i.e. Northeast, South, Midwest, etc.) The narrowest frame depends on our theories about what is driving segregation. If peoples' residential choices and social networks are to blame for increasingly segregated neighborhoods, then we definitely need to look at the county level, and perhaps even closer, at the municipality or even precinct level, considering that counties can house many different urban, suburban, and rural enclaves where political opinions could differ greatly. Scholars studying social capital have remarked that the typical U.S. county is too large – and thus too heterogeneous – a geographic unit to effectively measure local community or neighborhood context (Martin and Newman, 2015).

Unfortunately, it is difficult to apply such a narrow focus. Most of the data we need does not break down to such a small spatial frame like the precinct, or even the municipality. The best we can do at the moment is to use data at the county level. The studies we have already mentioned perform their analysis at the county level, and the emergent narrative appears to be that segregation is occurring, but not at a magnitude or rate that should worry us. Yet, the aforementioned studies do not take the frame problem seriously enough. Doing so would require us to also study the trends at the district, state, and regional level. Not only that, we ought to investigate if the trends in some counties, states, or districts differ from others depending on the region within which they are located.

Improved Evidence for Political Segregation

To put it another way, the studies we have mentioned thus far analyzed counties as one large clump, not taking into account the possibility that counties in some regions of the country are becoming more segregated, but counties in other regions or states are not. This technique is referred to as multilevel analysis (see endnote), and this is where the research is more telling.[1]

A comprehensive analysis shows that segregation has been occurring at the regional, state, and county level since at least 1976. Regional segregation increased the most, at 29 percent, whereas state and county segregation lagged at 12 and 14 percent respectively. In 1992, the difference between the greatest and least Democratic turnout at the state level was 25.8 percent. In 2012, this range opened up to 46.3 percent, meaning that states going Democratic became much more dominated by Democrats, while Republican-dominated states became much more dominated by Republicans (Johnston et al., 2016).

Multilevel analysis gives us more detailed insights. Twenty-nine states saw significant changes in segregation, whereas 17 saw no change, and only three saw a decrease in segregation. If we group states together into regions that share a history of similar socio-political dynamics, then the trends become even clearer. The New England states saw no changes in segregation, whereas the Mid-Atlantic states saw only a marginal rise (Lang and Pearson-Merkowitz, 2015; Johnston et al., 2016). The states on the West Coast also saw increased segregation between counties, although this occurred in the 1970s and '80s and slowed down in the 2000s. The opposite occurred in the South, where political segregation did not gain steam until the 2000s (Lang and Pearson-Merkowitz, 2015).

We can also categorize counties as urban, suburban, and rural and ask which landscapes have experienced more segregation. Not surprisingly, this analysis validates many of our preconceptions about how parties dominate certain landscapes. Democrats have become the undisputed party of the urban centers, the metropolis, as well as the low-income and immigrant-dense suburbs and post-industrial towns. Republicans on the other hand tend to thrive in rural areas, but also in suburbs not yet experiencing an influx of foreign immigration. This has led some researchers to call the suburb the "interface" of American political diversity (Rodden, 2015; Scala and Johnson, 2017).

Here also, the story has some chronological nuance. Modern political segregation happened earlier in urban areas, beginning around 1996. Suburban areas became increasingly segregated starting in 2000, whereas rural areas finally caught up in 2004 (Lang and Pearson-Merkowitz, 2015). Yet segregation was stronger in non-urban areas and in conservative areas than in urban and liberal ones (Bishop, 2009; Johnston et al., 2016).

We then have to go back and ask how these changes are happening – is migration or the composition of our social networks driving segregation? Or both? The data we have does not measure the influence of social networks directly. We can, however, measure migratory patterns with some precision using census and IRS data. Studies show that sorting (presumably as a consequence of social networks) is usually a greater influence on segregation than migration, although migration does play a role (Lang and Pearson-Merkowitz, 2015). A county with a 60–40 Democratic advantage in 1996 would turn their advantage into 61.18–38.82 in 2000 without any change in migration. A 1 percent change in migration from 1996 to 2000 would broaden that advantage to 62.34–37.66. It would be interesting to analyze this data on migration in its regional context. Did every region or state or county see similar changes in migration? Was migration a driver of segregation in the West Coast, whereas sorting might have been responsible for the gradual but eventual segregation in the South? Future studies will have to tease out the answers.

This is all to say that the issue of segregation is complex and depends upon geographic and chronologic context, which should not be surprising. Different parts of the country contend with different socio-economic situations where migration might not be so easy, or social networks not so robust. Political parties may also be more active in some areas than others, which could also be the cause of more or less sorting, and therefore more or less segregation and polarization. Looking at the power of media gives us an idea of how influential political parties can be in geographic space. We know, for example, that the Republican vote share increased wherever FOX News was first introduced in the 1990s (DellaVigna and Kaplan, 2007). Similarly, campaigns ought to influence partisan sorting and therefore segregation.

A Psychological Approach

We hope the preceding discussion has thus far offered some insight into the research regarding political segregation – the theories involved, respective counterarguments, and methodological issues. All things considered, we believe the research indicates that political segregation is occurring. We do not intend to be alarmist – our situation is not irredeemable. But we are observing a trend that needs to be monitored carefully because it is corroborated by yet another piece of evidence which implicates a fundamental aspect of human identity: personality. We emphasized earlier in the chapter the diverse preferences Republicans and Democrats have about where they choose to live. As it turns out, these preferences are correlated to what psychologists call the "Big Five" personality traits (see endnote).[2]

A simple example will illustrate the point. We have already noted that liberals tend to occupy urban areas. But why? Urban areas offer much more cultural and intellectual diversity. The people more likely to seek out and enjoy such diversity are people with high "openness," which is essentially a preference for new experiences, unconventional lifestyles, or unconventional ways of doing things (Verhulst et al., 2012). Not surprisingly, studies in the geography of psychology have concluded that people living in urban spaces tend to have higher levels of openness than the people living in non-urban areas (Rentfrow et al., 2008). And, not surprisingly, liberals tend to exhibit higher levels of openness (Verhulst et al., 2012). The syllogism is clear. Liberals are more open; people who are more open prefer to live in cities; therefore liberals prefer to live in cities. More extensive research on the relationship between geography and personality has corroborated this relationship between personality, politics, and place (Rentfrow et al., 2013; Rentfrow and Jokela, 2016; Elleman et al., 2018). People's residential choices are driven not so much by their politics, but by their personalities and lifestyle choices.Yet these choices have political consequences because our politics and personalities are tied together. In fact, research has shown that statewide personality traits predicted outcomes in the 1996, 2000, and 2004 presidential elections (Rentfrow et al., 2009).

But not all of the Big Five are associated with political ideology or partisanship, however. Openness, for example, has a long history in the literature as a measure of liberalism. Neuroticism has also been implicated as a predictor of liberal attitudes. Conscientiousness, on the other hand, predicts conservatism (Xu et al., 2013).[48] But of the other two traits, extraversion and agreeableness, the former does not seem to be relevant while the latter has a more complex relationship with ideology. Like each personality trait, Agreeableness can be broken down into two factors – in this case, compassion and politeness. Compassion seems to be associated with liberalism, whereas politeness appears to be a conservative trait (Hirsh et al., 2010).

We ran a small set of statistical analyses to see how data from a reputable political survey stands up to previous results. Using the American National Election Survey from 2016, we found as expected that liberalism can be predicted by openness and neuroticism. In keeping with previous research we also found that conservatism was predicted by conscientiousness, but also by measures of conventionalism and extraversion. While the result on extraversion is not supported by the literature, these results seem intuitive to us because they fit nicely with some of the data we discussed previously.

Consider that conservatives prefer to live in neighborhoods where people openly share a preference for conventional and traditional modes of being, like religious belief. Extraversion also makes sense within this context. In a neighborhood with less diversity and a defined set of social norms and expectations, individuals would feel it easier to be extraverted without fear of rejection because they know what to expect from the social landscape. Conversely, liberals may be more open, but also more neurotic. An urban landscape offers a great deal of cultural and intellectual diversity which would appeal to someone with high openness, but the constant novelty and presence of unknown cultures and ideas may also spark more anxiety than usual. In a landscape where values, cultures, and norms differ from one neighborhood to the next, a fear of social rejection may inhibit extraverted behavior.

Another result from our analysis shows that liberals believe less conventional lifestyles are good for society, which again ties them to urban areas where greater diversity is present.We also found that liberals tend to favor political correctness, which also fits into our geographic analysis: political correctness is a linguistic method meant to facilitate relationships between people whose views may differ greatly, which would be helpful in urban spaces where such cultural and intellectual diversity prevails.

We believe the evidence presented thus far validates a certain conception of political identity. The core of what we are suggesting is that our political preferences are essentially expressions of our personality and our culture. Our politics are informed by our cultural interests and psychological attitudes. Our political preferences are largely the manifestations of our socio-cultural identity interacting with our temperament. As one study puts it, people's personality traits seem to move them towards specific cultural practices which mold their political interests (Xu et al., 2013). A person with more openness may watch more foreign films in their adolescence and early adulthood, orienting them towards a more liberal conception of immigration, for example. A person with high conscientiousness may grow up very thrifty and careful with their money, orienting them towards fiscal conservatism.

People's personalities and lifestyle preferences are tightly wound up with their politics, and because culture happens in space and not a vacuum, it is not surprising that politics can play itself out with geographic consequences, like political segregation. The next step is to ask whether those geographic consequences have any knock-on effects, like political polarization.

So How About Polarization?

As already mentioned, it seems reasonable to assume that segregation may contribute to polarization by creating insulated pockets of partisans whose ideas and preferences go unchallenged. Over time, their ideas and preferences become radicalized. Conservative pundits point to cities like Portland, Oregon, and San Francisco, California, as examples of segregated liberal spaces that have bred far-left ideologues. But leaving these cities aside from particular scrutiny, a proper analysis would look at every city or county rather than isolating convenient samples. From this broader frame, one might be surprised to find that heterogenous districts actually tend to house more polarized voters, whereas more homogenous districts do not (McCarty et al., 2013). A district may appear to be moderate because candidates only tend to win by small margins, but in fact be composed of highly partisan Democrats and Republicans (Rodden, 2015).

Studies like this measure the margin of victory in a given geographic space, but they also measure citizens' ideological and policy preferences, which help researchers gauge how people truly feel beyond the Democrat–Republican binary of an electoral choice. As it turns out, the closer a district is to a 50–50 electoral margin, the more likely the partisans of that district will harbor extreme political preferences.

One possible explanation is that partisans in more heterogenous districts must interact with opposing partisans on a more consistent basis. Because peoples' political identities are largely based on their cultural preferences and personality traits, which do not change easily, they are unlikely to alter their political preferences despite consistent exposure to opposing ideas. Instead, the constant antagonism with opposing partisans drives people to reinforce their political identities by adopting more extreme versions of their original ideological positions.

We should stress, however, that the results discussed in this section were obtained at the district level. Thus far, no nationwide study has explored the connection between segregation and polarization at the level of the county, the state, or the region. The importance of such a study is key for political geography, especially if we want to understand how space influences social networks and the movement of ideas. Congressional districts tend to be too large, encompassing several different rural, suburban, and urban locales, making the county a better frame in which to isolate and understand the influence of different landscapes and cultures on the dynamics of socio-political interaction.

Conclusion

We would have liked to have ended this chapter offering assurances, although it ought to be clear there are none to offer. An optimist would point out that political segregation has not reached fever pitch when compared to the 1920s, or the Civil War. This is true, although the rapid increase of political segregation since the 1990s ought to give us pause. The question of political polarization cannot be decisively linked to the increase in political segregation, and perhaps some might feel uneasy about the lack of clarity on the issue.

Scholars of political geography still have several questions to contend with at many levels of the debate. Take for example the issue of social media. How much does our connection to people across the country or across the world blur the influence of geographic space? How might instant and unlimited access to news and punditry negate the opinions of our friends and family with whom we interact in our neighborhoods and cities?

And how about the geography of the American lifestyle? How does it contribute to political polarization? Our reliance on automobiles to get around isolates us in transit, while our homes offer an increasing sense of reclusion, particularly thanks to suburban sprawl. The public spaces we do share with others are now dominated by consumerist performance, to the point where political activity in most public spaces is experienced as a nuisance. From such a myopic view, the startling discovery might be the isolation and insulation of the American citizen and their political preferences. In a world like this, individuals can curate their own diet of political ideas without scrutiny from others. The geography of our cities, towns, public spaces, homes, and streets may be creating echo chambers we unconsciously inhabit in which we are safe from each other, but vulnerable to ourselves.

Notes

1 Multilevel analysis in this case is the process by which data from smaller geographic units is measured within the context of the larger geographic units to which they belong. For example, rather than analyzing all the counties in the United States as one group, counties are grouped according to the states they belong to and analyzed

within those groups. The idea is that counties from one state may exhibit a particular trend, whereas counties in another state exhibit a different trend. These differing trends would not be visible if the counties were analyzed altogether as one group.

2 The Big Five traits are *openness* (receptivity to new ideas or experiences), *conscientiousness* (adherence to norms, responsibilities, and organization), *extraversion* (preference for consistent social interaction), *agreeableness* (the inclination to be polite, kind, or non-confrontational), and *neuroticism* (the inclination towards anxiety, negative feelings, and doubt).

References

Abramowitz, A.I., Alexander, B. and Gunning, M., 2006. Incumbency, redistricting, and the decline of competition in US House elections. *The Journal of Politics*, *68*(1), pp. 75–88.

Abrams, S.J. and Fiorina, M.P., 2012. "The big sort" that wasn't: A skeptical reexamination. *PS: Political Science and Politics*, *45*(2), pp. 203–210.

Altman, M. and McDonald, M., 2015. Redistricting and polarization. *American Gridlock*, pp. 45–67.

Bishop, B., 2009. *The Big Sort: Why the Clustering of Like-Minded America Is Tearing Us Apart*. Houghton Mifflin Harcourt.

Carson, J.L., Crespin, M.H., Finocchiaro, C.J. and Rohde, D.W., 2007. Redistricting and party polarization in the US House of Representatives. *American Politics Research*, *35*(6), pp. 878–904.

DellaVigna, S. and Kaplan, E., 2007. The FOX News effect: Media bias and voting. *The Quarterly Journal of Economics*, *122*(3), pp. 1187–1234.

Elleman, Lorien G., Condon, David M., Russin, Sarah E. and Revelle, William, 2018. The personality of US states: Stability from 1999 to 2015. *Journal of Research in Personality*, *72*, pp. 64–72.

Florida, R., 2019. *The Rise of the Creative Class*. Basic Books.

Gimpel, J.G. and Hui, I.S., 2015. Seeking politically compatible neighbors? The role of neighborhood partisan composition in residential sorting. *Political Geography*, *48*, pp. 130–142.

Glaeser, E.L. and Ward, B.A., 2006. Myths and realities of American political geography. *Journal of Economic Perspectives*, *20*(2), pp. 119–144.

Hawkins S, Yudkin D, Juan-Torres M, and Dixon T, 2019. *Hidden Tribes: A Study of America's Polarized Landscape*. New York: More in Common.

Hirsh, Jacob B., DeYoung, Colin G., Xu, Xiaowen and Peterson, Jordan B., 2010. Compassionate liberals and polite conservatives: Associations of agreeableness with political ideology and moral values. *Personality and Social Psychology Bulletin*, *36*(5), pp. 655–664.

Hui, I., 2013. Who is your preferred neighbor? Partisan residential preferences and neighborhood satisfaction. *American Politics Research*, *41*(6), pp. 997–1021.

Johnston, R., Manley, D. and Jones, K., 2016. Spatial polarization of presidential voting in the United States, 1992–2012: The "big sort" revisited. *Annals of the American Association of Geographers*, *106*(5), pp. 1047–1062.

Lang, C. and Pearson-Merkowitz, S., 2015. Partisan sorting in the United States, 1972–2012: New evidence from a dynamic analysis. *Political Geography*, *48*, pp. 119–129.

Martin, D.C. and Newman, B.J., 2015. Measuring aggregate social capital using census response rates. *American Politics Research*, *43*(4), pp. 625–642.

McCarty, N., Poole, K.T. and Rosenthal, H., 2009. Does gerrymandering cause polarization? *American Journal of Political Science*, *53*(3), pp. 666–680.

McCarty, N., Rodden, J., Shor, B., Tausanovitch, C. and Warshaw, C., 2013, September. Geography and polarization. In: *Annual Meeting of the American Political Science Association*, Chicago, IL (Vol. *47*).

Motyl, M., Iyer, R., Oishi, S., Trawalter, S. and Nosek, B.A., 2014. How ideological migration geographically segregates groups. *Journal of Experimental Social Psychology*, *51*, pp. 1–14.

Nall, C. and Mummolo, J., 2013. Why partisans don't sort: How neighborhood quality concerns limit Americans' pursuit of like-minded neighbors. *Journal of Politics*. *PAGE \# "'Page: '#'"" 79* (1), pp. 45–59.

Pew Research Center. 2014. Political polarization in the American public: How increasing ideological uniformity and partisan antipathy affect politics, compromise and everyday life.

Rentfrow, P.J., Gosling, S.D., Jokela, M., Stillwell, D.J., Kosinski, M. and Potter, J., 2013. Divided we stand: Three psychological regions of the United States and their political, economic, social, and health correlates. *Journal of Personality and Social Psychology*, *105*(6), p. 996.

Rentfrow, P.J., Gosling, S.D. and Potter, J., 2008. A theory of the emergence, persistence, and expression of geographic variation in psychological characteristics. *Perspectives on Psychological Science*, *3*(5), pp. 339–369.

Rentfrow, P.J. and Jokela, M., 2016. Geographical psychology: The spatial organization of psychological phenomena. *Current Directions in Psychological Science*, *25*(6), pp. 393–398.

Rentfrow, P.J., Jost, J.T., Gosling, S.D. and Potter, J., 2009. Statewide differences in personality predict voting patterns in 1996–2004 US presidential elections. *Social and Psychological Bases of Ideology and System Justification*, *1*, pp. 314–349.

Rodden, J., 2015. Geography and Gridlock in the United States. *Solutions to Political Polarization in America*, pp. 104–120.

Scala, D.J. and Johnson, K.M., 2017. Political polarization along the rural–urban continuum? The geography of the presidential vote, 2000–2016. *The Annals of the American Academy of Political and Social Science*, *672*(1), pp. 162–184.

Thurber J, Yoshinaka A (eds)., *American Gridlock: The Sources, Character, and Impact of Political Polarization*. Cambridge U.K.: University of Cambridge Press, pp. 45–67.

Verhulst, B., Eaves, L.J. and Hatemi, P.K., 2012. Correlation not causation: The relationship between personality traits and political ideologies. *American Journal of Political Science*, *56*(1), pp. 34–51.

Walsh, K.C., 2012. Putting inequality in its place: Rural consciousness and the power of perspective. *American Political Science Review*, *106*(3), pp. 517–532.

Xu, X., Mar, R.A. and Peterson, J.B., 2013. Does cultural exposure partially explain the association between personality and political orientation? *Personality and Social Psychology Bulletin*, *39*(11), pp. 1497–1517.

Yudkin, D.A., 2019. *Hidden Tribes: A Study of America's Polarized Landscape*.

2

DEMOGRAPHIC CHANGE

Susan A. MacManus and Anthony A. Cilluffo

Rep. David Jolly: As national demographics change, major parties have a decision to make. Do they adapt to reflect those changes, or do they resist those changes by trying to simply expand participation among their natural political constituency? In my experience, the Democratic Party has chosen the former, Republicans the latter. And this political decision has public policy implications as well.

As the nation's demographics have trended toward great cultural and racial diversity, so too have our national priorities become more complex and more representative of our multiculturalism. While the vast majority of policy issues we face impact all cultures and all races universally as one American people, we know that some policy issues like health care, education, and immigration uniquely and often adversely impact different cultures and races more than others, as certain policy decisions have a disparate impact on people based on their socioeconomic position.

Our politics too often are slow to respond to the policy demands of shifting demographics, arguably because for three decades politicians have diligently worked to expel accountability and competition from our Congressional elections through big data gerrymandering to protect the major parties, closed primaries that silence independent voters, the acceptance and influence of big money, and other modern-day electoral hijinks.

As a lifelong Republican who left the party shortly after leaving Congress, I believe that the danger in the GOP's strategy of largely ignoring today's demographic changes is fraught with risk. The numbers are the numbers. The nation is becoming more diverse, not less. Communities of color and communities of culture are collectively becoming the majority. The issues often championed by these vital communities are becoming more central to the nation's future. Simply put, the party that champions the demographic changes of the nation and demonstrates convictions most aligned with our nation's vibrant diversity will find great success in the coming decades. The party that resists those changes will find great challenge.

Rep. Patrick E. Murphy: There is little disagreement that demographic change will have a profound impact on our democracy – it is just a matter of when. It's important for readers to consider the facts outlined in this chapter and consider why certain politicians – in the current era, Republicans – are making it harder to vote with stricter ID laws, voter restoration restrictions, and fewer polling stations in minority areas. It goes unspoken, but clearly politicians pushing for these changes see them as a partisan benefit to their side (and an advantage that must be removed from the opposition). It is the unnerving flipside of tactics that conservative white southern Democrats employed in the early 20th century to prevent blacks from voting, with a plethora of Jim Crow laws like poll taxes and literacy tests that urged disenfranchisement.

It will be interesting to see how Republican politicians adapt to these demographic changes. Will the party begin to embrace diversity and seek Hispanic and African-American votes using shared cultural or religious beliefs? Or will they double down on the rural–urban divide that is largely centered around rural and small-town white voters? Generational, demographic, and educational changes are all working against Republicans at the same time that white voters without a college degree are moving away from Democrats. Yet we only need to look back at recent history to see how quickly parties can adapt and grab a large segment of voters previously seen as unattainable.

Over the past few decades, major demographic and socioeconomic trends – namely, those affecting race and ethnicity, age, and geographic redistribution – have reshaped America and its politics. Immigration and generational replacement have brought millions of new voices into the political process. At the same time, economic remaking and geographic sorting have changed where many Americans live, how they earn a living, and which political issues matter most to them.

These trends show every sign of continuing. The impact will be felt on voter registration, political party membership (including No Party Affiliation or NPA), voter turnout, politicians and government officials, and their approach to issues such as immigration and health care. One wonders whether these trends will lead to greater polarization or greater bipartisanship. Understanding and adapting to these trends will be key to anyone who expects to participate in the political process.

Major Demographic Changes Remaking America

The America of today looks much different than it did just 50 years ago. In 1970, the population was still overwhelmingly white, the post-World War II generation was in grade school or college, more than half of Americans lived in the Midwest or Northeast, and only about one in ten Americans had a college degree. It was not long before things changed.

Sharp Increases in Racial and Ethnic Diversity

In 1970, more than nine in ten Americans were either white or black. The vast majority of the U.S. population consisted of non-Hispanic whites (84 percent), and the largest racial and ethnic minority group was blacks at 11 percent of the population (see Figure 2.1). Only 5 percent of the total U.S. population was foreign-born (Pew Research Center, 2015b). That would change as new immigration laws took effect.

Influx of Immigrants

The Immigration and Naturalization Act of 1965 – major legislation signed by President Lyndon Johnson that overhauled the U.S. immigration system – led to long-term changes in immigration patterns and demographics. Previously, immigration was based on a national-origins quota system that heavily favored immigrants from European countries. The 1965 law gave strong preference to immigrants with family ties in the United States and to skilled workers (Chishti et al., 2015). In the 50 years between 1965 and 2015, nearly 59 million immigrants came to this

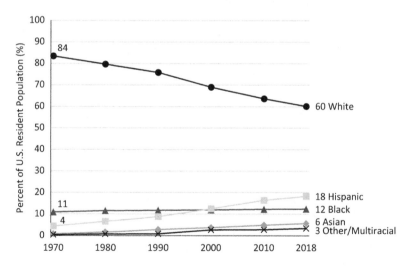

FIGURE 2.1   U.S. Population by Race and Ethnicity, 1970-2018. Note: Figures may not sum to 100% due to rounding. White, black, and Asian are single-race non-Hispanics only. Asian includes Pacific Islanders. Hispanics are of any race. Source: Authors' analysis of 1970, 1980, 1990 and 2000 decennial censuses and 2010 and 2018 American Community Survey (Ruggles, et al., 2020).

country, with just more than half coming from Latin America and a quarter from Asia. Together, these immigrants accounted for 55 percent of the U.S. population growth during that period (Pew Research Center, 2015b).

The reasons immigrants come to the United States are varied. Some come to escape poverty, war, or oppression. Others come to rejoin their families. Still others come seeking highly skilled jobs that are not available in their home countries. The reasons they come affect their socioeconomic outcomes. For example, among Asian Americans, many Burmese came to this country as refugees with low educational attainment; thus, they have one of the lowest median household incomes ($35,000). Conversely, many people from India arrived as highly skilled workers on H-1B visas; they have a much higher median household income – $100,000 (López et al., 2017).

Visa type also affects the rate at which immigrants attempt to become naturalized U.S. citizens. Refugees and asylum seekers – those allowed to come or stay to avoid political, social, religious, or other forms of persecution in their country of origin – are the most likely to naturalize as U.S. citizens. Those with family members of U.S. citizens are much less likely (U.S. Citizenship, 2016).

Immigrants are also more concentrated in some states than others. By 2018, nearly half (45 percent) lived in three states – California, Texas, and New York. Two-thirds lived in the West (34 percent) and South (33 percent), followed by the Northeast (21 percent) and Midwest (11 percent). Nearly two-thirds (65 percent) resided in 20 major metropolitan areas, the largest being New York, Los Angeles, and Miami (Radford, 2019). These areas have long been "immigrant magnets," drawing new arrivals to already-established immigrant communities.

Partially as a result of this modern wave of immigration, whites accounted for 60 percent of Americans in 2018. Hispanics surpassed blacks as the second-largest racial and ethnic group as of the 2000 decennial census and are now 18 percent of the population. The black share has held roughly steady since 1970 at 12 percent. Asians, the fastest-growing racial and ethnic group in the country, are now 6 percent of the U.S. population, up from less than 1 percent in 1970 (López et al., 2017). In 2018, 14 percent of the population was born in another country – roughly triple the share in 1970 (U.S. Census Bureau, 2019c).

Link Between Racial and Ethnic Diversity and Age

Minority populations have grown not only because of their immigration patterns, but also because of their relative youth. This factor is apparent in the rapid rise in the population share that identifies with multiple racial groups. Although still relatively small, it increased from 2.4 percent in 2000 (Jones and Bullock, 2012) to 3.4 percent in 2018 (U.S. Census Bureau, 2019b) – a 65 percent increase in 18 years. This trend is projected to increase with the growth in interracial marriage and the diversity of younger generations.

Another example is the sharp difference in fertility rates between different racial and ethnic groups. Fertility rates for Hispanic women are highest, followed by non-Hispanic black women, and non-Hispanic white women (Matthews and Hamilton, 2019). This means that the racial and ethnic composition of babies born in the United States will be less white than the population overall.

The U.S. Census Bureau projects that the non-white portion of the U.S. population will continue to grow. They expect that non-Hispanic whites, with their lower fertility and higher mortality rates, will no longer be a majority of the resident population by the year 2045 (Vespa et al., 2020). The reality is that America's minority population is younger than its white population. Demographer William Frey summarizes the link between race and ethnicity and age this way: "Clearly it is the growth of the nation's youthful minority population – attributable to a combination of past and present immigration and births among younger minority groups – that is keeping the nation from aging even faster than would otherwise be the case" (Frey, 2018).

Changes in the Age of Americans: Getting Grayer

The United States experienced a historic rise in fertility rates in the period after the end of World War II. The 76 million children born during this period, from 1946 to 1964, are known as Baby Boomers (Pollard and Scommegna, 2014). As the Boomers head toward their retirement years – the oldest Boomer turned 65 in 2011, and the youngest will do so in 2029 – they are dramatically altering the age composition of the country.

In 1970, 35 percent of Americans were younger than 18 (see Figure 2.2). Only one in ten was 65 or older. The rest of the population, 55 percent, was in their working years, ages 18 to 64. Since then, the share of the population younger than 18 has been steadily falling, a product of lower fertility rates for all racial and ethnic groups (Chappell, 2019).

According to Census Bureau projections, by 2035 those 65 and older will outnumber those younger than 18 for the first time in U.S. history (U.S. Census Bureau, 2019a). The gap will widen even more by 2060 – 23 percent of Americans will be 65 or older, while only 20 percent will be younger than 18, a difference of 14.5 million people.

Where Americans Live: More in Sunbelt and Metro Areas

Different generations have been drawn to certain geographical areas, even within the same state or locality. Contributing factors include vibrant economies and jobs, immigration (particularly of Hispanics and Asians), in-migration from other states, higher educational attainment, rising incomes, and the quality of life (MacManus and Cilluffo, 2019).

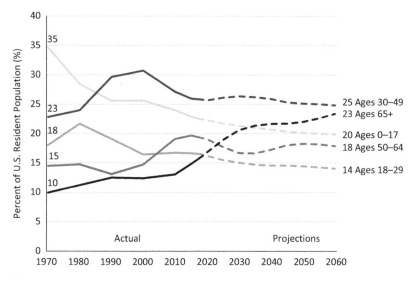

FIGURE 2.2   Age Composition of the U.S. Population, 1970-2060. Source: Authors'
analysis of 1970, 1980, 1990 and 2000 decennial censuses and 2010 and
2018 American Community Survey (Ruggles, et al., 2020) and 2020-
2060 U.S. Census Bureau population projections (U.S. Census Bureau,
2018a).

Rise of the South and West

In 1970, a majority of Americans lived in the Midwest (28 percent) and Northeast
(24 percent). The South was the most populous region by a slight margin (home
to 31 percent of Americans), while just 17 percent lived in the West.

Fifty years later, fewer than four in ten Americans live in the Midwest (21 percent) and Northeast (17 percent). The fast-growing regions of the South and West
are now home to more than six in ten Americans. The South is clearly the most
populous region, where 38 percent of Americans live, followed by the West with
24 percent of the population (see Figure 2.3).

New York, New Jersey, and Illinois have been the big losers in population,
while California, Texas, and Florida have led the way in growth. Signifying this
change, Florida passed New York as the nation's third-most populous state in 2014
(Overberg and Toppo, 2014). In 1970, only three of the ten largest metro areas
were in the South or West (Los Angeles, San Francisco, and Washington, D.C.) By
2019, seven were (Los Angeles, Dallas, Houston, Washington, D.C., Miami, Atlanta,
and Phoenix). All ten of the fastest-growing metropolitan areas are in the South
or West (U.S. Census Bureau, 2020).[1]

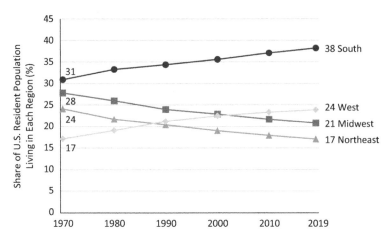

FIGURE 2.3 Share of U.S. Population Living in Each Region, 1970-2019. Source: U.S. Census Bureau, 1970-2010 decennial censuses and vintage 2019 population estimates.

What accounts for these differences in growth rates? Immigrants are more likely to settle in the South and West than in the past, partially reflecting the shift from mainly European immigrants to immigrants from Latin America and Asia. Until 1940, more than 80 percent of the foreign-born population lived in the Midwest and Northeast. More recently, more than two-thirds lived in the South and West (Jacobs, 2019). Higher shares of the population in the South and West are non-whites, who overall have higher fertility rates than whites (Passel et al., 2012).

In addition, the manufacturing base has declined in the Midwest and Northeast and new, professional, and service-industry jobs have relocated to the South and West. Others have chosen to move to these regions for a milder climate, lower cost of living and tax rates, or proximity to family. Many blacks fled the South's racist Jim Crow society in the Great Migration starting in the 1910s for a new life in the North. A reverse Great Migration began after 1990 as many blacks, led by college graduates and retirees, began moving back to the South (Toppo and Overberg, 2015). Atlanta, nearly destroyed in the Civil War, is now the de facto capital of the New South, a popular destination for young professionals and families, and home to the world's busiest airport (Airports Council, 2019).

Urbanization

Urbanization is nothing new. It has been underway, globally, since the Industrial Revolution (United Nations, 2018). The share of the resident population living in an urban area (which includes suburbs) rose from 74 percent in 1970 to 81 percent in 2010. These urban Americans live in 3,741 urban areas, which together cover just 3 percent of the country's land area. More than half (52 percent) of Americans live in an urban area with 500,000 people or more (U.S. Census Bureau, 2012).

Rural areas experienced an absolute decline in the several years after the Great Recession. However, the past few years have seen a modest rural revival, with counties outside metropolitan areas undergoing a slight population gain. This was largely driven by domestic migrants moving into rural counties that are next to metropolitan areas often because of more affordable housing. Rural counties farther from metro areas have continued to see a loss (Johnson, 2018).

The Changing Economy and Increasing Educational Attainment

Underlying these geographic movements were changes in the economy. The country's economic base has shifted from manufacturing to professional and service-providing industries. According to Bureau of Labor Statistics data, 28 percent of U.S. workers were employed in manufacturing in 1960. By 2020, that had fallen to just 8 percent. The number of manufacturing workers peaked at 19.6 million in mid-1979. By early 2020, it had dropped to 12.8 million – a loss of 6.7 million. In place of manufacturing, new jobs have arisen in professional and business services and the education and health services industries. In 1960, these two industry categories accounted for 12 percent of U.S. employment. By 2020, their share more than doubled, to 30 percent. Together, these industries employ more than 46 million workers.[2]

These changes in the economy have had a major impact on where people live and the jobs they hold. Manufacturing jobs were once concentrated in towns across the Midwest and Northeast near transportation networks. They often provided good-paying, steady work with benefits for those without a college degree. Those jobs have all but disappeared, giving rise to the Rust Belt of abandoned or decaying communities. In contrast, the new professional jobs are often located in cities and largely demand workers with at least a bachelor's degree. Improvements in technology mean that these jobs are less tethered to any particular place, which has helped companies start up or relocate to growing cities in the South and West.

Educational attainment has risen as the economy has created more jobs for college graduates, leaving fewer jobs for those with less formal education. In 1970, few Americans 25 and older had a bachelor's or advanced degree (11 percent), or some college experience (10 percent). By 2019, 36 percent of adults 25 and older had a bachelor's degree or higher, and 26 percent had some college experience. These gains came from improved high school completion rates. In 1970, about a third (34 percent) had only a high school diploma or equivalent, and 44 percent had not completed high school. Nearly 50 years later, a mere 10 percent had not completed high school.[3]

Changes in educational attainment have occurred by gender and race and ethnicity in recent years. Women are now more likely than men to enroll in college and, once there, to complete a degree. Students from poorer backgrounds and racial and ethnic minorities are going up the education ladder (Semuels, 2017). Among recent high school graduates, blacks and Hispanics have made significant progress in closing the gap in the share of recent graduates who enroll in college, although differences remain (Fry and Cilluffo, 2019).

Changes in education and employment patterns have become visible in household incomes. In 2018, the median U.S. household income was $63,179 – at or near the highest it has ever been. Significant racial and ethnic differences remain, however. Households headed by an Asian earn a median of $87,194, compared with $70,642 for whites, $51,450 for Hispanics, and $41,361 for blacks. Incomes are also higher in metropolitan areas ($66,164) than in the areas outside them ($49,867) (Semega et al., 2019). Among workers, wages are much higher for those with at least a bachelor's degree than for those with lower educational attainment (Torpey, 2018).

What do all these demographic changes mean?

Impact of Demographic Changes on Politics and Policies

A recent Pew Research Center study of the country's changing demographics documented the strong link between demographics and politics. The report concluded that "America's demographic changes are shifting the *electorate* – and American politics" (Cohn and Caumont, 2016). It is important to note here that the major demographic changes detailed thus far in this chapter (increasing racial and ethnic diversity, aging, and geographic mobility) are for the total U.S. population – formally known as the *resident population*. The *electorate* – U.S. citizens 18 and older who are eligible to vote – is a subset of the resident population.

Understanding the Electorate

The non-white share of the electorate is smaller than that of the resident (total) population because a higher proportion of minority populations are not eligible to vote either because they are not 18 or were born outside the United States and have not yet become citizens.[4] For example, a larger share of Hispanic and Asian adults was born outside the United States and are not yet naturalized, so they make up a smaller share of the electorate than that of the total U.S. resident population.[5] Specifically, Hispanics are 18 percent of the total U.S. population, but 13 percent of the electorate. Similarly, while Asians make up 6 percent of the population, they are 5 percent of the electorate.[6]

On top of this, eligibility to vote does not equate with *actually* registering to vote. In nearly all states, those who meet citizenship, age, and other requirements must register to vote. Those less likely to register include first- and second-generation immigrants (Trevelyan, 2016) and persons with lower educational attainment (U.S. Census Bureau, 2019d). Language issues, administrative barriers (Wright, 2012), and disinterest in or distrust of politics (Creek and Ueyama, 2017) also deter eligible voters from registering. Additionally, a few states have laws making it difficult for felons who have completed supervised release to restore their voting rights (National Council of State Legislatures, 2019), which disproportionately affects racial minorities (Sentencing Project, 2020).

Diversity Can Beget Polarization on Key Issues

Candidates and political parties must contend with shifts in the makeup of their constituencies and the issues they regard as most important. The three major demographic shifts already discussed are strongly associated with increasing political polarization – that is, a deeper divide between parties, which lessens the odds of reaching bipartisan agreement.

Major Racial and Ethnic Issue Conflict: Immigration

Given the impact that immigration has had on shaping the country's racial and ethnic composition over the country's history, it is no surprise that immigration frequently ranks as one of the most important problems facing the country (Gallup, Most Important). The U.S. immigration law has not been significantly changed since 1965, leading many to call for either significant revisions or comprehensive reform. Emotions run high on all sides of the issue, however, making bipartisanship and compromise elusive.

A good example is the 2013 debate around comprehensive immigration reform. The Border Security, Economic Opportunity, and Immigration Modernization Act of 2013 was co-sponsored in the U.S. Senate by the "Gang of Eight," a bipartisan group of eight senators, four Republicans and four Democrats, who together crafted the bill (Cox, 2013). Its hallmarks were offering a pathway to citizenship for unauthorized immigrants, increasing border security, and promoting highly skilled workers. The bill passed the Senate in June 2013 but was never considered in the U.S. House. Speaker John Boehner and House Republicans refused to act on it, effectively blocking passage. Conservatives took issue with the provisions offering a path to citizenship on terms they felt were too lenient. The backlash led Senator Marco Rubio, R-FL, member of the Gang of Eight and a co-sponsor, to distance himself and say it was never meant to become law before House conservatives made it "even better" (NBC News, 2016).

An earlier bill – narrower in focus – failed in 2011. Consequently, President Barack Obama took unilateral action in 2012 to grant "deferred action" to unauthorized immigrants who arrived in the country while children. The program, Deferred Action for Childhood Arrivals (DACA), enrolled about 800,000 persons who received work permits and protection from deportation (López and Krogstad, 2017). Extending support to "Dreamers" is overwhelmingly popular – one Gallup poll from June 2018 found that 83 percent of Americans favor creating a path to citizenship for them (Newport, 2018). Some Republicans oppose the program not for its protections of Dreamers, but for what they see as an unconstitutional abuse of executive power. On these grounds, President Donald Trump announced a six-month drawdown to the program starting in September 2017 (Shear and Davis, 2017). The Trump Administration's attempts to stop the program were challenged in multiple courts. Notwithstanding the legal challenges, the National Immigration Law Center reports that "individuals who have or previously had DACA can apply to renew it" (National Immigration Law Center, 2019).

Another immigration-related issue remains starkly polarized – border security. Trump campaigned on a promise that he would build a wall along the U.S.–Mexico border. When a bill funding part of the federal government, including the Department of Homeland Security, failed to include money for a border wall, Trump refused to sign it, touching off a 35-day partial government shutdown in December 2018 and January 2019 (Restuccia et al., 2019). Unable to secure funding from the budget process, Trump attempted to transfer money from several military accounts, resulting in a lawsuit in federal court by the Democratic-controlled House of Representatives for violating the separation of powers (Hsu, 2019). In June 2019, a federal judge blocked the use of $2.5 billion from the Department of Defense for building the wall (Del Real, 2019). Although a border wall proved unpopular with Americans overall, significant partisan differences existed on the question. In January 2019, 82 percent of Republicans favored substantially expanding the wall along the U.S.–Mexico border, compared with only 6 percent of Democrats (Pew Research Center, 2019). The issue is destined to form a major battle in the 2020 presidential election.

Different Reactions to Changing Racial Composition

Overall, Americans have mixed views about whether minorities forming a majority of the population by the year 2050 is a good or bad thing. According to a 2018 Pew Research Center survey, 35 percent say it will be very or somewhat good, compared with 23 percent who say it will be bad and 42 percent who say it will be neither good nor bad. These differences break down by demographics. Blacks and Hispanics are about twice as likely as whites to say the change will be good. Younger Americans are more positive about it, as are those with a bachelor's degree or higher. But the biggest difference is by party: Half of Democrats and independents who lean Democratic say the change will be good, compared with only 16 percent of Republicans. More than a third of Republicans (37 percent) say it will be at least somewhat bad, compared with only 12 percent of Democrats (Parker et al., 2019b).

Similar questions also show wide party differences. Republicans are more likely than Democrats to say that the change will lead to more conflicts between racial and ethnic groups (59 percent vs. 42 percent) and that it will weaken American customs and values (59 percent vs. 22 percent) (Parker et al., 2019b). A later survey found that Democrats are far more likely to say that the U.S. population being made up of people of many different races and ethnicities has a positive impact on the country's culture (77 percent vs. 50 percent). About half of white Republicans say it would bother them at least somewhat to hear people speak a language other than English in public, compared with a majority of white Democrats saying it would not bother them at all (Horowitz, 2019).

But will the U.S. become a *majority minority* nation by the year 2050? Some demographers question the Census Bureau's projections (Tavernise, 2018). For one thing, identity changes across generations. A quarter of third-generation immigrants[7] and half of fourth-generation immigrants with Hispanic ancestry consider themselves *non-Hispanic* (Lopez et al., 2017). Among Asians, those who were born in the United States are far more likely to describe themselves as "American" (instead of their family's country of origin or as "Asian American") than those born abroad (Pew Research Center, 2013).

Additionally, rising rates of interracial marriage (Livingston and Brown, 2017) and the growing multiracial population (Jones and Bullock, 2012) complicate how identity is understood. Instead, some demographers argue that current projections show complex demographic changes as a zero-sum game, with whites losing and other groups winning. The 2045 projection thus becomes a doomsday clock. It enables those who fear an undermining of the American way of life to resist, thus increasing emotions and making compromise harder (Tavernise, 2018). It is possible that, instead, our concept of race and ethnicity will radically change in the future to accommodate more complex notions of racial origin and ancestry.

Another consequence of racial and ethnic population changes is the rise of *identity politics*. Broadly speaking, identity politics is what happens when members of a particular social group focus on and organize around their shared characteristics and experiences, often perceived as injustices (Heyes, 2016). For example, advocates in the LGBT (Lesbian, Gay, Bisexual, Transgender) community have challenged laws, regulations, and other actions that discriminate against them. While many of the issues raised are legitimate, some argue that this focus on different identities increases polarization and makes bipartisanship harder (Brick and van der Linden, 2018). Some race-based identity movements are committed to issues for which compromise is either impossible or politically unfeasible (Zakaria, 2016).

Major Aging-Related Conflict Issue: Health Care

Health care has ranked as the most stressful topic on a wide-ranging list of potential issues for the past five years (Norman, 2019). Its importance will continue to increase as the U.S. population rapidly ages. Americans are not satisfied with how the nation's health care system works, with costs their biggest concern (Kenen, 2019). Spending is concentrated among older adults, with those 65 and older accounting for 36 percent of health care spending in 2016, but only 16 percent of the total population (Sawyer and Claxon, 2019). Older generations, particularly the Silent Generation (those born between 1928 and 1945), spend three times as much (15 percent) of their total spending on health care compared with Millennials (5 percent) (U.S. Bureau of Labor Statistics, 2018). Total spending on health care has far outpaced the overall increase in costs over time. In 1970, health expenditures per capita were about $1,800 in 2017 dollars; in 2017, they were $10,700 – a nearly 500 percent increase (Kamal et al., 2019).

While Americans across party lines agree that health care is a major issue facing the country and that the government has a role in solving it, health care policy is incredibly partisan. According to one poll from 2013, feelings toward the federal law nicknamed Obamacare were stronger (both positive and negative) than feelings toward the same law when referred to as the Affordable Care Act (Liesman, 2016). As of late 2018, less than half of Americans approved of the ACA, although feelings were sharply partisan: 84 percent of Democrats approved of the law, but only 9 percent of Republicans did (Brenan, 2018). Far from being a policy area for bipartisanship and compromise, health care is often a political prize. In the 2010 midterm elections, Republican challengers ran against the then-recently passed ACA and made major gains in reclaiming Congress. After the failed 2017 push by President Trump and Congressional Republicans to replace the ACA, Democrats ran on the issue of preserving and expanding health care in the 2018 midterm elections that helped them reclaim a House majority.

The aging population and rising health care costs contribute to projections of sharply increased federal spending on health care programs. The Congressional Budget Office projects overall federal health care spending to increase from 28 percent of non-interest spending in 2019 to 41 percent in 2049. Medicare, federal health insurance provided to the elderly, is the largest federal health care program and will account for about three-quarters of the increase (Congressional Budget Office, 2019).

At the same time, fewer workers will be paying payroll taxes that fund the program. This will lead to an increase in the dependency ratio – the number of people (young and old) dependent on others for care per worker. The increased dependency ratio, especially in the context of an aging population, will likely lead to workers needing to pay a higher share of their income to support other people. Some predict this will lead to intergenerational conflicts or even a "generation showdown" (Taylor, 2016). The sharp partisan differences on health care between younger and older generations mean it will continue to be a challenge to reach bipartisan solutions.

Generational Political Differences

Generational differences in political preferences have always been a fact of American politics. Each generation experiences different major events growing up that subsequently shape their political beliefs (see Table 2.1). For example, the Silent Generation grew up during the Era of Conformity (work hard and stay quiet) in the 1950s and is still one of the most conservative generations. Conversely, the Great Recession happened during the early adulthood or childhood of the Millennials, which helps explain why that generation is suspicious of big business and is generally more favorable toward government intervention in the economy and a socialistic bent.

Today's generational partisan gaps are wider than they have been in decades. In fact, some scholars argue that "the generation war is the best frame for understanding the ways that the Democratic and Republican parties are diverging" (Ferguson and Freymann, 2019). Only minor differences across the generations existed in the first-year presidential approval ratings for Bill Clinton and George W. Bush. Approval ratings for presidents Obama and Trump were much more divergent. While 64 percent of Millennials approved of Obama's job performance during his first year, only 49 percent of the Silent Generation did. In contrast, 46 percent of the Silent Generation but just 27 percent of Millennials approved of Trump's first year in office (Pew Research Center, 2018).

TABLE 2.1 America's Living Generations and Major Political Events

Generation	Born	Age in 2020	Major Events	Presidents
Greatest/GI Generation	Before 1928	93+	Great Depression, New Deal, World War II	Franklin Delano Roosevelt (D)
Silent Generation	1928–1945	75–92	Postwar happiness, Era of Conformity, Korean War	Truman (D); Eisenhower (R)
Baby Boomers	1946–1964	56–74	Civil Rights Movement, 60s Youth Culture—Save the World Activism, Drugs, Free Love, Vietnam War	Kennedy (D); Johnson (D); Nixon (R); Ford (R); Carter (D)
Generation X	1965–1980	40–55	MTV, 24-hour news, latch-key kids, transition to computers, AIDS	Reagan (R); GHW Bush (R), Clinton (D)
Millennials	1981–1996	24–39	9/11, social media, Iraq and Afghanistan conflicts, Great Recession, BP oil spill	GW Bush (R); Obama (D)
Generation Z	After 1996	23 and younger	Brexit, #BlackLivesMatter, #MeToo, Parkland school shooting; cancel culture	Obama (D); Trump (R)

Source: Generations from Pew Research Center, Events and Presidents from authors.
Note: "Presidents" column shows the sitting president when a member of the generation turned age 18.

These differences span opinions on political issues as well. In 1994, only minor generational differences occurred in the shares saying that immigrants strengthen the country. By 2017, Millennials were far more likely than Silents to say immigrants strengthen the country (79 percent vs. 47 percent). The other generations were in the middle (Gen X: 66 percent, Boomers: 56 percent) (Pew Research Center, 2018). Differences are also visible on issues such as same-sex marriage, marijuana legalization, racial issues, and government involvement. Although it is still early, indications are that Generation Z, the youngest adult generation, holds opinions broadly similar to the Millennials (Parker et al., 2019a). As opinions move further apart, intergenerational compromise may be harder to reach.

The varying composition of the generations helps explain some of the political differences between them. While 79 percent of the Silent Generation and 72 percent of the Boomers are white, only 61 percent of Gen X and 56 percent of Millennials are (Pew Research Center, 2018). Millennials are much more likely to have a college degree than older generations (Fry et al., 2018). Millennials are also far more likely to be religiously unaffiliated than older generations (Pew Research Center, 2015a). All of these compositional differences are closely related to holding more liberal opinions. The Democrat–Republican partisan divide is morphing into the left–right or conservative–liberal divide. Each party is feeling the effects of this generational segregation: "The dominant age cohort in each party recognizes its newfound power to choose candidates and set the policy agenda" (Ferguson and Freymann, 2019) – Democrats, the young; Republicans, the old.

Geographic Segregation and Conflict

As discussed in Chapter 1, we cannot overemphasize the increasing importance of geography on American political dynamics. Over the past decade, polarization escalated in every geographic category – urban, suburban, and rural (Gould and Bryan, 2018), leading some observers to say that "the political divide is increasingly a geographic divide" (Maxwell, 2019). Compromise and agreement are becoming more elusive as political, economic, and social forces remake urban and rural areas. For example, in the 2016 election, Hillary Clinton won the nation's urban areas, while Trump handily won rural areas and a plurality of suburban areas – where about half of all voters lived (CNN, 2016). In the 2018 midterm elections, Democrats won all but two of the 81 most urban U.S. House districts, while Republicans won 82 percent of the 184 most rural districts.

Driving these political shifts are changes in the socioeconomics of different geographies. With the decline of American farming and manufacturing, the best paid and most stable jobs are often located in cities. The economic decline of rural areas relative to urban areas has varied implications. Highly talented young rural residents migrate to urban areas in search of academic and employment opportunities, leading to population decline in rural areas (Kumar, 2018). About three in ten rural counties have at least a fifth of their population in poverty – higher than in urban or suburban areas and higher than the share of rural counties in 2000 (Parker et al., 2018). The incidence of opioid overdose deaths is rising most rapidly in rural areas, surpassing urban areas (U.S. Department of Agriculture, 2020). And the life expectancy of rural residents is about three years shorter than for residents of large urban areas, with the disparity wider than in the past (Singh and Siahpush, 2014).

These demographic differences between city and countryside impact political preferences, but so does geographic self-segregation, which drives polarization. Called "the big sort," Americans are increasingly likely to live near people who have similar opinions (Bishop, 2009). Polarization within states and counties has increased over time (Johnston et al., 2016). The idea is that as people live near only those with similar opinions and world views, it becomes easier for them to caricature the beliefs of others and to suffer from group polarization bias. One study found that the most politically intolerant Americans are highly educated whites living in urban areas – who are also least likely to have people with different political opinions in their social networks (Ripley et al., 2019).

One big question for the future is the degree to which workplace automation will impact these divides. Routine jobs – those that call for applying explicit rules to work situations, such as cashiers, janitors, and truck drivers – are at the greatest risk of being automated in the future. In the 2012 presidential election, areas with a higher share of routine jobs were more likely to have voted for the Republican candidate (Kolko, 2016). In the 2016 election, counties that voted for Trump had both a greater history of automation and were more likely to be impacted in the future (Muro et al., 2019). This has profound implications for future political polarization, as one study concluded that "automation in recent years tilted the electorate into opting for radical political change" (Frey et al., 2018). Some states are further along this path than others.

Major Cross-Cutting Conflict Issue: Coronavirus

The outbreak of coronavirus (COVID-19) that became a crisis in the U.S. in March 2020 exposed the political fault lines of the major demographic transformations and American politics at its best and worst. As the severity of the crisis first became clear, government officials took unprecedented actions to slow the spread of the virus, bringing the country to a virtual standstill. The U.S. Congress showed a rare moment of bipartisanship, when both houses unanimously passed a relief bill worth over $2 trillion (U.S. Congress, 2020). In the early moments of the crisis, many Americans put politics aside, listened to public officials, and took actions that helped save hundreds of thousands of lives in a show of shared sacrifice for the public good.

Yet, barely a month into the pandemic, politics began to re-emerge. Health officials warned that a false "sense of invulnerability among Millennials" put them and, especially, older people around them, at risk from the disease (Gunia,

2020). The virus's origins in China led to an increase in hate speech and racism toward those of perceived East-Asian descent (Timberg and Chiu, 2020). By mid-April 2020, as once-ascendant urban areas were gripped by severe outbreaks caused by high population density, residents of rural areas in at least ten states protested for governments to relax restrictions on social and economic activity (Jeffery, 2020).

Mixed with all of this are marked differences by socioeconomic status in how the economic shutdown has affected Americans. Higher-income Americans are more likely to have a job where they can work remotely during stay-at-home orders, while lower-income Americans are more likely to be shut out of work by workplace closures. In the pandemic's first months, about half of lower-income adults said that they or someone in their household lost a job or took a pay cut as a result of the coronavirus outbreak, compared with only about a third of upper-income adults (Parker et al., 2020).

It is too early to know what long-term effect coronavirus will have on the country. Will the shared memory of our linked fate bring in a new era of bipartisanship? Or will partisans "not let a crisis go to waste" and seek to score points for their side, at the expense of losing a rare moment of coming together? Raising the stakes during the early crisis response was the rapid approach of the 2020 presidential election, with both sides desperate to win the White House.

Case Study: Florida

No state reflects the challenges associated with significant changes in racial and ethnic and generational makeup as much as Florida – the nation's largest swing state and a microcosm of the United States at large. The Sunshine State's high growth rate, largely driven by domestic and foreign in-migration, has changed the state's politics from a one-party to a highly competitive two-party state in presidential and gubernatorial elections. At the same time, younger, more diverse voters are increasingly registering as independents (NPA), sending the two major political parties scrambling for ways to remain relevant.

Diversity Within Racial and Ethnic Groups

The overall racial and ethnic composition of Florida closely mirrors the nation overall. Florida's resident population is 53 percent non-Hispanic white (compared with 60 percent in the country overall), 26 percent Hispanic (U.S. 18 percent), 15 percent black (U.S. 12 percent), and 3 percent Asian (U.S. 6 percent).[8] While these racial and ethnic groups differ politically and socioeconomically, significant differences exist *within* each group as well (see Table 2.2).

Florida Hispanics, as a group, are notable in that no one origin group dominates the population. Twenty-eight percent are Cuban, 21 percent Puerto

TABLE 2.2 Diversity of National Origin Within Racial and Ethnic Groups in Florida, 2018 (Percentages are share of all Florida Hispanics/Asians that are of that origin group)

Hispanics	Asians
Cuban: 28 percent	Asian Indian: 29 percent
Puerto Rican: 21 percent	Chinese: 19 percent
Mexican: 13 percent	Filipino: 18 percent
Colombian: 7 percent	Vietnamese: 12 percent
Dominican: 4 percent	Korean: 5 percent

Source: Authors' analysis based on U.S. Census Bureau, Table B03001 Hispanic or Latino Origin by Specific Origin, 2018 American Community Survey 1-year estimates and Table B02015 Asian Alone by Selected Groups, 2018 American Community Survey 1-year estimates.

Rican, and 13 percent Mexican, while smaller shares are Colombian (7 percent), Dominican (4 percent), or some other origin. Cubans, one of the few racial and ethnic minority groups to lean Republican, are concentrated in Miami. Puerto Ricans, who are unique among Hispanic groups in that they are already U.S. citizens, frequently settle in Central Florida, around Orlando. By contrast, Mexicans are spread around the state (Wang and Rayer, 2016).

The origins of the Florida Asian population are also diverse. Twenty-nine percent are Indian, 19 percent Chinese, 18 percent Filipino, 12 percent Vietnamese, and 5 percent Korean. The Asian population overall is scattered across the state but is centered in areas near large cities, universities, and other hubs for industries requiring highly skilled workers (Wang and Rayer, 2016). Of course, the socioeconomic outcomes for Asians vary, as for all racial groups, and not all are well off, highly educated, professional workers.

Changes in Florida Voter Registration

Long-term changes in the party affiliation of Florida's registered voters tell the story of the changes that remade the state. In Florida, voters can choose to affiliate with a political party when they register, or they can choose to register as NPA. In 1972, a large majority of Florida voters were registered as Democrats (69 percent), compared with 28 percent who were Republican and only 3 percent who were registered as either NPA or with a minor party.[9] The share of Florida voters registered as Democrats has been falling continuously since then (with a brief jump in 2008), to 37 percent in 2020. The share of voters who were Republican rapidly rose from 1982 to 1994, when 42 percent of voters were registered Republicans. The share has gradually fallen since then, to 35 percent in

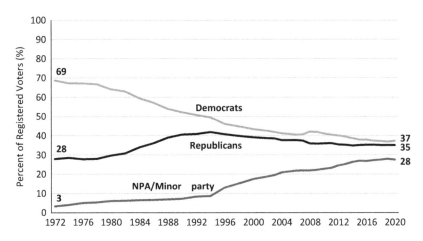

FIGURE 2.4 Florida Registered Voter Party Affiliation, 1972-2020. Note: Data for 2020 as of February 29, 2020.. Source: Florida Division of Elections.

2020. Since 1994, only NPAs have been growing as a share of Florida voters, from just 9 percent in that year to 28 percent in 2020[10] (see Figure 2.4).

Some of this change is due to the changing demographic composition of the state. Hispanics and Asians – the two fastest-growing racial and ethnic groups – are the most likely to register as NPAs. A plurality of Asians (42 percent) are registered NPA, while Hispanics are slightly more likely to register as Democrats than NPA (39 percent vs. 36 percent). The share of blacks among Florida's registered voters has risen only modestly in recent decades, from 11 percent in 2000 to 13 percent in 2018. This has meant that although 80 percent of black registered voters are registered as Democrats, it has not greatly impacted the statewide partisan composition. A plurality of non-Hispanic white voters is registered as Republicans (46 percent), while 28 percent are Democrats and 25 percent are NPAs.

Age is also closely related to likelihood of registering NPA. Among Gen Z registered voters, 38 percent are NPAs – higher than the share registered as Democrats (35 percent) or Republicans (25 percent). The share registering NPA declines with older generations: 35 percent of Millennials, 29 percent of Gen X, 21 percent of Baby Boomers, and 17 percent of the Silent Generation. These disparities speak to a general distrust of the major parties by younger voters as well as the challenge the parties face in remaining relevant to younger voters.

Today, those moving from other states to Florida bring their politics with them. Floridians who formerly lived in the Northeast tend to lean Democratic and are turning the areas they settle in bluer – from traditional Democratic strongholds, such as Broward and Palm Beach counties, to historically red counties, such as Hillsborough, Pinellas, and Orange. New residents from other regions – notably the Midwest – tend to lean Republican and have turned areas into which they move redder – suburban areas such as Pasco County, north of Tampa, and The Villages, a large retirement center northwest of Orlando. In 2016, The Villages gave Trump his largest margin of victory of any place in the state. The point is that Florida's designation as a purple state is not because the state's residents are unusually independent in their opinions, but because the red and blue areas roughly balance out.

Racial and Ethnic Composition of the 2016 Electorate and Voters

In analyzing the racial and ethnic political composition of Florida's over 21 million residents, it is important to distinguish between a group's resident and eligible populations, registered voters, and actual voters. Using Florida's Hispanics as an example, their share of the state's resident population is 25 percent, but only 19 percent of the voting-eligible population (see Table 2.3). It drops to 16 percent once only registered voters are included. (In Florida, those who are eligible must register to be able to vote.) This decline is partially attributable to the fact that first- and second-generation immigrants, with lower educational attainment, are less likely to register. Finally, not all registered voters turn out to vote. Generally, turnout is higher among older, highly educated, and economically well-off adults – a lower share of which is Hispanic, which helps explain the 15 percent Hispanic share of actual voters. The fall-off between these voter participation measures among Hispanics is far flatter among the state's other racial groups due to their lower immigration rates.

TABLE 2.3 Racial Composition of Florida Population, Electorate, and Voters in 2016 Presidential Election (Percentages are share of each population that are of that racial/ethnic group)

	Resident population	Voting-eligible population	Registered voters	Actual Voters
White	55	63	64	67
Black	15	14	13	13
Hispanic	25	19	16	15
Asian	3	2	2	2
Other	2	2	3	2
Unknown	--	--	2	2

Source: Resident population and voting-eligible population from authors' analysis of 2016 American Community Survey (Ruggles, et al., 2019). Registered voters and actual voters from Florida Division of Elections, Florida Voter Registration System (FVRS) extracts.

Note: Columns may not sum to 100% due to rounding. White, black, and Asian are single-race non-Hispanics only. Asian includes Pacific Islanders. Hispanics are of any race. Racial/ethnic identity is not available for a small share of registrants in FVRS data.

Conclusion: Are Demographics Destiny?

With major demographic and socioeconomic trends reshaping America and its politics, one asks: What will happen to the parties?

Both Democrats and Republicans face serious challenges to staying relevant among racial and ethnic minority and younger voters, a higher share of whom identify as independents than older white voters. Both parties are facing another headwind – a rising distrust of, and disengagement from, the two-party system. Some ebullient Democrats see racial changes and generational replacement as ushering in a new, permanent Democratic majority, labeled the "Rising American Electorate" (Voter Participation Center, 2020). In this view, the Democratic Party represents the "coalition of transformation," which welcomes demographic changes. The Republican Party, on the other hand, represents a "coalition of restoration" drawing support from those uncomfortable with those changes (Brownstein, 2012). Further inroads for Republicans, however, may be hard to come by. Some Republicans are pushing to redefine the party as its current base continues to shrink in some states and localities more than others (Republican, 2013). Suburban women, often swing voters, are a key target for the GOP as candidates and voters.

What about partisan polarization? When Americans feel that they are being left behind – or that what they think they deserve is being given to someone else less deserving – they are more susceptible to a zero-sum, us-versus-them platform that increases polarization. Even labeling demographic trends as "problems" needing a "solution" is a framing choice that risks increasing partisanship. Actually, each trend presents both opportunities and challenges for policymakers and Americans together to address.

Looking ahead, observers generally agree that that the U.S. population will continue to age, become more racially and ethnically diverse, and continue transitioning to a more pluralistic population. Less certain is the impact future racial and ethnic changes will have because of "the fluidity of racial and ethnic identity" and the "difficulties of unifying the numerous and widely diverse constituencies referred to as minorities or people of color" (Wilson, 2016).

At a minimum, one thing is sure – the nation's demographics will continue to change. Some changes will be predictable, but others will not. Some will dig deep divides among the populace, while others will bring the nation closer together. Parties and politicians will have to adapt to remain relevant … and in office.

Notes

1 This comparison is based on numeric change in population. Metropolitan areas include all counties within the core urban area and nearby counties with strong commuting ties to it. Therefore, differences in the size of counties are not as much of a concern. Although the exact metro areas in the top ten fastest-growing by percent change are different, all ten are also in the South and West.

2 This is from Bureau of Labor Statistics data for civilian, non-farm employment. All years are as of January 1.

3 Authors' analysis of 1970 and 2019 Current Population Survey, Annual Social and Economic Supplement (Flood et al., 2020).

4 The median age – the age at which half the population is older, and half is younger – for non-Hispanic whites was 43.6 years old in 2018, compared with 37.3 for Asians, 34.4 for blacks, and 29.5 for Hispanics.

5 This analysis includes those born outside the United States to U.S.-citizen parents and those born in U.S. territories (such as Puerto Rico) as being born in the United States.

6 Authors' analysis of 2018 American Community Survey (Ruggles et al., 2020). Whites, blacks, and Asians are single-race non-Hispanics. Asian includes Pacific Islanders. Hispanics are of any race.

7 A third-generation immigrant's grandparents were born in another country. Both they and their parents were born in the United States.

8 Authors' analysis of 2018 American Community Survey (Ruggles et al., 2020). Whites, blacks, and Asians are single-race non-Hispanics. Asian includes Pacific Islanders. Hispanics are of any race.

9 Nearly all those in the NPA/minor party category are registered as NPAs. For example, in 2020, 26 percent of Florida voters were NPAs, compared with just 1 percent registered with a minor party. For this reason, the remainder of this analysis will refer to this group as NPAs.

10 Unless otherwise cited, all figures in this section are based on the authors' analysis of Florida Voter Registration System (FVRS) data from the Florida Division of Elections. The demographic analysis is based on the October 2018 general election book closing extract.

References

Airports Council International, 2019. Preliminary World Airport Traffic Rankings Released. *ACI World*, 13 March.

Bishop, B., 2009. *The Big Sort: Why the Clustering of Like-Minded America Is Tearing Us Apart*. Houghton Mifflin Harcourt.

Brenan, M., 2018. Approval of the Affordable Care Act Falls Back Below 50 Percent. *Gallup*, 30 November.

Brick, C. and van der Linden, S., 2018. How Identity, Not Issues, Explains the Partisan Divide. *Scientific American*, 19 June.

Brownstein, R., 2012. The Coalition of Transformation vs. the Coalition of Restoration. *The Atlantic*, 21 November.

Chappell, B., 2019. U.S. Births Fell to a 32-Year Low in 2018; CDC Says Birthrate Is in Record Slump. *NPR*, 15 May.

Chishti, M., Hipsman, F. and Ball, I., 2015. Fifty Years on, the 1965 Immigration and Nationality Act Continues to Reshape the United States. *Migration Policy Institute*, October, 15.

CNN, 2016. Exit Polls: National President. *CNN Politics*, updated 23 November, https://www.cnn.com/election/2016/results/exit-polls [Accessed 25 April 2020].

Cohn, D. and Caumont, A., 2016. 10 Demographic Trends Shaping the U.S. and the World in 2016. *Pew Research Center*, 31 March.

Congressional Budget Office, 2019. *The 2019 Long-Term Budget Outlook*.

Cox, R., 2013. Schumer Introduces Comprehensive Immigration Reform Bill. *The Hill*, 17 April.

Creek, H. and Ueyama, K., 2017. Why Are Millions of Citizens Not Registered to Vote? *The Pew Charitable Trusts*, June.

Del Real, J.A., 2019. U.S. Judge Blocks Trump Plan to Shift $2.5 Billion to Pay for Border Wall. *New York Times*, 28 June.

Ferguson, N. and Freymann, E., 2019. The Coming Generation War. *The Atlantic*, 6 May.

Flood, S., King, M., Rodgers, R., Ruggles, S. and Warren, J.R., 2020. *Integrated Public Use Microdata Series, Current Population Survey: Version 7.0 Dataset*. Minneapolis, MN: IPUMS.

Frey, C.B., Berger, T. and Chen, C., 2018. Political Machinery: Did Robots Swing the 2016 US presidential election? *Oxford Review of Economic Policy*, 34(3), p. 418.

Frey, W.H., 2018. The US Will Become 'Minority White' in 2045, Census Projects. *Brookings*, 14 March.

Fry, R. and Cilluffo, A., 2019. A Rising Share of Undergraduates Are From Poor Families, Especially at Less Selective Colleges. *Pew Research Center*, 22 May.

Fry, R., Igielnik, R. and Patten, E., 2018. How Millennials Today Compare with Their Grandparents 50 Years Ago. *Pew Research Center*, 16 March.

Gallup. Most Important Problem. https://news.gallup.com/poll/1675/most-important-problem.aspx [Accessed 25 April 2020].

Gould, S. and Bryan, B., 2018. The Diverging Midterm Results Show There's a Growing Political Chasm in America and Both Parties Look Like They're Digging In. *Business Insider*, 12 November.

Gunia, A., 2020. Millennials Aren't Taking Coronavirus Seriously, a Top WHO Official Warns. *Time*, 20 March.

Heyes, C., 2016. Identity Politics. *Stanford Encyclopedia of Philosophy*. Revised 23 March 2016. https://plato.stanford.edu/entries/identity-politics/ [Accessed 25 April 2020].

Horowitz, J.M., 2019. Americans See Advantages and Challenges in Country's Growing Racial and Ethnic Diversity. *Pew Research Center*, 8 May.

Hsu, S.S., 2019. House Appeals Ruling Rejecting Lawsuit to Block Spending on Trump Border Wall. *Washington Post*, 10 June.

Jacobs, P., 2019. Where the Nation's Foreign-Born Live Has Changed Over Time. *U.S. Census Bureau*, 8 May.

Jeffrey, A., 2020. Scenes of Protests Across the Country Demanding States Reopen the Economy Amid Coronavirus Pandemic. *CNBC*, 18 April.

Johnson, K., 2018. Domestic Migration and Fewer Births Reshaping America. *University of New Hampshire Carsey School of Public Policy*, 22 March.

Johnston, R., Manley, D. and Jones, K., 2016. Spatial Polarization of Presidential Voting in the United States, 1992–2012: The "Big Sort" Revisited. *Annals of the American Association of Geographers*, 106(5), pp. 1047–1062.

Jones, N.A. and Bullock, J., 2012. The Two or More Races Population: 2010. *U.S. Census Bureau, 2010 Census Briefs, C2010BR–13*. U.S. Census Bureau, September.

Kamal, R., McDermott, D. and Cox, C., 2019. How Has U.S. Spending on Healthcare Changed over Time? *Peterson-KFF Health System Tracker*, 20 December.

Kenen, J., 2019. Obamacare Fight Obscures America's Real Health Care Crisis: Money. *Politico*, 3 April.

Kolko, J., 2016. Republican-Leaning Cities Are at Greater Risk of Job Automation. *FiveThirtyEight*, 17 February.

Kumar, D., 2018. Rural America Is Losing Young People–Consequences and Solutions. *University of Pennsylvania Wharton Public Policy Initiative*, 23 March.

Liesman, S., 2013. What's in a Name? Lots When It Comes to Obamacare/ACA. *CNBC*, 26 September.

Livingston, G. and Brown, A., 2017. Intermarriage in the US 50 Years after Loving v. Virginia. *Pew Research Center*, 18 May.

López, G. and Krogstad, J.M., 2017. Key Facts About Unauthorized Immigrants Enrolled in DACA. *Pew Research Center*, 25 September.

López, G., Ruiz, N.G. and Patten, E., 2017. Key Facts About Asian Americans, a Diverse and Growing Population. *Pew Research Center*, 8 September.

Lopez, M.H., Gonzalez-Barrera, A. and López, G., 2017. Hispanic Identity Fades Across Generations as Immigrant Connections Fall Away. *Pew Research Center*, 20 December.

MacManus, S.A. and Cilluffo, A., 2019. The Changing Demographics of the South and Its Impact on National Politics. In: Charles S. Bullock III, Susan A. MacManus, Jeremy D. Mayer, and Mark J. Rozell, eds. *The South and the Transformation of American Politics*. Oxford: Oxford University Press.

Matthews, T.J. and Hamilton, B.E., 2019. Total Fertility Rates by State and Race and Hispanic Origin: United States. *Centers for Disease Control and Prevention. National Vital Statistics Reports 68*(1), 10 January.

Maxwell, R., 2019. Why Are Urban and Rural Areas so Politically Divided? *Washington Post*, 5 March.

Muro, M., Whiton, J. and Maxim, R., 2019. Automation Perpetuates the Red-Blue Divide. *Brookings*, 19 March.

National Council of State Legislatures, 2019. Felon Voting Rights. *Elections and Campaigns*, 14 October.

National Immigration Law Center, 2019. Status of Current DACA Litigation. Updated 7 June 2019, https://www.nilc.org/issues/daca/status-current-daca-litigation/ [Accessed 25 April 2020].

NBC News, 2016. Rubio: Gang of 8 Bill Never Intended to Become Law, 15 February.

Newport, F., 2018. Americans Oppose Border Walls, Favor Dealing With DACA. *Gallup*, 20 June.

Norman, J., 2019. Healthcare Once Again Tops List of Americans' Worries. *Gallup*, 1 April.

Overberg, P. and Toppo, G., 2014. Census: Florida's Population Overtakes New York's. *USA Today*, 23 December.

Parker, K., Horowitz, J.M., Brown, A., Fry, R., Cohn, D. and Igielnik, R., 2018. What Unites and Divides Urban, Suburban and Rural Communities. *Pew Research Center*, 22 May.

Parker, K., Graf, N. and Igielnik, R., 2019a. Generation Z Looks a Lot Like Millennials on Key Social and Political Issues. *Pew Research Center*, 17 January.

Parker, K., Morin, R. and Horowitz, J.M., 2019b. Looking to the Future, Public Sees an America in Decline on Many Fronts. *Pew Research Center*, 21 March.

Parket, K., Horowitz, J.M. and Brown, A., 2020. About Half of Lower-Income Americans Report Household Job or Wage Loss Due to COVID-19. *Pew Research Center*, 21 April.

Passel, J., Livingston, G. and Cohn, D., 2012. Explaining Why Minority Births Now Outnumber White Births. *Pew Research Center*, 17 May.

Pew Research Center, 2013. The Rise of Asian Americans. *Pew Research Center*, Updated 4 April.

Pew Research Center, 2015a. America's Changing Religious Landscape. *Pew Research Center*, 12 May.

Pew Research Center, 2015b. Modern Immigration Wave Brings 59 Million to U.S., Driving Population Growth and Change Through 2065. *Pew Research Center*, September 28.

Pew Research Center, 2018. The Generation Gap in American Politics. *Pew Research Center*, 1 March.

Pew Research Center, 2019. Most Border Wall Opponents, Supporters Say Shutdown Concessions are Unacceptable. *Pew Research Center*, 16 January.

Pollard, K.M. and Scommegna, P., 2014. Just How Many Baby Boomers Are There? *Population Reference Bureau*, 16 April.

Radford, J., 2019. Key Findings About U.S. Immigrants. *Pew Research Center*, 17 June.

Republican National Committee, 2013. Growth and Opportunity Project. Released 18 March. https://online.wsj.com/public/resources/documents/RNCreport031820 13.pdf [Accessed 25 April 2020].

Restuccia, A., Everett, B. and Caygle, H., 2019. Longest Shutdown in History Ends After Trump Relents on Wall. *Politico*, 25 January.

Ripley, A., Tenjarla, R. and He, A.Y., 2019. The Geography of Partisan Prejudice. *The Atlantic*, 4 March.

Ruggles, S., Flood, S., Goeken, R., Grover, J., Meyer, E., Pacas, J. and Sobek, M., 2020. *IPUMS USA: Version 10.0 Dataset*. Minneapolis, MN: IPUMS.

Sawyer, B. and Claxon, G., 2019. How Do Health Expenditures Vary Across the Population? *Peterson-KFF Health System Tracker*, 16 January.

Semega, J., Kollar, M., Creamer, J. and Mohanty, A., 2019. Income and Poverty in the United States: 2018. *U.S. Census Bureau, Current Population Reports, P60-266*. U.S. Census Bureau.

Semuels, A., 2017. Poor Girls Are Leaving Their Brothers Behind. *The Atlantic*, 27 November.

Shear, M.D. and Davis, J.H., 2017. Trump Moves to End DACA and Calls on Congress to Act. *New York Times*, 5 September.

Singh, G.K. and Siahpush, M., 2014. Widening Rural–Urban Disparities in Life Expectancy, US, 1969–2009. *American Journal of Preventive Medicine*, 46(2), pp. E19-E29.

Tavernise, S., 2018. Why the Announcement of a Looming White Minority Makes Demographers Nervous. *New York Times*, 22 November.

Taylor, P., 2016. *The Next America: Boomers, Millennials, and the Looming Generational Showdown*. New York: PublicAffairs.

The Sentencing Project, 2020. Felony Disenfranchisement. https://www.sentencingproject. org/ issues/felony-disenfranchisement/ [Accessed 25 April 2020].

Timberg, C. and Chiu, A., 2020. As the Coronavirus Spreads, so Does Online Racism Targeting Asians, New Research Shows. *The Washington Post*, April 8.

Toppo, G. and Overberg, P., 2015. After Nearly 100 Years, Great Migration Begins Reversal. *USA Today*, Updated 18 March.

Torpey, E., 2018. Measuring the Value of Education. *U.S. Bureau of Labor Statistics, Career Outlook*, April.

Trevelyan, E., 2016. Immigrant Voting in the United States. *U.S. Census Bureau Random Samplings*, 30 November.

United Nations Population Division, 2018. *World Urbanization Prospects, The 2018 Revision*.

U.S. Bureau of Labor Statistics, 2018. Spending Patterns of Millennials and Earlier Generations in 2016. *U.S. Bureau of Labor Statistics, the Economics Daily*, 1 August.

U.S. Census Bureau, 2012. United States Summary Population and Housing Unit Counts. *2010 Census of Population and Housing, Report CPH-2-1*.

U.S. Census Bureau, 2018a. 2017 National Population Projections Tables: Main Series. https://www.census.gov/data/tables/2017/demo/popproj/2017-summary-tables.ht ml [Accessed 25 April 2020].

U.S. Census Bureau, 2019a. Older People Projected to Outnumber Children for First Time in U.S. History. *Release Number CB18-41*.

U.S. Census Bureau, 2019b. *Table B02001: Race, 2018 ACS 1-Year Estimates*. Released 26 September [Accessed 25 April 2020].

U.S. Census Bureau, 2019c. *Table B05001: Nativity and Citizenship Status in the U.S., 2018 ACS 1-Year Estimates*. Released 26 September [Accessed 25 April 2020].

U.S. Census Bureau, 2019d. Voting and Registration in the Election of November 2018. *Release No. P20*.

U.S. Census Bureau, 2020. Most of the Counties with the Largest Population Gains Since 2010 Are in Texas. *Release Number CB20-53*.

U.S. Citizenship and Immigration Services, Office of Policy and Strategy, 2016. *Trends in Naturalization Rates: FY 2014 Update*, November.

U.S. Congress, 2020. H.R. 748, Coronavirus Aid, Relief, and Economic Security (CARES) Act.

U.S. Department of Agriculture, 2020. Opioid Misuse in Rural America. https://www.usda.gov/topics/opioids [Accessed 25 April 2020].

Vespa, J., Medina, L. and Armstrong, D.M., 2020. Demographic Turning Points for the United States: Population Projections for 2020 to 2060. *U.S. Census Bureau, Current Population Reports, P25-1144*. U.S. Census Bureau, Updated February.

Voter Participation Center, 2020. The Rising American Electorate. The Voter Participation Center. https://www.voterparticipation.org/our-research/ [Accessed 25 April 2020].

Wang, Y. and Rayer, S., 2016. Foreign in-Migration to Florida, 2005–2014. *University of Florida Bureau of Economic and Business Research*, 15 April.

Wilson, V., 2016. People of Color Will Be a Majority of the American Working Class in 2032. *Economic Policy Institute*, 9 June.

Wright, B., 2012. Why Are 51 Million Eligible Americans Not Registered to Vote? *Demos*, 1 November.

Zakaria, F., 2016. It's No Longer the Economy, Stupid: Our Identity Politics Are Polarizing Us. *Washington Post*, 15 September.

3

THE POLARIZATION OF THE MEDIA

Sara Gorman

Rep. Patrick E. Murphy: The impact of media, both mainstream and social, on our political climate is one of the most important to understand and one of the hardest to address or fix. Taking this chapter a step further and connecting it to a political campaign is alarming. Ms. Gorman notes that there is more polarization among the most politically active individuals, who are the people who tend to vote in primary elections. As a result of gerrymandering (addressed in a subsequent chapter), most congressional districts are basically pre-determined to be either Democratic or Republican, so the only election that truly matters is the primary. In a primary – where voter turnout is almost always lower – less than 15% of the population determines the next member of Congress from that district. If this small percentage is more polarized, influenced by "fake news," hyper-partisan media personalities, and living in an echo chamber, the politicians elected will reflect these views.

Once in office, the member basically has no choice but to continue spewing outlandish beliefs and conspiracies in order to get re-elected. That is because in two years, that same 15% of hyper-partisan voters will be dependably showing up to the polls. As this plays out cycle after cycle, both Democrats and Republicans are losing moderates to more extreme members of their parties. With fewer moderates there is less meaningful compromise and debate, and instead more grandstanding about politically buzzy topics. Politicians have an incentive to say more controversial and outlandish things as a way to appeal to the most politically active members of their party. Not only does this lead to more followers and articles and tweets, but it typically leads to more fundraising as well. The more money a candidate has, the better their chances at re-election and moving up in party leadership. So while there is an honest debate to be had as to the effect of media polarization on the broader population, there is no doubt those who are voting in primaries and determining a majority of congressional elections are becoming more polarized and politically impactful.

Rep. David Jolly: The media's influence on today's politics and the decisions made by today's politicians cannot be overstated. Not because of the professional scrutiny and investigations that defined journalism of past generations, but instead because we now live in an age of information where television networks and social media platforms deliver to politicians a relatively highly informed audience with predictable and narrowly tailored political viewpoints. The audience of today's media platforms is typically not looking for the news; the audience is looking to be told their politicians agree with their perspective on the news. Thus, the reward for politicians to deliver to that audience a highly energized, partisan message is clear – more votes, more contributions, more national exposure among the respective ideological constituency. Conversely, there is simply little electoral reward for the politician who delivers to that audience a more sober, cross-partisan message, and thus little reason for those politicians to step out in the spotlight with a message that may otherwise be of critical importance to the national conversation.

My time in politics provided a few takeaways regarding how to approach and study the media's handling of political issues. As a baseline matter, consider whether the platform is engaged in news reporting or editorializing. The clearest example of this is often found in your local print newspaper. The news stories are obvious – for example, the local school board meeting, a criminal activity report, a transportation challenge or solution, or a human-interest matter. Editorials or opinion columns in newspapers often sit in their own section and are labeled as such. The challenge in print, digital, and network media is to spot the crossover areas and to then determine whether it is a deliberate trait of that particular news product, or whether it is candidly poor journalism, in which the author may even fail to recognize their own subjectivity.

An example of the latter follows. Suppose a politician runs on promising to increase education spending by $10 over the previous year. After getting elected, the politician manages to increase education spending by $5. Is the story that the politician managed to increase spending on education, or is the story that the politicians misled the public with their campaign promise and instead cut education by $5 from the target? This is a real example that plays out in Congress almost annually during consideration of federal spending. If the current trajectory for Medicare is to increase spending by $600 billion over the next five years, but a party instead wants to increase it by $500 billion, are they raising spending by $500 billion, or cutting it by $100 billion?

Politicians can deliver a political message on the above examples with broad license. But the challenge for reporters has traditionally been how to contextualize the news without too much subjectivity. Not so much anymore. Most of the leading news sources on politics unapologetically take the subjective approach to confirm the natural political biases of their audiences. Media in the United States, after all, is a for-profit endeavor. Until a media outlet finds a profit motive in objectivity that appears greater than the subjective, we likely will remain burdened by and reward media platforms that merely align with our natural political biases rather than challenge them.

It may seem evident that the American public is more politically polarized today than ever before. Partisan debates seem to rage in person and especially online in various forms of social media. Yet before discussing ways in which the traditional media may be polarized and may be having a polarizing effect on the American public, it will be important to understand the extent of the polarization problem in the first place.

On the one hand, there is some evidence that the American public has become more divided on a wide array of political issues. The percentage of people who hold consistently liberal or conservative views, as opposed to some combination of the two, has risen from 10 percent to 20 percent over the course of the past two decades (De-Wit et al., 2019). This is of course not an insignificant shift in the political composition of the general public. It means that it has become significantly less common for Americans to hold views from one party on some political issues and views from the other on other issues. Instead, people are falling in line with a single party more consistently across a range of issues. There is certainly anecdotal evidence that a certain type of polarization called "affective polarization," in which dislike of the other group increases, is on the rise, given the kind of vicious debates we often see on social media among people of different political parties.

On the other hand, there are many who argue that the idea that the American public has become extremely segregated into different ideological groups that live in their respective "echo chambers" has been exaggerated (Prior, 2013; Wong, 2016). The argument here is that the vast majority of Americans are still moderate and that even if political parties have become more extreme, most Americans still occupy an ideological space that lies somewhere in the middle. On most issues, according to this argument, the vast majority of Americans continue to take moderate positions (Prior, 2013). Along with this argument comes the notion that there is really no evidence that mainstream media sources themselves have become more polarized, even if political party members who appear in mainstream media have become more polarized (Prior, 2013).

The reality is probably somewhere in between these two viewpoints. While the vast majority of Americans most likely hold on to more moderate beliefs, the people at the extreme ends of the political spectrum on both sides have become significantly more polarized. This is important because these people tend to be the most politically engaged and the people who are most likely to vote and actually influence elections (Mitchell and Weisel, 2014). A recent year-long study looked at ways people got information about politics and government on news media, on social media, and how they talked to friends and family about it. The study categorized individuals as "consistently liberal," "consistently conservative," or as having mixed views. The authors found that those who were categorized as consistently liberal or consistently conservative had very different information streams than those with mixed views. In addition, as might be expected, their information streams were distinct from each other, with basically no overlap in sources accessed to get news and other information (Mitchell and Weisel, 2014).

There were some interesting differences in the media diets of consistent conservatives and consistent liberals. Consistent conservatives were found to be tightly clustered around a single news source, with 47 percent citing Fox News as the main source of their information about politics and the government; express greater distrust than trust of 24 of the 36 news sources mentioned in the study; be more likely to have friends who shared their political views; be more likely to hear political opinions in line with their own when on Facebook. Consistent liberals were found to be more likely to be less unified in their media loyalty, relying on a wider array of news outlets; express more trust than distrust of 28 of the 36 news sources presented in the study; be more likely than those in other political groups to block or "defriend" someone on Facebook due to political views; be more likely to follow issue-based groups rather than political parties or candidates on Facebook (Mitchell and Weisel, 2014). It is not quite clear why these differences between avid followers of these two political parties differ in these ways. Nonetheless, it is important to note how these highly politically engaged members of the American public consume information about political issues. The extreme media loyalty to only several news sources and vast distrust of most mainstream media outlets seen among consistent conservatives is concerning and suggestive of more of an "echo chamber" existence, as is the tendency of consistent liberals to "block" or "defriend" people who do not share their political views.

Overall, this study did seem to show that those on the extreme left and extreme right (consistent liberals and consistent conservatives) basically live in echo chambers. Consistent conservatives and consistent liberals are both more likely to follow politicians and political groups on social media, which makes their feeds much more polarized. In personal conversations, those on the far left and far right are more likely to consistently hear views that align with their own thinking. Only 25 percent of people with mixed views agreed with this statement as compared to 52 percent of consistent liberals and 66 percent of consistent conservatives. The vast majority of people with mixed views reported seeing a variety of viewpoints reflected on their social media feeds – only about 23 percent of those with mixed views say the posts they see are nearly always or mostly in line with their own political views. On the other hand, 47 percent of consistent conservatives say the posts they see are nearly always or mostly in line with their own political views and 32 percent of consistent liberals say the same. Sixty-six percent of consistent conservatives and 52 percent of consistent liberals report that their friends share their political views, compared to 36 percent of those with mixed views. Of those with mixed views, 79 percent report disagreeing about politics at least sometimes with their closest discussion partners, compared to only 53 percent of consistent conservatives and 41 percent of consistent conservatives (Mitchell and Weisel, 2014).

What we see here is certainly more polarization among the most politically engaged individuals. This polarization has led to a situation in which the extreme ends of the political spectrum are less and less likely to even have exposure to the arguments and ideas of the other side. They surround themselves in person and on social media with like-minded individuals only. They remain mostly loyal to several news sources that are distinct from the news sources with which the other side engages. At the same time, the political parties themselves have become increasingly polarized and even people with more moderate views tend to stick to one side in voting behaviors. This has meant that politics have become more polarized, with elite politicians on either side holding very distinct views from each other. Even if the media is simply reflecting the elite politicians' views, because those views have become so polarized, the media will naturally become more polarized as a result. So while not every member of the American public may be more polarized now than before, it is safe to say that the overall political scene has become more polarized, that the most politically engaged members of the populace have become more extreme, and that even our mainstream media sources have become more polarized insofar as they are reflecting an increasingly polarized political scene.

Does Media Polarization Cause Political Polarization?

Once we have established that Americans are more politically polarized now than in previous decades, at least among the most politically engaged members of each party, it is tempting to believe that the media, which we see as increasingly polarized, is a major cause here. But whether or not media polarization causes political polarization is still an open question. A recent Reuters Institute study found that American media sources are more polarized than media sources in other countries (Edkins, 2017). But what effect does this actually have on the general public?

Some scholars have suggested that highly partisan media is the primary incubator and disseminator of disinformation today. That is, partisan media may do more than polarize people – it may even lead to misperceptions that cause people to be misinformed. As Mitchell and Weisel put it, partisan media sources are "combining decontextualized truths, repeated falsehoods, and leaps of logic to create a fundamentally misleading view of the world" (Mitchell and Weisel, 2014). This pattern may not be entirely new. Some have suggested that the American far right has a history of exploiting new media to advance an ideological agenda from anti-communist radio in the 1950s to right-wing talk radio in the 1990s (Mitchell and Weisel, 2014). Some of the most well-known far-right hyperpartisan media sources today include *Breitbart*, *The Daily Caller*, *Infowars*, *The Gateway Pundit*, and *The Washington Examiner*. Hyperpartisan sources do of course also exist on the left. Some of the most well-known far-left hyperpartisan media sources today include *Occupy Democrats*, *Addicting Info*, *Daily Newsbin*, and *Bipartisan Report*. However, it is well-documented that these far-left media sources are less influential among liberals than center-left or mainstream news sources (Mitchell and Weisel, 2014). The U.S. media environment is therefore asymmetrically polarized. The far right is a dense, tightly-linked network of sources that are generally isolated from mainstream media sources, whereas the far left is much more integrated into mainstream media (Mitchell and Weisel, 2014).

In many ways, hyperpartisan news is more important to understand than fake news. Hyperpartisan news is much more likely to be shared on Facebook and much more influential than fake news (Mitchell and Weisel, 2014). Encountering hyperpartisan news is not limited to the hyperpartisan news sources listed above. Indeed, mainstream news can have polarizing effects. As Arceneaux and Johnson point out, news sources spend a lot of their time reporting on where parties stand on particular issues (Arceneaux and Johnson, 2013). If the political elites are highly polarized on a particular issue, the mainstream news will report these polarized views, even if the news source itself is not partisan. In this way, the media can act as megaphones of politically polarized viewpoints. This gives people the impression that their parties are extremely polarized and pushes their personal viewpoints to the extremes (Mitchell and Weisel, 2014). What is important to recognize here is first that party elites may be more responsible for polarization than the media is on its own. That is, without the polarization already occurring among party elites, it would be difficult for the media on its own to cause polarization in the general population. But also, and perhaps more importantly, the news practice of giving equal voice to both sides might actually be working against us in this case. While normally we might think that it is essential that the media represent all sides of an issue to ensure a thoroughly informed general public, in the case of many political issues today, the media's harping on the divides in and extremes of political elites may be creating a situation in which the general public is becoming more polarized.

It may seem logical that exposing people to ideas from the other side might ultimately make them less polarized and that therefore the media's practice of always giving equal voice to both sides of the debate is instrumental in reducing polarization. However, this is not always the case. In fact, several studies have shown the opposite to be true. In one study, engaging with both pro- and counter-attitudinal websites was positively associated with stronger "in-group mentality" than exposure to pro-attitudinal websites alone. This is to say that people who saw both attitudes that agreed with theirs and those that did not were more likely to become more entrenched in their original views. Users who hear both sides of the argument are more likely to become even more convinced of their own opinions than users who are exposed only to views confirming their opinions (Mitchell and Weisel, 2014).

A 2013 study by Druckman and colleagues demonstrates how people tend to respond to polarization (or non-polarization) among political elites. In this study, subjects were shown a strong argument and a weak counter-argument and then placed in different conditions regarding what they were told about political elites' polarization on the relevant issue. When subjects were told that elites were not polarized, they changed their opinions toward the stronger argument they had been shown. When subjects were told that political elites were moderately polarized, they first agreed with the stronger argument but after being shown the weaker argument tended to revert to their party's position. When subjects were told that elites were deeply divided on the issue, they tended to align their attitudes consistently with whatever they were told was their party's position regardless of strength of argument (Mitchell and Weisel, 2014). These results suggest that the perception of polarization among elites has a major effect on actual polarization among the general public. When people perceive that political elites are deeply divided, they tend to dig their heels into the views of their party even more. When this happens, people are less likely to carefully evaluate arguments and respond to factual information. To be certain, the media has a large role to play in the perception people have of elite polarization. The more the media harps on the divided political situation among political elites, the more extreme the general public becomes. In this way, a partisan media slant is not necessary for polarization (Prior, 2013). All that is required is strong and frequent representation of a situation of dividedness among political elites.

In many cases, the media may not be able to change the way people think about an issue. On deeply divided issues such as climate change, people take their cues from what the political elites in their parties say and the content of what the media reports on these issues may have very little influence and very little ability to change people's minds. Nonetheless, there is research to suggest that the media can affect policy by influencing which topics the public and policy-makers focus on. In a recent study by King and colleagues, groups of two to five mostly small online U.S. media outlets wrote stories on broad subjects chosen by the experimenters, such as climate, immigration, and education policy. Each cluster of stories ran on these outlets for one or two consecutive weeks. The authors then assessed the influence of the stories by comparing outcomes in the treatment week in which the stories ran to the control week in which they did not run. The authors focused on the discussion of the chosen topic on Twitter during the time the story ran. Each cluster of stories in the study generated more than 13,000 additional Twitter posts by more than 7,000 unique authors in the week following publication. This represented a 10 percent increase relative to the typical weekly volume of posts on these topics on Twitter in general. The suggestion here is that even "small media" can have a major influence and that the media is extremely influential in determining which topics get discussed in the policy environment.

How Do People Absorb Information from the Media and Online?

In thinking about how people may become polarized by what they are exposed to in the media and online on social media, it is important to have a clearer understanding of how people absorb this kind of political information, what sorts of biases get in the way of pure understanding of the content, and what psychological mechanisms might influence our response.

It turns out that Americans are exquisitely sensitive to political symbols and that even suggesting the possibility of a partisan viewpoint on a particular issue can completely change the way we interpret information. For example, in one study, subjects were randomized to a social media anonymous group, a social media explicit political identity group, and a social media "symbolic" identity group. In the anonymous group, information was presented as is with no suggestion of political stance. In the explicit identity group, information was presented as being either Democratic or Republican in nature. In the symbolic identity group, information was presented along with a symbol of a political party, such as a donkey or elephant, in a subtle place at the bottom of the screen. All subjects were then exposed to a NASA graph about sea level changes by 2025. They were then asked to forecast sea ice-level changes by 2025 using the information from the graph. In the anonymous group, users correctly predicted changes by 2025, thereby essentially reinforcing the existence of climate change. But as soon as subtle cues of party affiliation were shown at the bottom of the screen, more than half of people changed their answers and responded incorrectly. This suggests that even subtle cues of party affiliation can interfere with our ability to correctly analyze and absorb facts and information (AAAS, 2018).

As discussed above, it is not at all clear that simple exposure to ideas from the other side is enough to reduce polarization. In fact, in some cases, this kind of exposure can increase polarization. In one study of 1,220 Republican and Democratic Twitter users, subjects followed bots retweeting elected officials, media sources, and opinion leaders from the other side. They then filled out surveys about partisan political issues and ranked their views on a seven-point scale from most conservative to most liberal. The study found an increase in issue-based polarization after a month of exposure to ideas from the other side. The suggestion here is that it is not *any* contact with the other side that can change minds. It has to be positive contact, there needs to be shared goals, and there needs to be a reason for cooperation. Forcing people to encounter views from the other side is much more likely to backfire than to change their minds (Klein, 2018). In addition, it has been shown that when counter-attitudinal and pro-attitudinal messages are consumed at the same time, the effects of counter-attitudinal messages are diluted. Thus, if people are consuming a lot of partisan media and then get exposed to counter-attitudinal messages, the effect of this exposure is limited (Garrett et al., 2014).

We have also seen how sensitive people are to the suggestion that something might be political. When a story on something non-political is suddenly framed in a political way, people change the way they absorb the information about the fundamentally non-political issue. For example, in one experiment, participants were shown one of three stories about Zika: one that focused purely on public health information, one that asserted that climate change could accelerate the virus's spread, and one that linked Zika to illegal immigration. The stories affected subjects' views of Zika depending on their pre-existing worldview. People who were concerned about illegal immigration but not climate change became concerned about Zika when it was linked to immigration but less concerned when it was linked to climate change. People who saw climate change as high-risk but illegal immigration as low-risk were equally worried about Zika when given the public health story or the Zika-global warming story but were less concerned when confronted with the illegal immigration story. All of this suggests that the framing of any story within policy-related or political issues can completely change the way people interpret the facts in the story. Rather than being able to see Zika for what it is – a public health threat that should be taken seriously no matter what – people's response to the same set of facts completely changes when the story is framed in different ways that touch on policy issues that are of more and less importance to them.

Suggestions of partisanship can radically alter the way people approach scientific information as well. In a 2015 experiment, Bolson and Druckman found that subjects tend to disbelieve scientific evidence when it is presented as being highly subject to partisan disputes. On the other hand, when subjects are told there is a scientific consensus and the issue is not highly partisan, they tend to agree with the scientific consensus (Mitchell and Weisel, 2014). This of course suggests that our reaction to and interpretation of even straightforward, factual information is subject to a great deal of manipulation based on our understanding of the potential political context. The more polarized the political context, the farther we often get from simply wanting to understand the facts and the more prone we are to falling prey to misinformation.

There are also other, superficial signals that can drastically change the way we evaluate information, especially in a complex policy environment. For example, repetitive exposure to false information can make it more credible. In one study, investigators found that subjects who were exposed to fake news headlines repeatedly were much more likely to think they were true than those who were exposed to them for the first time. This effect persisted for several weeks after the initial repeated exposure to the headlines, even when subjects were told that the contents were disputed (Mitchell and Weisel, 2014). There are also recency effects, in which people believe that the most recent information is automatically the most accurate. This has been shown to be the case in experiments utilizing Twitter. In these cases, subjects exposed to different Twitter feeds were most likely to trust the ones that were most recently updated (Mitchell and Weisel, 2014). These two phenomena of recency and frequency are significant because they represent the tactics of many fake news sources and even highly partisan, heavily ideological sources. These sources tend to repeatedly expose people to the same ideas and do so frequently. They may therefore be particularly convincing to people.

Perceptions of how other people are responding to particular news items can also be very influential and shape a lot of what people see in their social media feeds. The "endorsement heuristic" is the phenomenon in which people trust particular pieces of information more because they have the perception that other people trust that information. Internet users in particular tend to rely heavily on this heuristic in making sense of the many pieces of information they are regularly exposed to online. In one study, Li and Sakamoto found that suggesting to users that others were very likely to endorse and share a particular piece of information made them much more likely to share it themselves, regardless of whether they actually believed the information was true, false, or debatable. This last point is particularly important. It essentially tells us that social cues are so strong that they have the ability to override people's sense of what is true and what is false. That is, social influence is so powerful that most people are willing to put aside their general perception about the basic quality of the information (e.g., whether it is true or false) in service of fitting in better with the endorsement of a larger social group (Mitchell and Weisel, 2014).

The emotional salience of different messages also has the capacity to change the way we approach their basic information. Messages that evoke anger often result in less scrutiny and more "motivationally directed" interpretation. That is, when our anger is evoked, we are more likely to interpret information in a way that agrees with what we already believe and is in line with the political party we support. When anxiety is evoked, on the other hand, we tend to more carefully scrutinize messages, attempting to understand accuracy. In these cases, we are less prone to politically motivated, partisan reasoning (Mitchell and Weisel, 2014). This is especially important to understand, as messages that evoke anger are more likely to become viral.

What Role Does Social Media Play?

Now that we understand how the media impacts polarization and how people absorb information and the various psychological influences on that process, we would be remiss not to address the specific case of social media in examining this concept of media polarization. It is common to hear the refrain that social media has made us more polarized and more extreme. However, it is not entirely clear that this is borne out by the evidence. For one thing, polarization is often highest among groups that use social media the least, who tend to be elderly individuals (De-Wit, et al., 2019). It is likely too simplistic to blame social media for the polarizing effects we are seeing today, when much more complex factors are probably at play, including increasing income inequality and diverging political leaders (Boxell et al., 2017).

Nonetheless, there is some convincing evidence that social media can play a role in extreme political views, in spreading misinformation, and in polarizing the general public. This is especially important because some have suggested that social media may be influencing traditional media, and not just the other way around (De-Wit, et al., 2019). As with traditional media, exposure to more partisan material on social media and the perception of highly partisan debates may lead to a very different interpretation of factual information. In one 2015 study looking at tweets surrounding the UK parliamentary elections, exposure to partisan tweets shifted voter assessment of information about the economy and immigration in a direction that was favorable to their preferred party's platform. Non-partisan tweets on the same subjects led to more factually accurate assessments of the content (Mitchell and Weisel, 2014).

Other studies have confirmed that when individuals are exposed to partisan information on social media, affective polarization, the phenomenon in which negative views of the opposing side are exacerbated, tends to increase (Mitchell and Weisel, 2014). Even though social media may lead to exposure to more diverse views, many of these encounters with the "other side" tend to be highly negative and lead to increased feelings of disdain, which is the essence of affective polarization. Indeed, people are more likely to share highly emotional and moral messages on social media, which have a greater capacity for increasing bipartisan disdain and affective polarization. Researchers have found that moral–emotional words in tweets on polarizing issues, such as gun control and climate change, make those messages significantly more likely to be shared on Twitter (Mitchell and Weisel, 2014).

There is no question that social media has the capacity to increase feelings of disdain for the "other side" and therefore contributes to affective polarization especially. To the extent that social media may influence traditional media and to the extent that more and more people get their news on social media, these are important considerations for any examination of media polarization and the increasing political divides among members of the general public.

Conclusion: What to Do About Polarization

In trying to formulate responses to polarization, it is essential but nonetheless challenging to first establish what an ideal solution might look like. It is understood, of course, that the objective is not to eliminate differences of opinion or to create complete homogeneity. We recognize that people will join groups that hold particular points of view and that there will be vigorous debate and disagreements among people in any open society.

We might decide, however, that the inability to consider other points of view is the pernicious element of polarization. Furthermore, the characterization of those who hold different points of view as somehow "evil" is regrettable. Essentially, without discouraging people from holding strong points of view, a reasonable goal might be to encourage tolerance of others and sufficient flexibility so that minds can change when a sufficiently strong argument is presented that merits a shift in opinion or belief.

Given that as a goal, the next, and equally difficult, challenge is to understand how tolerance and flexibility might be accomplished. We can attempt to apply some of the principles and empirical research described so far in this chapter to formulate approaches that will promote flexibility and tolerance.

First, it is essential to change the usual focus from those with hardened views on either side of an issue and concentrate on the large majority of people who are undecided or deciding. For example, we are unlikely to influence someone who has made a career of claiming that vaccines are harmful and attempting to do so invariably involves engaging in rancorous debate. Similarly, an individual who heads an anti-nuclear energy organization is not the person who will be influenced by scientific evidence about nuclear energy's benefits and safety. But most people do not write articles, lead partisan organizations, or picket in front of corporate headquarters. According to Ferber, "On any given issue, a group of people will contain 20 percent at each end of the spectrum who are so deeply dug in they'll never be convinced" (Ferber, 2018). Focusing on the 60 percent of individuals who are either followers of such people or potential followers is more likely to help develop a substantial group of people who are open to listening to both sides of an issue and making decisions based on the best available evidence.

Next, despite frequent warnings that "facts alone" are insufficient to sway opinions, evidence suggests that *both* facts and stories are necessary to sway public opinion toward the middle ground. With regard to the former, fact-checking and providing accurate and timely information that counteracts fake news and misinformation is effective in helping people sort out what is actually known about an issue from mere opinion (Motta et al., 2018). It is also the case, however, that facts must be presented in language that people understand, free of jargon and inflammatory language (Lee, 2017).

At the same time, it is definitely the case that we respond strongly to stories. Journalists know this, and frequently begin their articles with a gripping depiction of one individual's experience (van Laer and Gordon, 2017). This sometimes irritates scientists, who decry drawing conclusions from small samples. Although they are correct that a single example is always insufficient to make valid conclusions, that stance ignores the simple fact that stories are a persuasive method for attracting attention to an issue. The obvious conclusion is that an effective method for presenting issues to people is to combine emotional stories with clearly and simply presented facts. In doing so, it is important to keep in mind that the job of the journalist is not to drive people toward one pole or the other but to provide sufficient information that permits people to accept the reality that there may be multiple, well-intentioned points of view about an issue.

Another important innovation is to use the power of charismatic and celebrated individuals to portray the ability to change one's mind in the face of evidence as a positive attribute. In political campaigns, candidates are often accused of "flip-flopping" and criticized if a current position or statement differs from something once held, even if in the candidate's distant past. This creates the impression that complete consistency in viewpoint is essential and virtuous. It is indeed extremely difficult for individuals to admit they are wrong (Wong, 2017). We know from science, on the other hand, that the ability to change conclusions and beliefs in the face of new evidence is the only path toward ascertaining truth. The example of Albert Einstein's repudiation of a theory he developed about a "gravitational constant" is often used in science to show that highly respected individuals can change their minds without suffering permanent reputational damage.[1] We advocate the presentation to the public of many more instances in which people who have gained widespread respect acknowledge that new evidence has resulted in a change of belief.

There also needs to be a reconsideration of what we mean by "fair balance." Once again, presenting all sides of a complex and controversial issue is clearly a virtue, but as we have noted above, it also inadvertently gives voice to iconoclasts who hold clearly spurious beliefs. Today, in a discussion of environmental risks for cancer, no respectable journalist would dedicate space to anyone claiming that cigarette smoking is safe, even though there are actually still such individuals extant. To do so might mislead readers into thinking that there is a legitimate debate about the carcinogenic effects of tobacco use. In a similar vein, journalists need to reconsider whether "fair balance" in some instances entails promoting ideas about which there is a clear consensus. At the very least, when presenting outlier ideas, we need to do a much better job at explaining that not only are these not accepted by most experts, there is good reason they are not.

Finally, we need to have heightened respect for the power of social affiliation in the formation and maintenance of ideas and beliefs. Let us imagine an individual who is a member of a hypothetical group that believes that a particular food additive – we will call it Compound A – is dangerous and should be banned. This individual spends a great time communicating and socializing with other members of the group. If strong evidence emerges that Compound A is not only not harmful but in fact beneficial to human health and should in fact be added to more foods, our anti-Compound A individual is in a difficult position. As an individual, if he changes his position and now believes Compound A is safe, he will have very little ability to increase the amount of Compound A that actually winds up in food. But changing his mind gives him great power to aggravate the members of his social group and result in his losing friends and becoming isolated. One way of dealing with this is to help people see that there are other people facing the same dilemmas and thus providing the possibility of alternative social groups.

To summarize, we suggest several possible media-driven solutions to polarization. First, concentrating efforts on people who are not iconoclastic leaders of opinion groups but still open to tolerance and flexibility. Second, using both clearly and simply put facts and emotionally driven stories to make the case for alternative points of view. Also, the media ought to provide examples of respected people changing their minds about an issue when new and convincing evidence is presented. And lastly, we must respect the power of social affiliation in belief formulation and maintenance and highlight alternative social groups that hold more tolerant and flexible opinions. All of these solutions hinge on a proper understanding of the concept of "fair balance" so that it continues to mean the presentation of all sides of an issue without giving pulpits to those who hold clearly spurious ideas that violate the consensus of experts.

Note

1 In fact, Einstein's gravitational constant turned out not to be the mistake he came to believe it was, and is now incorporated into theories of dark energy.

References

AAAS, 2018. Can social media networks reduce political polarization on climate change? *EurekAlert*, 13 September. https://www.eurekalert.org/pub_releases/2018-09/uo p-csm 082918.php.

Arceneaux, K., and Johnson, M., 2013. *Changing Minds or Changing Channels? Partisan News in an Age of Choice*. Chicago, IL: University of Chicago Press.

Boxell, L., Gentzkow, M., and Shapiro, J.M., 2017. Is media driving Americans apart? *The New York Times*, 6 December.

De-Wit, L., Brick, C., and Van Der Linden, S., 2019. Are social media driving political polarization? *greatergood. berkeley. Edu.*

Edkins, B., 2017. Report: U.S. Media Among most polarized in the world. *Forbes*, 27 June.

Ferber, D., 2018. Fighting back against 'alternative facts': Experts share their secrets. *Science. Mag.org*, 17 February.

Garrett, R.K., Gvirsman, S.D., Johnson, B.K., Tsfati, Y., Neo, R., and Dal, A., 2014. Implications of pro-and counterattitudinal information exposure for affective polarization. *Human Communication Research*, 40(3), pp. 309–332.

King, G., Schneer, B., and White, A., 2017. "How the News Media Activate Public Expression and Influence National Agendas," *Science*, 358, pp. 776–780.

Klein, E., 2018. When Twitter users hear out the other side, they become more polarized: Echo chambers aren't what's polarizing America. *Vox*, 18 October.

Lee, B.Y., 2017. Study re-emphasizes: If you want to advance science, try explaining it more simply. *Forbes*, 26 March.

Mitchell, A. and Weisel, R., 2014. Political polarization and media habits. *Pew Research Center*, 21 October.

Motta, M., Stecula, D., and Haglin, K., 2018. Countering misinformation about flu vaccine is harder than it seems. *The Conversation*, 6 December.

Prior, M., 2013. Media and political polarization. *Annual Review of Political Science*, 16(1), pp.101–127.

Van Laer, T. and Gordon, R., 2017. How telling the right stories can make people act on climate change. *The Conversation*, 6 November.

Wong, K., 2017. Why it's so hard to admit you're wrong. *The New York Times*, 22 May.

Wong, M., 2016. Matthew Gentzkow on the media, political polarization and the power of data. *Stanford SIEPR*, 14 July.

4

GERRYMANDERING

Brian Amos

Rep. Patrick E. Murphy: After serving in the House of Representatives for four years, I believe gerrymandering is the single biggest driver of partisanship in our country today. There are around 50 swing districts in the country right now, which means that about 90% of congressional districts are already predetermined to be Republican or Democratic. And as has been analyzed in previous chapters, the most politically active voters, or that small percentage of about 15% who vote in primaries, are becoming more ingrained in their political beliefs. Therefore, roughly 15% of our country is determining about 90% of our members of Congress! So if you're a candidate running for office, your first job is to pander to that small group of voters because ultimately, they will decide your fate.

Much of the extremism we see in our politics starts with this perverse incentive to only target a small group of voters with a message that will resonate with them. As partisan media outlets help prop up more extreme messages and personalities, it follows that candidates will raise more money by generating more followers or airtime – and the enticement to be more partisan actually increases. There were numerous instances during committee hearings I sat in where members of Congress were asking identical partisan questions to those testifying. I didn't realize it at first, but they were all simply trying to have the press capture the same soundbite of divisive attacks that would appeal to those ultra-partisan voters in their districts; the actual substance or bigger picture hardly mattered. I've seen members of Congress ask colleagues how they did after a line of questioning as if they had just been acting onstage and were curious about their performance.

This process actually played out seamlessly during the impeachment hearings of President Trump. I've spoken to numerous Republican members of Congress who acknowledge his actions toward Ukraine were dangerous to our foreign policy goals and believe he should be impeached and removed from office. But they willingly admit that the small group of primary voters in their districts nonetheless "adore" President Trump. So if these members display anything short of absolute support, their vote to impeach will cost them their jobs. If we can expect members of Congress to act like any ordinary American with a job, they will do almost anything to keep it – even if that means risking our democracy or their integrity.

Rep. David Jolly: The first time a student of any age learns about gerrymandering, there is often an intuitive resistance to the idea. It just seems wrong. As adults, many still think it so. But the federal courts have largely considered gerrymandering a "political question," where questions of fairness are to be wrestled over by voters and politicians, each of whom bring their own self-interest to the debate.

But we must not limit our studying of gerrymandering to questions of basic fairness. Instead, consider how gerrymandering influences the decision-making of candidates and elected officials once in office. How gerrymandering disrupts democracy.

If a member represents a highly gerrymandered district in an otherwise fairly competitive geographical region, they will make decisions consistently out of line with their greater community, choosing instead to reflect the viewpoint of their deliberately gerrymandered constituency within that competitive community. Why? Because there is greater electoral reward for taking the more polarized position. Conversely, if a member represents a highly competitive district, they will find greater electoral reward in taking a more balanced approach to their legislating. In any line of work, one does the things that will keep them employed. In a district gerrymandered along partisan lines, that means acting like a partisan. In a competitive district, that means representing more diverse political thought.

I know. I represented a 50–50 district before gerrymandering reform required the lines to be redrawn to better reflect the geography of our local community. I felt the natural electoral pressure every day to be thoughtful in my approach, reasonable in working with both sides of the aisle, and to make decisions that I thought would best represent a majority of my community regardless of party. Hyper-partisan behavior would not be rewarded.

The question of how to draw lines is one that will forever be faced by voters and their representatives. It is easy to identify when lines are drawn strictly to advance a partisan interest, and some voters will always opine that map drawing is a proper function of a majority party. To the victor go the spoils. The harder question, however, is among those who reject partisan line drawing and instead aspire to a greater fairness. What is fair? Is it geography? Is it partisan balance? Is it more competitive districts? Is it in protecting majority minority districts? Or is it as the courts have indicated a political question to ultimately be determined from time to time by the opinions of an evolving and informed electorate and their shifting partisan majorities?

There is a long history in making fun of the odd-looking legislative districts that politicians draw to help their own parties, and the term we still use today for this practice – gerrymandering – was coined by someone riffing on one of these examples in 1812. During a dinner party, a group of Federalists in Massachusetts named the district after Elbridge Gerry, the governor of the state. The map containing Gerry's salamander eventually squeezed out a 29-to-11 majority for his party in the 1812 elections, despite them winning just under half the votes cast (Dean, 1892). One 19th-century observer noted that

> The form of the district was a subject of remark, and it was said that it resembled some horrible animal, and only wanted wings to make a frightful political dragon. Mr. [Elkanah] Tisdale took his pencil and sketched the wings, and there was a discussion about the name, some suggesting that of Salamander. Mr. [Richard] Alsop proposed that of Gerrymander, which was adopted.
>
> *(Dean, 1892)*

The similes may have changed since then, but our surprise at these "frightful political" creations has not:

> Yesterday, we asked everyone to tell us what they thought the new 7th district of Illinois looked like. The response was overwhelming and, often, quite clever. Say whatever else you want about Fix readers; they are creative. Bondosan, though, took the cake, with his suggestion that the new 7th district "looks like Beavis eating a slice of pizza (New York style, not Chicago deep dish)."
>
> *(Blake, 2011)*

Gerrymandering is a tactic still used by politicians today, but the landscape has shifted. The legal requirements have changed, disallowing some forms of unfair districting, but increasing the value of unusually shaped, non-compact districts. Technology has developed rapidly over the past 30 years for redistricting, allowing block-by-block data to influence where lines are drawn. We are at some of the highest levels of partisan polarization in the nation's history, which is likely due in part to redistricting (Figure 4.1).

By one measure of gerrymandering, the efficiency gap, the maps first used in 2012 on average were the most extreme in the modern era (Stephanopoulos and McGhee, 2015: 836), and the Democrats managed to win just 193 seats (45%) in the U.S. House despite receiving more total votes than the Republicans in that election (Haas, 2019). Unfortunately for reformers, the federal courts stepped out of the partisan gerrymandering debate in 2019 in the Supreme Court's ruling on *Rucho v. Common Cause*, removing the possibility of an instant, national

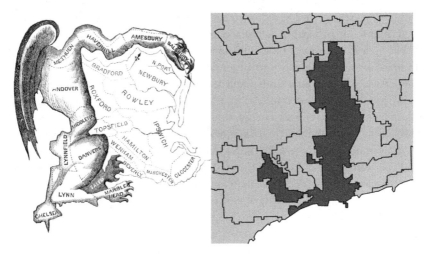

FIGURE 4.1   Left: Elkanah Tisdale's "gerrymander." Right: Illinois's 7th district, passed in 2011, rotated 90 degrees clockwise.)

remedy. However, there have been recent successes at the state level, ones that could potentially spread to other states in the post-2020 census redistricting cycle.

The Reapportionment Revolution

Even though the act of redistricting in America is older than the United States itself, having been practiced even in the colonial era (Griffith, 1907), the modern era of redistricting only began in the 1960s; this dividing line represented one dimension of the Civil Rights Era and its transformation of suffrage and representation in the United States. Prior to several key decisions made by the U.S. Supreme Court under Chief Justice Earl Warren, the drawing of legislative districts was outside the realm of what the federal courts considered themselves able to rule on. While Congress occasionally exercised its constitutional right to put guidelines on the process for U.S. House districts, in general, states themselves had sole discretion over where to place their lines.

Despite the lack of federal rules in this era, salamander-shaped districts like the original gerrymander were relatively rare. Congressional districts were often compact and followed existing political and administrative boundaries where possible, as most anti-gerrymandering reformers would prefer. However, a major problem was one of *malapportionment*: districts that were unbalanced in population across a state. This occurs today between censuses, as births, deaths, and movements across a state compound and lead to imbalanced districts. In this pre-modern era, though, redrawing every decade was not required, and in some cases, states chose not to update lines for multiple consecutive decades. Malapportionment in other cases was present regardless of how recent the redistricting: some states took their lead from the U.S. Senate when drawing state legislative lines, and treated counties as units that deserved individual representation. Even in states that attempted to grant extra representatives to larger counties, the gaps in population between the largest and smallest counties still led to massive disparities. Both routes to malapportionment tended to lead to urban underrepresentation and, along with the cracking of racial minority communities across two or more districts to dilute their influence, were tools to weaken minority voices in the political process.

This situation changed with the Supreme Court decision *Baker v. Carr* in 1962 and the related 1964 cases *Wesberry v. Sanders* and *Reynolds v. Sims* (citations in References). In these decisions, the Court declared redistricting questions to be within the domain of the federal courts, and with that power, it laid down the principle of "one person, one vote" based on the Equal Protection Clause of the 14th Amendment. Put simply, districts across a jurisdiction should have roughly the same population. This decision was so significant that some scholars refer to it as the "Reapportionment Revolution" (Cox et al., 2002). As an example of how fault-shifting this was, the state legislature of Florida was unable to deal with the new requirements to the point of them being the catalyst for a new state constitution, passed by voters in 1968 (Adkins, 2016). Today, every legislature with districts, from the U.S. House to state legislatures to city councils, must redraw their lines every ten years after a census to rebalance population.

Data and Technology

The reapportionment revolution and its equal population requirement raised the need for more detailed geographic data from the U.S. Census. Prior to this point, the Census Bureau provided tabulations for relatively large areas, with census tracts and county subdivisions like townships being on the smaller end of consideration (Turner and LaMacchia, 1999). For the 1970 census, tabulations were provided at the block level in larger cities and their denser neighboring areas, and via "enumeration districts" that were larger than blocks for more rural areas. Over the following decades, the data provided became more detailed, easier to obtain, and digital. In 1975, President Ford signed what became Public Law 94-171, which provided timeframes for data collection and release for the decennial census. Because of issues with mismatched geography in the 1970 census, the Census Bureau allowed states to submit boundaries for which tabulations would be provided; this continues today in the form of suggestions for block boundaries and the voluntary submission by states of their voting district maps (U.S. Census Bureau, 2019). Furthermore, to give states enough time to redistrict before the following general election, the Census Bureau is required by PL94-171 to have basic population and race data available to states within a year of Census Day, which falls on April 1 of the census year.

The 1990 census and its data release were the first to resemble the present state of redistricting. Every piece of the country was divided into census blocks; in 2010, there were just over 11 million of these blocks nationwide (U.S. Census Bureau, 2010 Census Tallies). This was also the first census where computers played a major role in the redistricting process. Though the first states were using computers for redistricting in the post-1970 cycle, this was likely only for limited purposes, and definitely not for direct drawing (Altman et al., 2005). The first modern geographic information systems (GIS) that allowed for the drawing of districts on screen were developed in the 1980s, and the census provided its wealth of digital boundary cartography to states through its TIGER/Line program (Turner and LaMacchia, 1999: 24). At this stage, redistricting software was relatively expensive and required computers more powerful than the average household possessed, but by the post-2010 redistricting cycle, technology had progressed to the point where full-fledged redistricting could be done using a web application through a user's browser. Dave's Redistricting App (davesredistricting.org) is one such example that is available to the public.

Mapmakers are not just limited to Census Bureau population counts, however. Election results can be broken down from the precinct level to the census block, allowing for on-the-fly voting reports of districts as they're being drawn. Voter registration lists can be geocoded, making each voter a dot on the map, allowing for partisanship and voter turnout predictions. Companies exist which collect a wide range of data on as many people as they can, and while some of this information may not be directly political, it may be valuable in modeling what sort of candidate that person would vote for, or even how they might behave ten years later, in the last election held under the map (Daley, 2016: 60). While mapmakers can't tilt maps to their advantage using malapportionment today, they can instead tweak their lines down to the city block level based on a broad range of data.

Gerrymandering Strategy

Each state handles the redistricting process slightly differently, but most states pass new mapping plans like any other bill they'd consider in the legislative process; other states' map-drawing processes are mostly conducted by politicians themselves in some form (Levitt, 2008: 20). Therefore, the expectation is that if one party controls both chambers of the legislature and the governor's seat, there will be a strong incentive for them to draw a partisan gerrymander to their benefit. To do so, their goal is to be efficient with the placement of their own voters and inefficient with the voters of the other party (Stephanopoulos and McGhee, 2015). The common strategy is referred to as packing and cracking. The party drawing the map would pack as many of their opponents' voters as possible into a small number of districts, thereby "wasting" those voters in elections with overwhelming wins. This leaves the rest of the state with a greater share of the majority party's voters, who are then drawn into districts where they win safely, but not by

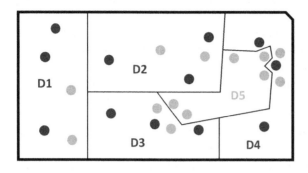

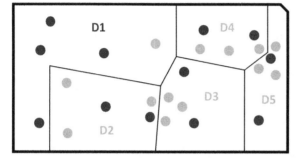

FIGURE 4.2   A hypothetical state with 13 grey dots representing voters of one party, and 12 black dots representing voters of another. Top: A pro-black dot gerrymander. Bottom: a pro-grey dot gerrymander

overwhelming margins; they "crack" their opponents' voters across districts to not be a majority anywhere else.

Figure 4.2 is an illustration of how two parties might approach a hypothetical state with nearly an even balance of voters. The top and bottom maps both have 13 grey dots and 12 black dots needing to be divided into five districts of five dots apiece. In the top map, the black dot party is in charge, and packs district five with grey dots, needing an odd shape to do so. By efficiently drawing the remaining four districts as 3–2 black dot victories, the black dot party – a minority in the state – can win four of the five districts. Likewise, in the bottom map, the grey dot party packs district one, and wins 3–2 in the remaining four districts.

Geographic Sorting Versus Gerrymandering

If the key to gerrymandering is packing your opponents' voters and not packing your own, this raises the question of whether it's easier for one party to adhere to this strategy than the other. There is reason to believe that's the case: city centers tend to be overwhelmingly Democratic, with no comparable dense hotspots of Republican voters (Chen and Rodden, 2013). If a map drawer were to stick to a strategy of drawing compact districts and not cracking cities across districts, this can lead to "natural" gerrymandering that favors the Republican Party.

The question, though, is how much of the gap we see in vote share won by Democrats across all U.S. House races versus the share of seats they win is due to natural gerrymandering and how much is artificial. One issue is that, though a map of compact districts may have a slight Republican advantage, many of the maps drawn by Republicans were not made up of compact districts (Azavea, 2012). While the party may argue that the natural bias is the main factor in some of its litigation (*Gill v. Whitford*, 2018), the party organization doesn't always echo that. The Republican State Leadership Committee, an organization created to help the party in its state legislative races, started the Redistricting Majority Project (REDMAP) to target state legislative chambers in 2010 that were close to giving Republicans full control of the process in a state or preventing Democrats from having that power in others. The RSLC raised $30 million for the project, and the 2010 election was a landslide for the party; they subsequently controlled both chambers of the legislature in 25 states, up from 14 states prior to the election. REDMAP's website takes credit for winning the House in 2012 despite only winning 49% of the nationwide vote, and highlights some of the states with the largest imbalances.[1] Democrats have created a similar organization with an eye towards 2019 and 2020 state legislative races headed by Obama Administration Attorney General Eric Holder called the National Democratic Redistricting Committee.[2]

Polarization

Another open debate is how much of a factor redistricting plays in the trend of increased partisan polarization that Congress has seen over the past 50 years. Polarization is almost certainly the product of multiple causes, but there is a pathway for partisan gerrymandering to have played a role (Altman and MacDonald, 2015b). Firstly, there is a clear pattern of members matching their districts: Democrats from highly Democratic districts tend to be more liberal, and likewise for Republicans and being more conservative. Secondly, while the magnitude of the effect may vary depending on how it is measured, there is evidence of a decline in the number of competitive districts immediately after the last three redistricting cycles, from a very small effect in 1992 to a considerably more pronounced one in 2012 (Altman and MacDonald, 2015b). Taken together, redistricting is likely a contributor to recent polarization, and making a concerted effort to draw competitive districts may alleviate this effect.

Case Study: Florida's Congressional Districts

Florida state legislators entered the redistricting process in 2011 under a new set of rules than what had been in place in previous decades. The transition from being a solid Democratic state to a solid Republican state had completed in the 1990s, leaving the GOP able to draw the map of their choice in 2001 after finally taking control of the state legislature. Their resulting congressional plan was one of the most gerrymandered in the country by one measure (Altman and MacDonald, 2015a: 163). In 2010, though, two citizen-initiated constitutional amendments referred to as the "Fair District Amendments" were approved by voters. Among other guidelines, these banned the drawing of districts to benefit a political party or incumbent.[3] Thus, the Republicans – at least on paper – would be constrained in what they would be able to accomplish.

On its face, the redistricting committees in both chambers were running an open process that relied heavily on public input. Over the summer of 2011, members of the committees made 26 stops around the state to hold public listening sessions, which were attended by nearly 5,000 people in total (MacManus et al., 2015). The committees also took input through mail, fax, email, and social media. Senate President Don Gaetz bragged on the chamber floor, "So if you are counting, if you are keeping track, the redistricting plans before you today were developed only after receiving the oral and written testimony of over 3,000 Floridians. No one in American redistricting history has been more inclusive" (Florida Senate, 2012: 48).

While Senator Gaetz's first sentence was technically true, there were also more partisan actions happening behind the scenes. For instance, if one digs through the public input released by the Senate, at least 30 of the emails received by the committee followed the same three-line message nearly word for word. An example, sent by his colleague Brady Thompson of Tallahassee, read, "I like your Senate Plan. I think the districts look fair and balanced. Thank you for following county lines and having an open process."[4] This suggests that there was some coordination behind the scenes to tilt the tone of the public input.

The partisanship of the process ran deeper, though, and was only revealed later in litigation. Shortly after the 2010 elections and the passage of the Fair District Amendments, Republican leaders and legislative staff held meetings with a small group of Republican consultants who, "prior to passage of the [new constitutional standards], would have generally been involved in the redistricting process" (*League of Women Voters*, 2015: 22). Included among these consultants was Frank Terraferma, who was described as a "genius map drawer" by national Republicans (*League of Women Voters*, 2015: 23). In testimony, those present at the meetings generally stated that they could not remember what was discussed, beyond the message that they would not have a seat at the table during the process because of the new constitutional restrictions. Trial court judge Terry Lewis remarked in one of his opinions, "there was really no reason to convene two meetings just to tell active political partisans" that (*League of Women Voters*, 2015: 12).

Because many of the emails were destroyed after the completion of the redistricting process, we will likely never know the true extent of the contact between these consultants and legislators or legislative staff during the drafting process.

Some of what survived suggests that these consultants did have more of a seat at the table than the average citizen, however. For instance, the Speaker of the House's chief of staff, Kirk Pepper, was sharing maps with Marc Reichelderfer, one of the consultants present at those meetings, as they were being drafted by staff. Commenting on a draft plan sent to him by Pepper, Reichelderfer commented that it was "a bit messed up," to which Pepper responded, "Performance or geography?" (*League of Women Voters*, 2015: 28). Pepper later explained that this was a sarcastic comment and not one relating to the partisanship of the plan, but Judge Lewis also expressed skepticism about this (*League of Women Voters*, 2015: 29).

While there was no direct evidence of a flow of mapping ideas from consultants to the legislature, there are a couple of pieces of circumstantial evidence that suggest this was happening. Firstly, in an email sent by Frank Terraferma to a Republican legislator, he commented that he saw Kirk Pepper "huddled on a computer" at the state Republican headquarters with Rich Heffley, another consultant present at those post-election meetings; he further said in the email that this was in relation to "[c]ongressional redistricting if I had to guess?" (*League of Women Voters*, 2015: 26). Pepper denied that the two were meeting about redistricting.

What was not denied was that Terraferma was drawing draft plans with a strong Republican advantage, and that some of these districts somehow ended up being submitted as public input under the name of Alex Posada, a student a Florida State University and a member of the College Republicans there. Furthermore, one of these maps, labeled with the code "HPUBC0132," saw more attention from House staff than any other publicly submitted map. Fourteen of the draft maps produced by the House in the discovery process of litigation had filenames beginning with "Cong 132 rev," suggesting staff developed the ideas from the public submission. There were also plans from the production with the names "frank cong plan," "forMarc," and "MarcR2" that were highly similar to the HPUB0132 map, which suggests that the people working on it knew that Frank Terraferma was involved, and that Marc Reichelderfer would see the changes the staff made (*League of Women Voters*, 2015).

Regardless of who had input into the drawing process, by the numbers, the map that passed the state legislature and was signed by the governor clearly advantaged Republicans. Barack Obama, who won Florida by nearly a 3% margin in 2008, only won ten of the 27 districts, and Democratic gubernatorial candidate Alex Sink, who narrowly lost the state in 2010, also won just ten. These proved to be good gauges for the first set of elections held under the map: Obama won the state again, but only ten Democrats were elected to the House.[5]

One of the strategies taken by the Republicans in drawing the plan was one taken by Republicans in other states, as well. An amendment to the Voting Rights Act in 1982, followed by the landmark Supreme Court case *Thornburg v. Gingles* in 1986, placed a new requirement on redistricting at every level of government: if there was a large enough racial or ethnic minority community in a geographically compact area such that if the community were drawn into the same district, they could elect the candidate of their choosing, and the racial majority in the area voted as an opposing bloc to the minority, then the district keeping them together should be drawn (*Thornburg v. Gingles*). The districts the *Gingles* test produces are often referred to as "majority-minority districts." However, since African American voters tend to overwhelmingly support Democratic candidates, a packed district with the stated purpose of adhering to the Voting Rights Act is nearly equivalent to a packed Democratic district in a pro-Republican redistricting strategy.

One example of this in the Florida congressional plan was the notorious fifth district, pictured in Figure 4.3, which stretched from Jacksonville to Orlando. The necessity of an African American district in the northern part of the state had been established after the 1990 census, in the period where the courts were still sorting out the *Gingles* test; a federal court adopted a district that was even less compact than 2012's district five (*DeGrandy and Wetherell*). However, the legislature had gone further than the previous decade in this case. In the post-2000 census redistricting, the voting-age population in the Jacksonville–Orlando district had been 46.8% African American, but those drawing the maps after the 2010

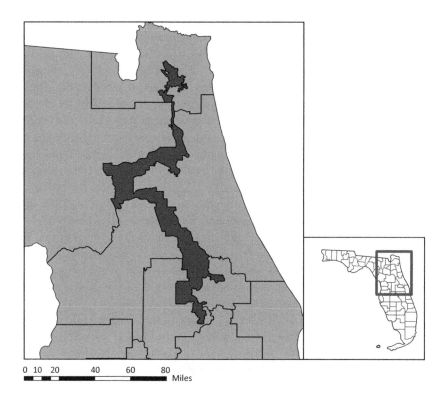

0 10 20   40   60   80
■■ ■□ ■■■■■■■■■■■■■■■■■■■■■■■■■■■ Miles

FIGURE 4.3   Florida's Fifth Congressional District

census claimed that they believed they needed to have that share exceed 50% in order to comply with the Voting Rights Act. The various "arms" grabbing up black voters around Orlando left just one other district in the area that was likely for Democrats to win, where a fairer map would be likely to have another.

Ultimately, the map was struck down by the Florida Supreme Court for being a partisan gerrymander. One of the key bodies of evidence for the decision was the draft plan that the redistricting staff had drawn in private on the way to the plans that were introduced in committee which were ordered to be released in the discovery process of the trial (*League of Women Voters*, 2015). The challengers to the gerrymander were able to piece together a timeline of what draft maps were drawn when, and a trend emerged. One of the very first maps drawn by the staff, labeled as "Congressional 1" and "Congress_11072011(1)," had a proportional 14-13 Democratic advantage for Obama in 2008 and a proportional 14-13 Republican advantage in 2010. This quickly dipped to a 15-12 Republican advantage on average in the following draft plans, and eventually to a 16-11 advantage in the last maps drawn (Amos, 2018). These were not matched with improvements in neutral redistricting criteria like district compactness, which suggested that partisanship was the main explanation for the edits. The map the courts chose as a replacement – after the legislature failed to pass one themselves in special session – elected 14 Republicans and 13 Democrats in the 2018 election.

Case Study: Maryland's Congressional Districts

Figure 4.4 shows the congressional district map for the state of Maryland. By some measures, the state has the least compact districts on average of any in the country, and several of the individual districts rate as the most non-compact, as well (Azavea,

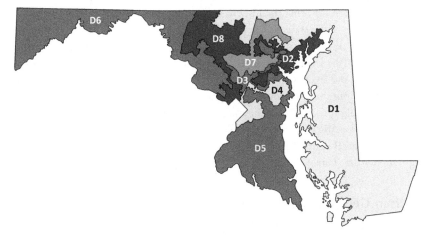

FIGURE 4.4 Maryland's Congressional Districts, 2013-2022

2012; Ingraham, 2014). Like Republicans in Florida, Democrats in Maryland tapped political consultants for help in 2011 to draw draft plans, namely the company NCEC Services (Whiting, 2018), and they successfully delivered a map that elected seven Democrats and one Republican. And, like in Florida, the map was challenged on the grounds of partisan gerrymandering; the state did not have its own ban on gerrymandering, so they relied on arguments rooted in the U.S. Constitution.

Interestingly, the case was not centered on the districts in the middle of the state that had some of the worst compactness scores. This is in large part because the bizarre shapes in this area were not primarily examples of partisan gerrymandering: drawing a much cleaner map in this area would still likely have resulted in Democratic victories (and a more compact eight-Democrat sweep map was also possible) (Wolf, 2016). Instead, the shapes resulted from requests by the incumbents who held those seats which were sometimes difficult to reconcile. Maryland Senate President Mike Miller was candid with the Baltimore Sun in explaining these considerations (Linskey and Fritze, 2011). On the Z-shaped district three: "We recognized that Congressman Sarbanes lived in Baltimore County, but wanted to continue to represent the capital city Annapolis, and that was challenging." On the T-shaped district two: "We recognized the fact that Congressman Ruppersberger, for example, is on the Intelligence Committee … We tried to be sure that he represented both Aberdeen [Proving Ground] and Fort Meade, which was kind of challenging." On district five: "Congressman Hoyer lives in St. Mary's County and wants to represent Pax River, but also wanted to represent his alma mater, College Park, and that was challenging."

The Democrats did go a step further, however, and looked for a way to improve their position from holding six of the eight seats in the state to seven. Initial attempts were made on the eastern side of the state with district one, with hopes of setting up a favorable situation for Democrat Frank Kratovil, who had narrowly won there in 2008 but lost in 2010 (Whiting, 2018). When this approach proved to make reelection for other incumbent Democrats more difficult, focus moved to the western side of the state. In the past, the sixth district ran across the panhandle and across the northern, more conservative parts of the state, and Republican Roscoe Bartlett had held that area for 20 years. In 2011, the Democrats broke the district up, and snaked two of the pieces to connect with portions of strongly Democratic Montgomery County. Bartlett went from winning the sixth in 2010 by 29% to losing it to businessman and political newcomer John Delaney by 20% in 2012. This specific change to the sixth was the basis of the partisan gerrymandering case the Republicans brought, one that made it all the way to the U.S. Supreme Court (*Lamone v. Benisek*).

Partisan Gerrymandering in Federal Court

As mentioned above, the Maryland gerrymandering case was a federal one. Stepping back, the extent to which the federal courts' power reached on redistricting was a matter of debate within the court in the wake of *Baker v. Carr*. Motivated by the Voting Rights Act and the 14th Amendment, racial discrimination in redistricting has been a regular issue taken up and ruled upon by the federal courts. Partisan gerrymandering was a separate issue, however, and one that a larger portion of the Supreme Court argued fell under the doctrine of being a "political question" better hashed out by the other two branches. Though the idea of partisan gerrymandering being something the courts could rule on and a violation of the Equal Protection Clause was hinted at as early as 1965 (Fortson v. Dorsey, 1965: 439),[6] it would not be directly addressed until 1986 in *Davis v. Bandemer*. Here, the Supreme Court did declare partisan gerrymandering to be within the federal courts' domain, but it failed to issue a majority opinion with a standard for the courts to follow. *Vieth v. Jubelirer* in 2004 hinted at a reversal of this decision, with the four-member plurality opinion arguing the impossibility of a manageable standard to judge the presence of a partisan gerrymander. Justice Anthony Kennedy remained the swing vote rejecting proposed standards for judgment, but not closing the door on the possibility of their existence. After his retirement in 2018 and his replacement by Justice Brett Kavanaugh, *Rucho v. Common Cause* in 2019 shifted the lingering plurality to a majority, moving partisan redistricting out of the realm of the federal courts.

For reformers interested in preventing partisan gerrymanders, the *Rucho* ruling was a setback: a decision by the Supreme Court could have enforced standards nationwide. However, redistricting is done by the states, so a patchwork of 50 state constitutions, laws, and courts also govern the process. Success in gerrymandering reform has been seen at this level, and with the federal courts out of the game, the states will be the main battlefield in the wake of the 2020 census.

Approaches to Stop Gerrymandering

There are two primary routes that reformers can take to rein in gerrymandering at the state level: placing restrictions on the process and changing who oversees the process. The second approach is usually accompanied by the first approach, while the reverse is less likely to be true. Both have seen some success in different states, but the evidence seems to point to the need to put the task of redistricting into the hands of a neutral group to consistently and effectively prevent a gerrymander.

Restrictions on the ability for state legislatures to enact a gerrymander can potentially be found at three levels: the state constitution, state laws, or nonbinding guidance for the process given by a full chamber or a committee within it. These are listed in order of likelihood to prevent a gerrymander. Non-binding guidance is just that, and the people to gauge whether the language is being followed is the legislative majority which likely had the largest say in the drawing of the map to begin with. For instance, South Carolina had guidelines produced in both chambers which said to consider district compactness in balance with other factors (South Carolina Senate, 2011; South Carolina House, 2011); the sixth congressional district is especially non-compact.[7]

Laws may seem more binding than guidelines, but one issue is that district maps are usually bills themselves, suggesting that if a legislature had the votes to enact a new map, they would also have the votes to rescind any laws that the map could potentially be in violation of. For instance, in Wisconsin prior to 2011, the normal timeline of redistricting was to allow local governments to redistrict first, after which state and federal district plans would be completed by the state legislature. A bill allowing a reversal of this timeline was passed and signed by the governor a couple weeks before the actual state and federal maps were put into effect (Wisconsin Legislature, 2011).

Constitutional requirements, therefore, have the most strength, since amending a state constitution requires public approval in every state but Delaware, and may require supermajority or multi-session votes in the legislature prior to that. This has been an avenue of reform: as mentioned above, in the 2010 general election, voters in the state of Florida approved a citizen-initiated constitutional amendment banning partisan gerrymandering (Fl. Const.), which led to the first districts being struck down for the reason of partisan gerrymandering in the country's history (*League of Women Voters*, 2018). In other states, reformers have targeted existing language in a state's constitution that does not explicitly ban gerrymandering, but implies that it is not allowed. For instance, the congressional plan in Pennsylvania was struck down in 2018 by the state's supreme court based on a clause guaranteeing "free and equal" elections.[57] Twelve additional states have identical language in their state constitutions, and another 13 have a clause guaranteeing "free and open" elections (Grofman and Cervas, 2018), which make them prime candidates for similar challenges in the future should partisan gerrymanders be drawn.

The weakness of relying on constitutional bans on gerrymandering is that unless a state also requires a court review of plans before they take effect, the protections are reactive and require significant legal resources to enforce. For instance, groups in Florida challenged the state's congressional plan immediately after it was signed by the governor in early 2012, but initial successes in court didn't occur until past the deadline to affect the 2014 elections, and the final replacement map wasn't chosen until December 2015, meaning that the unconstitutional map was in place for two full terms. Additionally, this approach depends on who is ruling on these cases. Florida's 4-3 liberal majority on the state supreme court turned into a likely 6-1 conservative majority in 2019 as three justices faced mandatory retirement and were replaced by appointees of Republican Ron DeSantis (Pratt, 2019). This new majority could show more deference to a Republican legislature in 2022 if they attempt another partisan gerrymander.

A more proactive approach already used in some states is to take the task of redistricting out of the hands of politicians and give it to an independent commission. In states like Idaho, Montana, and Washington, members of these committees are chosen by legislative leaders in an even partisan balance, but the members cannot be politicians themselves. In Arizona and California, the process is further insulated by having an initial pool of potential members nominated by nonpartisan groups from which legislative leaders can choose or make vetoes, requiring a balance of party registrants in the final selections (Levitt, 2008). The logic is that having non-politicians who need to compromise with members outside their party to pass a map will lead to fairer outcomes. And, when compared to plans drawn by legislatures or commissions made up of politicians, there is indeed evidence that plans drawn by these independent commissions lead to a greater degree of electoral competitiveness (Lindgren and Southwell, 2013; DeVault, 2019).

Many of the independent commission states created their processes through the normal legislative process, but the most recent ones, Arizona and California, did so through direct democracy processes, where a group of citizens qualified the issues for a vote by the public without the input of the state legislature.[8] Only about a third of the states have citizen-initiated constitutional amendments available as an option, though, so lobbying legislators to put the system into place is the primary option in the rest of the country.

Even though *Rucho* marked the federal courts getting out of the realm of partisan gerrymandering, the door is still open for Congress to step in. At various points in history, Congress has placed requirements on states in the drawing of their U.S. House districts, such as having them be contiguous and compact. Even today, federal law requires each member of the House to be elected from a single-member district. Recent introduced bills have gone further, though, with some proposing an explicit ban on partisan gerrymandering or requiring each state to use an independent redistricting commission to draw their congressional lines. After the Democrats won back the House in 2018, they designated a broad electoral reform package as H.R.1, which included both provisions; it passed the House but died quietly in the Republican-controlled Senate. There are explicit constitutional provisions allowing Congress to regulate elections for the U.S. House, but an argument can be made that Congress could create a ban on partisan gerrymandering for state elections as well, grounding it in 14th Amendment equal protection defenses (Stephanopoulos, 2019).

While the front lines of gerrymandering reform will be in state courts and state legislatures, there is a space for average citizens to get involved. As mentioned in the Florida case study, knowing what plans the legislature knew were possible was instrumental in striking down the enacted plan as a gerrymander. This evidence is key, because the number of possible plans that can be drawn using census geography is beyond astronomical; dividing 50 units of geography into two districts with 25 units apiece has 6×10^{31} possibilities (Altman, 1997), and the average state has hundreds of thousands of census blocks. Therefore, the legislature can plausibly plead ignorance if someone produces a fairer plan in later litigation: they may have just not come across it in their drawing process. Public input of full plans before the state legislature acts can remove this ignorance. State good government groups can incentivize public input that meets legal muster through the holding of redistricting contests, and the Public Mapping Project using open source software developed by Azavea has facilitated a number of these projects over the past decade.[9]

Conclusion

Although the term "gerrymandering" is nearly as old as the country itself, there is evidence that the practice has been amplified in recent decades. Some of the effect may be due to self-sorting by Democrats as mentioned previously in this volume, but it is likely that much of the effect is intentional and has been aided by improvements in technology. Furthermore, this has likely contributed to the growing polarization in the United States. In 2019, the Supreme Court ruled that it would not be stepping into the realm of partisan gerrymandering, but other recent initiatives and court cases have plotted a course for reformers to take at the state level to prevent the practice.

Notes

1 See redistrictingmajorityproject.com.
2 See democraticredistricting.com.
3 See Fl. Const. art. III § 20+21, on the ballot as Amendments 5 and 6.
4 See page 21 of the online document at ttp://www.flsenate.gov/PublishedContent/ SESSION/ HOME/REDISTRICTING2012/ PUBLICCOMMENTS/Email_ Comments_PCBs.pdf, 21.
5 Because uncontested races do not appear on the ballot in Florida, calculating House vote totals for each party is difficult.
6 Page 49 of the decision reads:"…our opinion is not to be understood to say that in all instances or under all circumstances such a system as Georgia has will comport with the dictates of the Equal Protection Clause. It might well be that, designedly or other-wise, a multi-member constituency apportionment scheme, under the circumstances of a particular case, would operate to minimize or cancel out the voting strength of racial *or political elements* of the voting population." (emphasis added)
7 Using the U.S. Census's 115th congressional district shapefile, it was among the top 20 least compact districts across the country under the Polsby-Popper measure. Additionally, district 1 placed in the top 40.
8 Ohio did pass an amendment in 2018 to create a commission made up of politicians for use in state legislative redistricting and as a backup for congressional redistricting that require a bipartisan vote for passage.
9 DistrictBuilder at districtbuilder.org.

References

Adkins, M.E., 2016. *Making Modern Florida: How the Spirit of Reform Shaped a New State Constitution.* Gainesville, FL: University Press of Florida.

Altman, M., 1997. Is Automation the Answer: The Computational Complexity of Automated Redistricting. *Rutgers Computer and Law Technology Journal, 23*, pp. 81–142.

Altman, M., MacDonald, K. and McDonald, M., 2005. From Crayons to Computers: The Evolution of Computer Use in Redistricting. *Social Science Computer Review, 23*(3), pp. 334–346.

Altman, M. and McDonald, M., 2015a. *Paradoxes of Political Reform: Congressional Redistricting in Florida. Jigsaw Puzzle Politics in the Sunshine State*. Gainesville, FL: University Press of Florida.

Altman, M. and McDonald, M., 2015b. Redistricting and Polarization. In: Thurber, J.A. and Yoshinaka, A. eds. *American gridlock: The sources, character, and impact of political polarization*. Cambridge: Cambridge University Press, 45–67.

Amos, B., 2018. *Detecting Gerrymandering: The Known Bias Test*. Ph.D. University of Florida.

Azavea, 2012. *Redrawing the Map on Redistricting 2012 Addendum*. Azavea. https://s3.amaz onaws.com/s3.azavea.com/com.redistrictingthenation/pdfs/Redistricting_The_N ation_Addendum.pdf.

Baker v. Carr, 369 U.S. 186, 82 S. Ct. 691, 7 L. Ed. 2d 663 (1962).

Blake, A., 2011. Name that District Winner: 'Beavis Eating Pizza'. *Washington Post*, 29 July.

Chen, J. and Rodden, J., 2013. Unintentional Gerrymandering: Political Geography and Electoral Bias in Legislatures. *Quarterly Journal of Political Science, 8*(3), pp. 239–269.

Cox, G.W., Katz, J.N. and Katz, J.D., 2002. *Elbridge Gerry's Salamander: The Electoral Consequences of the Reapportionment Revolution*. Cambridge: Cambridge University Press.

Daley, D., 2016. *Ratf** Ked: Why Your Vote Doesn't Count*. New York: WW Norton & Company.

Davis v. Bandemer, 478 U.S. 109 (1986).

Dean, J.W., 1892. The Gerrymander. *New England Historical and Genealogical Register, 46*, pp. 374–383.

DeGrandy v. Wetherell, 794 F. Supp. 1076 (N.D. Fla. 1992).

DeVault, J.M., 2019. *Independent Redistricting Commissions and Electoral Competition in the US*. House of Representatives.

Fl. Const. art. III § 20+21.

Florida Senate, 2012. Floor Debate, January 17, Volume I.

Fortson v. Dorsey, 379 U.S. 433, 85 S. Ct. 498, 13 L. Ed. 2d 401 (1965).

Gill v. Whitford, 138 S. Ct. 1916, 201 L. Ed. 2d 313, 585 U.S. (2018).

Griffith, E.C., 1907. *The Rise and Development of the Gerrymander*. Chicago: Scott Foresman.

Grofman, B. and Cervas, J.R., 2018. Can State Courts Cure Partisan Gerrymandering: Lessons from League of Women Voters v. Commonwealth of Pennsylvania (2018). *Election Law Journal: Rules, Politics, and Policy, 17*(4), pp. 264–285.

Haas, K.L., 2019. *Statistics of the Presidential and Congressional Election from Official Sources for the Election of November 8, 2016*. Office of the Clerk, U.S. House of Representatives. https://history.house.gov/Institution/Election-Statistics/Election-Statistics.

Ingraham, C., 2014. America's Most Gerrymandered Congressional Districts. *Washington Post*, 15 May.

Lamone v. Benisek, 139 S. Ct. 783 (U.S. 2019).

League of Women Voters of Fla. v. Detzner, 179 So. 3d 258 (Fla. 2015).

League of Women Voters of Pennsylvania et al. v. Commonwealth of Pennsylvania et al., Pa. 159 MM 2017 (2018).

Levitt, J., 2008. A Citizen's Guide to Redistricting. *Available at SSRN 1647221*.

Lindgren, E. and Southwell, P., 2013. The Effect of Redistricting Commissions on Electoral Competitiveness in US House Elections, 2002–2010. *Journal of Politics and Law, 6*, 13.

Linskey, A. and Fritze, J., 2011. GOP, Others Find Faults with Proposed Map. *The Baltimore Sun*, 13 October.

MacManus, S.A., Cheshire, J.M., Hill, T.L. and Schuler, S.C., 2015. Redistricting in Florida: Loud Voices from the Grassroots. In: Seth C. McKee, ed. *Jigsaw Puzzle Politics in the Sunshine State*. Gainesville, FL: University of Florida, 126–162.

Pratt, C., 2019. Governor Ron DeSantis Gives the Florida Supreme Court a Conservative Makeover. *Federalist Society Blog*, 29 January. https://fedsoc.org/commentary/blog-posts /governor-ron-desantis-gives-the-florida-supreme-court-a-conservative-makeover.

Reynolds v. Sims, 377 U.S. 533, 84 S. Ct. 1362, 12 L. Ed. 2d 506 (1964).

Rucho v. Common Cause, 139 S. Ct. 2484, 588 U.S., 204 L. Ed. 2d 931 (2019).

South Carolina House of Representatives, 2011, *2011 Guidelines and Criteria For Congressional and Legislative Redistricting*.

South Carolina Senate, 2011. *2011 Redistricting Guidelines*.

Stephanopoulos, N.O., 2019. H.R. 1 and Redistricting Commissions. *Election Law Blog*, 9 January. https://electionlawblog.org/?p=103123.

Stephanopoulos, N.O. and McGhee, E.M., 2015. Partisan Gerrymandering and the Efficiency Gap. *University of Chicago Law Review*, *82*, 831.

Thornburg v. Gingles, 478 U.S. 30, 106 S. Ct. 2752, 92 L. Ed. 2d 25 (1986).

Turner Jr, M.L. and LaMacchia, R.A., 1999. The US Census, Redistricting, and Technology: A 30-Year Perspective. *Social Science Computer Review*, *17*(1), pp. 16–26.

U.S. Census Bureau, 2019. *Redistricting Data Program Management*. U.S. Census Bureau. https ://www.census.gov/programs-surveys/decennial-census/about/rdo/program-manag ement.html.

U.S. Census Bureau, 2010. *Census Tallies*. U.S. Census Bureau. https://www.census.gov/pr ograms-surveys/decennial-census/about/rdo/program-management.html.

Wesberry v. Sanders, 376 U.S. 1, 84 S. Ct. 526, 11 L. Ed. 2d 481 (1964).

Wisconsin Legislature, 2011. Senate Bill 150.

Wolf, S., 2016. No, Maryland Is Not the Most Gerrymandered State. There Is More to Gerrymandering than Ugly Shapes. *Daily Kos*, 1 June.

Whiting, A., 2018. Political Insiders Plotted the Most Gerrymandered District in America— And Left a Paper Trail. *Washingtonian*, 20 May.

5

MONEY IN POLITICS

Sean D. Foreman

Rep. David Jolly: We have a part-time Congress in a full-time world. Why? Not because they only meet a few days a week. Members are otherwise consumed full-time by the responsibilities of their office and remaining in office. But because in today's politics the demands on fundraising are such that raising money is the primary responsibility of any member of Congress. If a member of Congress says otherwise, they're lying.

We often have debates about the role of money in politics. Those debates often center on the influence that money has on a member's decision-making. But consider the influence money has on a member's time.

If you notionally consider the average congressional race as requiring a member of Congress to raise at least $2 million per cycle, that's roughly $20,000 a week every week for two years that a member needs to raise, with two weeks off each year. That's $4,000 each workday, and if you miss a day, it's $8,000 the next day. Consider further that many races actually require $5 million or $10 million or more.

Now consider the amount of time it would take someone to raise $4,000 a day, every day. And if your reelection depended foremost on having those funds available to go on television, to run campaign ads, to pay staff, to print materials, to operate a campaign, are you more likely to attend a congressional hearing or a constituent meeting, or are you more likely to spend time dialing for dollars? Based on my experience, for most members of Congress it's the latter.

I was first elected in a highly competitive, very expensive special election. I was sworn in in March and faced my first reelection that November. After only about six weeks in office I was asked to meet with the House Majority Leader who I was told wanted to help me in my reelection effort. We met in a political office outside of the Capitol so we could discuss fundraising and other matters. I had two staff members with me. The Leader proceeded to tell me the pathway to my reelection relied solely on fundraising, not policy-making. He turned to one of my staff members and said, "Your problem is that you have a new member in office with aspirations of doing great legislative things, but what you have to do between now and November is make sure he's on the phone raising money. That's his only priority."

My experience is not unique. Money in politics is destroying representative government and destroying a functioning Congress. Why are some of our greatest policy needs going unmet? Because Congress wakes up every day focused on what will most assuredly get them ree- lected – money, not policy.

Part of addressing today's campaign finance system, for those who believe a change is war- ranted, requires a change in jurisprudence in our federal courts, including the Supreme Court. Still other changes can be made legislatively, including caps on giving, disclosure requirements, and rules that Congress could choose to put on itself.

Whatever one's opinion on our current campaign finance system and the many proposed reforms, it is an undeniable fact that our current system preoccupies the attention of members of Congress and distracts them from full-time policy-making. Our policy-making suffers because of it, and for many, including myself, it appears our democracy suffers because of it as well.

Rep. Patrick E. Murphy: At the time, my first campaign for Congress was the most expen- sive U.S. House race in history, with the combined spending total surpassing $24 million. My campaign for Senate a few years later would end up being a $40 million affair, not including the outside groups that formed on their own and put money into those races.

While I was serving in the House, I was called by a large donor and offered several million dollars if I would change my mind on a voting decision. Of course, I did not do this. But I imagine that other members would not be so honorable if given the choice. Money has become such a key component and easy indicator as to who will win the election. Saying no to money is essentially saying no to winning. Name ID, TV advertising, mailers, an email or digital program, consultants, staff – all of these crucial elements needed for winning take millions to make happen.

In having been the person sitting on the phone asking for campaign contributions for hours on end, I am strongly in support of any improvement or restrictions to campaign fundraising efforts. I sometimes felt more like a telemarketer than a member of Congress! This change needs to be even across the aisle. There is a strong argument to end Citizen's United, but without it you are single-handedly disarming with knowledge that the money may still be on the other side.

There is very little explicit deal-making on larger Super PAC donations (that I know of), simply because it is not needed. The basis for outside money and larger contributions is based solely on your voting record. The bigger groups make their stances clear and have ways to make sure you know where they stand. If you have the voting record they approve of, the check will be there – it's that simple. As most members are in fairly safe seats, this applies particularly to those in tough campaigns, or those running for higher office.

Money makes the world go around. It is especially so in politics. The money that is collected for campaigns, paid (or not paid) in taxes, and doled out from public purses is critical for understanding who has power, and who does not, in American politics. "Money is the mother's milk of politics" is an often-repeated quote attributed to Jesse Unruh, a powerful California politician. "True, Jesse Unruh may have benefited slightly. But hell, there's been a lot more benefits for California," he said in summing up what seems to be the definition of a successful political career in the United States: do good for yourself while doing good for your country (Uhlig, 1987). This idea is rooted in the classical liberal American concept of individualism itself.

With each successive cycle, the amount of money raised and spent for political campaigns increases. The cost of winning a seat in Congress has dramatically risen. There are more ads, polls, and staff with greater expertise and sophistication that add to costs. It was estimated that $6 billion was spent on the 2012 congressional and presidential elections. In 2016 it was $6.5 billion. In 2012 on average House members needed to raise nearly $1.7 million to win a seat and to raise nearly $2,315 each day of the election cycle. Senators needed around $10.5 million, averaging $14,351 raised each campaign day, to prevail (Costa, 2013).

Congressional midterm spending records were again broken in 2018 with approximately $5.2 billion spent – a 35 percent increase from 2014. Much of the increase came from outside spending which accounted for $1.3 billion, a 61 percent increase over 2014. There were more outside expenditures in the 2018 than the 2012 cycle, second only to 2016 (Mayersohn, 2018). Part of the spending was fueled by several high-profile U.S. House special elections and several competitive California races that outpaced the money spent in other races. The high-profile Texas U.S. Senate race between Republican incumbent Ted Cruz and Democratic challenger Rep. Beto O'Rourke saw the most individual money at $124 million raised and spent. O'Rouke spent $79 million, a record for congressional candidates while Cruz made use of $45 million – and Cruz won. Florida's contest between Democratic incumbent Sen. Bill Nelson and Republican Gov. Rick Scott witnessed the most individual and outside money combined, a whopping $209.3 million, with $92.8 million coming from outside spending.

While money buys access, it does not necessarily buy outcomes. The understanding is that campaign contributors will get their phone calls answered, meetings granted, and, at least, their voices heard on key issues. But do contributions effectively help contributors purchase the votes of legislators and buy outcomes by supporting enough legislators to get a bill passed? Answering this question requires a more detailed analysis (McKay, 2018). Whether it is favorable or not, the reality is that the current system essentially enables legal bribery in American politics, and there must be some reason why they spend all that money on campaigns.

Regardless of whether money buys access or not, the public perception is that it does. In a February 2019 poll by The Center for Public Integrity, 85 percent of Americans agreed that "elected officials often do favors for big campaign donors" while 7 percent disagreed and 8 percent did not know (The Center, 2019). Poll after poll show that a majority of Americans believe Congress is spending too much time raising money and paying attention to donors rather than making policy and meeting with more constituents. Part of the problem rests with a system of competitive elections with a win-at-all-costs strategy that requires endless fundraising to finance campaigns in the current political environment.

The idea that money can play a role in determining the political process is engrained from the Supreme Court decision of *Buckley v. Valeo* (1976), which equated money, and the ability to raise and spend it, with the freedom of speech. That decision was extended when SCOTUS, in *Citizens United v. FEC* (2010), equated corporations with individuals in their First Amendment right to speak loudly through their use of money in political campaign advertisements.

Congress and the Fundraising Treadmill

There are no term limits placed on members of Congress to be found in the original Constitution written by the Framers, nor in any subsequent amendments. It is said that there are natural term limits in that members of the House have to run for reelection and face voters every two years and the Senate each six years. But it is also known that incumbents have tremendous advantages and perks afforded by the position which make it easier to win reelection. One of the advantages is the access to campaign donors that incumbents can get as they move into their respective committees and policy specializations while serving in a public office.

Raising money early is important to seed a campaign's activities. It helps to gain staff, get organized, and raise more money. It requires significant funding to hire staff, rent space, travel, conduct polls, and run a competitive campaign. This is where it helps having personal wealth, or the early backing of a group like EMILY's List (Early Money is Like Yeast), or a national party organization to get ahead.

The amount of time that members need to spend fundraising as opposed to lawmaking is out of balance. It appears to be an inescapable part of the job. Members in surveys report having to spend four hours or more on making fundraising calls on a typical day on the job. They spend twice as much time on fundraising than on legislating. The more successful they are at raising money, the more they are asked to do. The less successful, the more pressure is placed to succeed or be replaced.

A January 2013 presentation given by the Democratic Congressional Committee (DCCC) said that incoming freshmen should spend four hours a day out of a ten-hour day making phone calls to raise money. There is another hour dedicated to strategic outreach which could also include some time spent raising money at various "meet and greet" or mealtime events. Meanwhile, there are about three to four hours of time dedicated to the work of Congress, committees, floor votes, meetings, and constituent services per day. Fundraising goals are set depending on the competitiveness of the district and can increase once members are close to meeting goals (Davidson et al., 2013: 71).

Congressman Chris Van Hollen (D-MD) served in the U.S. House from 2003 to 2017 and was the DCCC Chair from 2007–11. One of the DCCC chair's responsibilities is to help raise money for candidates nationwide as well as for the national party. "The Maryland congressman had no illusions about the power of money on Capitol Hill. He knew how much he had had to raise in his upset victory in 2002. He had watched his colleagues in both parties devote endless hours to fund-raising, much of it from lobbyists" (Gottlieb, 2015).

In June 2013 Ryan Lizza, then a *New Yorker* writer, overheard a sitting first-term U.S. House member making fundraising phone calls over multiple hours on a train ride from New York to Washington D.C. and tweeted about it without directly naming the individual. Lizza quoted the politician as sounding desperate and humiliated as he pleaded for money (Bump 2013; Graham, 2013; Gottlieb, 2015). The Twitter feed (since deleted) caused a variety of replies that indicated that people were not surprised to see that this is how members of Congress was spending their time.

The secrecy was further unveiled by co-editor David Jolly during a *60 Minutes* appearance in 2014. "Members of Congress spend too much time raising money and not enough time doing their job," Jolly said, in blowing the whistle on the political parties' fundraising schemes. Jolly had served as general counsel to his predecessor, Rep. C.W. "Bill" Young and had worked as a lobbyist for a Washington, D.C. firm, so he understood the donor game. But when he was told after winning the March election that he needed to raise $2 million for the November reelection bid, which worked out to $18,000 per day, he was further determined to work toward reforming the system.

As part of the story, CBS used a staffer to take hidden cameras into the National Republican Congressional Committee (NRCC) private operations to show the "sweat shop" telemarking environment faced by members of Congress. They disclosed flow charts with the scripts to follow when making calls to different donors. They exposed the small offices with phones, computers, and lists of donors and the white boards on the walls keeping tallies about how much each member raised for the party and how they were doing on their campaign goals.

"The House schedule is actually arranged, in some ways, around fundraising," said Jolly. "You never see a committee working through lunch because those are your fundraising times. And then in between afternoon votes and evening votes, that's when you can see Democrats walking down this street, Republicans walking down that street to spend time on the phone making phone calls" (O'Donnell, 2016).

"If members would be candid, there's a lot of frustration centered around it," said Rep. Reid Ribble (R-WI), who retired after six years in Congress, which was two years earlier than his self-imposed four-term limit. Rep. Rick Nolan (D-MN), who served in the 1970s and was elected again in 2012, noted that both parties told newly elected officials they needed to spend 30 hours per week on fundraising, and that the "telemarketing" part of the job discouraged good people from running for office. Nolan said that Congress "has hardly become a democratic institution anymore ... because of all of the money in politics" (O'Donnell, 2016).

The need to constantly raise money surely is one of the worst parts of the job in running for office. "Running for office, raising money is something that's very hard for me to do ... not difficult in results, but difficult for me internally, you know. I hate it," said Dave Reichert, who decided not to run for reelection in 2018 in a swing district (Brunner, 2019).

The corrupting force of campaign funding can extend beyond members of Congress to affect staffers as well. As notable congressional scholar Norman Ornstein pointed out, staffers who have friends who are lobbyists can help get money from the federal budget for their friends' clients. This facilitating of legislative results, it is expected, will help bring further campaign contributions. "Lawmakers, who need millions for expensive election campaigns, 'shake down' lobbyists for contributions. In return, the lobbyists expect easy access to lawmakers. The quid pro quo extends down the organizational ladder to the congressional staff" (Gottlieb, 2015).

Jolly introduced the Stop Act which would ban all federal elected officials from directly soliciting campaign funds. Under the proposal, members of Congress could attend fundraisers, but they could not themselves ask for money. The bill did have some co-sponsors, but ultimately did not advance. Jolly won in 2014, but lost reelection in 2016, despite drawing about even in individual spending at around $2 million with his opponent Charlie Crist. Crist is a Republican-turned-Democrat who benefited from nearly $2.9 million in outside spending, compared to Jolly's $715,313. Outside funding also provided $179,404 in support of Crist, with just $10,602 in support of Jolly.

Legislative Background

The current campaign finance legal framework in American politics emerged from the Federal Election Campaign Acts of 1971 and 1974. The 1971 law required stricter disclosure of the source of campaign funding and expenditures. It required campaigns to file quarterly reports and it provided the basic legislative framework for what became political action committees (PACs). This allows groups like corporations, unions, or public interest groups to establish committees to solicit funds that can be expended in campaign-related activities for federal elections. Administration and enforcement of the law was initially decentralized between the clerk of the U.S. House, secretary of the U.S. Senate, and the comptroller general of the U.S. General Accounting Office.

The 1974 law authorized the creation of the Federal Election Commission (FEC) to be a central and independent regulatory agency for campaign finance. The law also imposed both contribution and spending limits on campaigns. The Supreme Court in the *Buckley v. Valeo* (1976) decision struck down the spending limits while upholding the limits on contributions.

In the *Buckley* case, the Court found that placing limits on campaign contributions served Congress' compelling interest of "safeguarding the integrity of elections." They also, however, said that spending limits restricted the First Amendment right to free speech enjoyed by "individuals, groups, and candidates." The decision was 7–1 with one abstention.

While the FEC had clear reporting rules for funds given directly to a candidate, which is called *hard money*, there was also *soft money* that was given to the political parties in nearly unlimited amounts for party-building activities. These soft monies were also used by the party to endorse and support candidates.

However, the most problematic type of political donations are called *dark money contributions*. Dark money is the undisclosed donation and spending of money intended to influence voters. Money can be undisclosed through two main loopholes. First, political nonprofits who may run ads are not legally obligated to disclose their donors – sometimes they do and sometimes they do not. If they are not formally recognized on spending reports, then the money is not traceable to a particular source. Secondly, Super PACs can accept donations from these political nonprofits and also from corporations that may be established as "shells" formed solely as pass-through organizations for political donations with no names attached to their donations (Center for Responsive Politics, Dark Money Basics). In other cases, the timing of donations can allow them to be disclosed after the election date.

Outside spending that is not disclosed or shielded from disclosure until after the election has had mixed outputs since 2010. Spending subject to "no disclosure" went from 44.9 percent of total campaign spending in 2010 to 30.1 percent in 2012, to 31.4 percent in 2014, to 12.9 percent in 2016, and to 13.7 percent in 2018, according to Open Secrets. Meanwhile funding with "some disclosure" increased from 7.2 percent in 2010 to 29.5 percent in 2012, but then dropped to 8.6 percent in 2014 before rising to 15 percent in 2016 and 36.4 percent of total outside spending by disclosure status in 2018 (Center for Responsive Politics, Excluding Party Committees).

In 1907, Congress under the leadership of President Theodore Roosevelt passed a ban on corporate fundraising, albeit in the wake of Roosevelt's own campaign scandal in the 1904 campaign. Named for populist Sen. Benjamin Tillman of South Carolina, the Tillman Act explicitly prohibited corporations and banks from contributing money to federal campaigns. Eventually, groups like unions, trade organizations, and other special interests began to create their own associations to raise money for candidates, namely political action committees (PACs).

A 1990 ruling by SCOTUS in *Austin v. Michigan Chamber of Commerce* upheld the ban on corporate spending for political contributions. The Michigan Campaign Finance Act had prohibited corporate funds from state campaigns and classified chambers of commerce as business associations. By a 6–3 decision, SCOTUS ruled to uphold the Michigan law "that prohibited corporations from using treasury money for independent expenditures to support or oppose candidates in elections for state offices." The court held the Chamber to be akin to a business group rather than a political organization. The Chamber argued that they should be exempt from the limitations because they were a "nonprofit ideological corporation" that was acting more like a political association than a business firm. The Court, however, found that the law did not violate the First or Fourteenth Amendments and was narrowly tailored to achieve the goals of avoiding corruption or the appearance of corruption.

The *Buckley* case set the ground rules for what was permissible in campaign financing until the passage of the Bipartisan Campaign Finance Reform Act (BCRA) of 2002. The BCRA was the first significant update to the laws from the 1970s. Signed by President George W. Bush, the law was also known as the McCain–Feingold Act, in recognition of its bipartisan Senate sponsors, John McCain (R-AZ) and Russ Feingold (D-WI). It also had bipartisan House sponsors in Reps. Christopher Shays (R-CT) and Martin Meehan (D-MA), and was the culminating legislation from a negotiating process that began in 1995 (Foreman, 2008).

The BRCA has four main components and one unintended consequence. First, it doubled the hard money expenditure limit. The 1974 limits were $1,000 per person per election cycle and $5,000 for PACs. The individual limits would double to $2,000 for the 2004 election and then increase by $100 each election cycle. So in 2006 it would be $2,100 rising to $2,800 for 2020. The law doubled PAC contributions from $5,000 to $10,000 and increased limits on donations to national parties indexed to inflation to increase each election cycle.

Second, the BCRA banned soft money donations to national political parties. This was a main factor for the law, to try to decrease the outside influence that could occur by skirting the letter of the law by giving additional money to the national parties for generic "party-building" activities rather than as earmarked for party campaign support to candidates running in the current cycle. State parties were still permitted to accept up to $10,000 per donor in soft money funding for the use of specific voter outreach or registration efforts.

The third main change from BCRA was that candidates, political parties, PACs, and other interests engaged in electioneering advocacy must explicitly claim credit or identify who is responsible for presenting the content of the advertisement with the "Stand By Your Ad" clause. The public is familiar with these disclaimers that have been used in advertisements since the 2004 campaign cycle.

Fourth, it imposed funding restrictions on "electioneering communications" in the form of "issue ads" or "coordinated expenditures" such as broadcast ads naming candidates within 60 days of an election. This provision would be at the root of several court challenges.

While the BCRA attempted to eliminate soft money, it also provided the unintended consequence of prompting outside groups to organize and spend money on their own rather than give it to political parties. The rise of "527 groups," so-called because of the IRS tax line that allows political advocacy by these type of independent organizations, added another dimension to campaigns. In the 2004 presidential election, Swift Boat Veterans for Truth was created by Bush family allies to denounce Democratic nominee John Kerry and his war record by featuring men with whom he served in Vietnam. The group did not have to disclose its donors and could mask the origin of attack. These 527 groups have been used since 2004, but were surpassed in importance with the advent of Super PACs.

The first challenge to the BCRA was in the case *McConnell v. Federal Elections Commission* (2003). The case was brought by an odd political alliance of U.S. Senator Mitch McConnell (R-KY), then the majority whip, the California Democratic Party, the ACLU, AFL-CIO, and the NRA to challenge the constitutionality of the law.

The BCRA had an unusual provision that provided for bypassing the typical judicial process with an early federal trial and a direct appeal to the Supreme Court. In the McConnell case, the Court upheld Congress's authority to ban soft money as part of its constitutional authority to regulate elections. The Court also rejected arguments that regulations on the source, content, or timing of political advertising violated the First Amendment. The 5-4 decision was authorized by Justices Sandra Day O'Connor and John Paul Stevens and joined by Justices David Souter, David Breyer, and Ruth Bader Ginsburg. The majority found that because the law regulated soft money contributions that are largely used for party-related activities like voter registration and voter outreach, soft money spending was not tantamount to expressing political values. Therefore, they would deserve more protection but in this case the Court found the restrictions to be minimal and Congress had a legitimate interest in preventing corruption or the appearance of corruption.

O'Connor was replaced on the Court by Samuel Alito in early 2006, and he would be the swing vote that moved the Court toward overturning parts of the BCRA in 2007 and 2010 and reversing their decisions in *Austin* and on a key component of the *McConnell* case.

In the case of *FEC v. Wisconsin Right to Life, Inc.* (2007), the Court defined a distinction between issue ads and express advocacy in siding with WRTL, a pro-life non-profit corporation. WRTL ran ads that encouraged viewers to contact the state's U.S. senators and tell them to oppose filibusters of judicial nominees. The group intended to run the ads through the election but were prohibited from running them within 60 days of the election due to the BCRA. However, the Court sided 5-4 with WRTL, claiming that their ads were legitimate issue ads rather than sham issue ads or express advocacy efforts. The majority stated that unless an ad expressly encourages the support or defeat of a candidate, it could be considered an issue ad. Justice Souter in the dissent noted that the WRTL ads were indistinguishable from political advocacy.

The 2008 election was another record year in terms of money raised and spent, fueled by Barack Obama's campaign. Obama won and eventually replaced Breyer and Souter with Elena Kagan and Sonia Sotomayor. Campaign finance was a talking point along the campaign trail for Obama, but not a serious priority in office. With the ability to raise enormous sums of money and to encourage others to spend on his behalf campaign, finance reform was not a major focus.

The U.S. Supreme Court decision in *Citizens United v. Federal Election Commission* (2010) changed campaign finance rules by striking down parts of BCRA. The *Citizens United* decision provided that corporations have the same free speech rights as individuals protected under the First Amendment. The majority also found that the law was not too broad in regulating speech in advertisements paid for by corporations or unions. This ruling opened the door for corporations to spend exorbitant amounts of money on political advocacy speech, as long as they do not coordinate with or endorse a candidate or party. As a result, outside expenditures can become a larger part of campaign spending.

The *Citizens United* case originated in 2008 with a dispute over *Hillary: The Movie*, a 90-minute documentary made by the so-named conservative nonprofit organization funded by conservative interests describing why Hillary Clinton would not make a good president. Citizens United produced the movie for purposes of distributing it to cable networks to make available to their customers on-demand. They also arranged to air commercials advertising how the documentary could be viewed within 30 days of the 2008 primary election season. If deemed to be "electioneering communications" under FEC guidelines, the documentary and ads promoting it would be prohibited from being aired.

Citizens United anticipated they would be fined by the FEC in violation of the BCRA and the ban on direct corporate spending on political advocacy ads, so they sought an injunction in U.S. District Court in Washington, D.C. arguing that Section 203 was unconstitutional. They argued that the movie did not fit the law's definition of "express advocacy" in support or against a candidate following the *WRTL* precedent.

Justice Breyer perhaps foresaw what would occur with a Court decision in favor of Citizens United allowing essentially unlimited corporate political speech when he said in oral argument:"Would that leave the country in a situation where corporations and trade unions can spend as much as they want in the last 30 days on television ads, etc., of this kind, but political parties couldn't, because political parties can only spend their hard money on this kind of expenditure? Therefore the group that is charged with the responsibility of building a platform that will appeal to a majority of Americans is limited, but the groups that have particular interest, like corporations or trade unions, can spend as much as they want? Am I right about the consequence?" (*Citizens United v. Federal Election Commission*).

Indeed we appear to have witnessed Justice Breyer's concern in the 2016 and 2018 election cycles. "Increasingly we are seeing a tale of two fund raising stories – one story for Super PACs and outside groups which can accept unlimited contributions and which are thriving – and a very different landscape for political parties, which are forced to operate under strict contribution limits and prohibitions. Absent legislative action, this imbalance in the campaign finance system could become even more pronounced in future election cycles" (Toner and Trainer, 2019).

Citizens United essentially formalized a campaign finance structure built by the Supreme Court since *Buckley*. Individuals can spend an unlimited amount of funds as part of their First Amendment rights and so can corporations. Corporations are entities that are entitled to the same constitutional rights as individuals when it comes to participation in political campaigns.

The next piece to fall from Congress' efforts to regulate campaign spending was with the *McCutcheon v. FEC* (2014) decision. The Court removed the aggregate giving limits per election cycle in a challenge from an active, wealthy Republican donor. This allows an individual donor to give the maximum amount to an unlimited number of candidates. The Court issued a plurality decision of 4-3 with Justice Thomas concurring with the majority opinion but writing in concurrence that the limits in contributions upheld in *Buckley* should be overturned.

The Race for the 2020 Nomination

Democrats had a scattershot approach to campaign finance reform. There was a faction of Democrats who said they would not accept PAC money. They bashed corporations and corporate donors. On the evening when Joe Biden announced his 2020 presidential bid he held a fundraiser with corporate leaders. This was followed by his allies forming a Super PAC called For the People PAC to raise millions of dollars for Biden's bid. It may be necessary in the campaign finance arms race to have an aligned Super PAC, but it makes it difficult for a candidate to credibly talk about overturning *Citizens United* when they are benefiting from the system.

The importance of fundraising was seen in the Democratic National Committee's rules to qualify for their 2020 presidential debates. Candidates had to be polling at 1 percent in three of the qualifying polls *or* raise funds from 65,000 unique donors from at least 20 different states. There were 20 candidates that qualified for the first debates over two nights in Miami. For the third debate, the DNC raised it to 2 percent in four qualifying polls *and* 130,000 unique donors. These criteria demonstrate the importance of fundraising as a signal of standing within the party. Of course, early fundraising is already essential for any presidential campaign, but there now seems to be emphasis on showcasing one's fundraising abilities rather than publicizing policy ideas. The number of donors has become a marker, showing the breadth of support a candidate may have, especially among grassroots political participants.

Emphasizing the importance of focused fundraising, Democrats in May 2019 announced a Unity Fund to raise money for a PAC aimed at combining efforts of Democratic donors regardless of who is the nominee. Former President Obama was part of the rollout effort in an email appeal from the Democratic Party.

Campaign finance featured prominently in the DNC's lengthy 2016 platform. Under the entry of "Fixing Our Broken Campaign Finance System," Democrats pledged to "fight for real campaign finance reform now." That is followed by the bold pronouncement that "Democrats support a constitutional amendment to overturn the Supreme Court's decisions in *Citizens United* and *Buckley v. Valeo*" (Democratic, 2016: 23). It is likely that the 2020 platform will contain a similar statement.

On the other side, the Republican platform calls for repealing the existing campaign finance regulations. This plank has been part of both the 2012 and 2016 platforms. In 2016, the "Crony Capitalism and Corporate Welfare" section chastised cronyism and bashed bureaucratic favoritism (Gribbin, 2016: 28). In the Republican Party, campaign finance was not on the issue agenda with Donald Trump in 2016 and likely will not be with him at the top of the ticket in 2020. After the Trump era, another assessment of the political party environment will be warranted.

Possible Reforms

Now that the legal and policy environment is clearer, it is time to explore possible reforms to the system to lessen the importance of raising campaign funds by candidates for office. Some basic reforms include requiring more financial disclosure, lowering contribution limits, restricting issue ads, providing free TV air time, eliminating PACS, implementing public financing, overturning the Supreme Court's decisions, or amending the Constitution. Each has strengths and weaknesses, some of which are described below.

Overturn Citizens United

The 2010 *Citizens United* decision was a serious setback for campaign reform efforts. It set new precedence allowing corporations to spend unlimited amounts of money and often with shady disclosure. The only two ways to end this practice are to overturn the Court's decision or to amend the Constitution. With the selection of two more conservative justices by President Trump, the Court is not likely to revisit its decision or overturn it any time soon. Furthermore, Congress does not have the will to pass a law under these circumstances to challenge the precedent.

This means that a constitutional amendment to ban or limit corporate spending in political campaigns is the only available recourse to replace the *Citizens United* framework. Each election cycle, major candidates, mostly but not all Democrats, call for a constitutional amendment to end *Citizens United*. The list includes most presidential and many congressional candidates.

Constitutional Amendment

There is a popular movement behind proposing a 28th Amendment to the Constitution to essentially provide Congress with the authority to override the *Citizens* decision. There have been multiple proposals in each congressional session in recent decades. The number of these proposals has increased since 2010 after *Citizens*.[1] One proposal had more than 200 co-sponsors in the 114th Congress and enjoys the support of the nonprofit group American Promise. This particular proposal would permit Congress and the states to regulate and set reasonable limits on how much money candidates can raise and spend. Additionally, it would permit legislation to "distinguish between natural persons and corporations or other artificial entities created by law, including by prohibiting such entities from spending money to influence elections."[2]

In June 2019, New Hampshire became the 20th state to vote in support of an amendment that would provide some such remedy to the "corporation clause." Numerous local governments have passed resolutions that call for a campaign finance-related amendment or point to support for specific reform proposals. This includes 27 local resolutions in Maine, 64 in Vermont, 82 in New Hampshire, 207 in Massachusetts – a robust New England region – along with 144 in Wisconsin, 50 in California, and dozens in other states.[3]

Further Limits

The amounts of personal contributions and PAC contributions are already limited. While they are higher than what most Americans can afford to contribute, they are relatively low for wealthy individuals. It is not likely that Congress will vote to reduce the current limits, even if they could garner the votes.

It is possible that Congress could refuse to raise the limits further than currently permitted under BCRA to keep with inflation, as a way of placing limits. With limits on individual contributions, candidates would need to rely more on parties or find outside groups to support them. That would limit the amount candidates could raise and spend, but what would be needed are limits on corporate spending.

Public Finance

There is the public option to have taxpayers finance a partial or the full cost of political campaigns. Many countries and 14 U.S. states have a form of public campaign financing. The concept was proposed by Theodore Roosevelt in his 1907 State of the Union speech, but not enacted by Congress until it was introduced with the 1971 FECA.

The 1971 law mandated public financing for presidential elections, but this provision was struck down by the Supreme Court in the *Buckley* case. Use of public funding is voluntary, but candidates must meet three threshold criteria to qualify. These rules in primary elections include having raised money from donors in at least 20 states, agreeing to limit expenditures to an amount called the *national spending limit* that is adjusted for inflation each cycle, and limiting the spending of funds from their own personal accounts toward their campaign.

There is a box on the federal tax return form where a taxpayer can elect to donate $3 to the Presidential Election Campaign Fund, money that does not impact the amount of the tax liability. The amount of money in that fund helps determine how much public funding is available each cycle.

It may be the case that inequality in the financing of primary candidates may significantly impact the selection of a nominee, but the presidential candidate that raises and spends the most does not necessarily win the office. "Inequality in the resources available to candidates in presidential primary campaigns is likely to have a greater effect than in the presidential general election, in which public financing is available to both major-party candidates" (Theiss-Morse et al., 2018). However, most major party candidates eschew public financing. In 2000, both Bush and Gore skipped over it, as did Bush and Kerry in 2004. In 2008, Obama initially said he would take public matching funds, but then reversed course when he was able to outraise his opponents. John McCain, who ran a shoestring budget to win the nomination, did take public financing in 2008. Obama and Mitt Romney passed on public dollars in 2012, that being the first presidential election of the *Citizens United* era where supporters of both candidates and parties could give unlimited funds to Super PACs in support of or opposition to one of the candidates. In 2016, Trump spent around $66.1 million of his own money and did not raise as prolifically from traditional big Republican donors initially while doing well with new, small donors. Although Trump's opponents outspent him in 2016, his victory was aided by the enormous amount of free media he received (Theiss-Morse et al., 2018).

Of the 14 states that have public financing, each one requires a candidate to limit both their private donations and their campaign spending in exchange for a share of public financial support. There are two "clean" election states, Maine and

Arizona, that offer full campaign funding while the other states provide matching funds.

Several states also provide public money to political parties to help fund activities like conventions and voter registration drives. Some states allow taxpayers to donate a part of their tax refund to a fund that finances campaigns. In Florida, the state remits to the political parties 85 percent of the filing fees collected while reserving 15 percent for the general fund (National Conference, 2019a).

There are countries that have no limits on contributions or on expenditures. These are mostly medium to smaller sized European countries which have peculiar features in their campaign systems different to the U.S. They typically have limited timeframes for campaigns of about six weeks. They are either forbidden from advertising on television or in other cases given free air time for ads. Furthermore, they often are systems with strong political parties who have greater control over who occupies seats, thus weakening incentives to contribute to individual members (Waldman, 2014). These parameters, which limit the need for excess campaign spending, would not likely work in the U.S. due to our long, competitive campaigns.

One innovative idea used in Seattle is to issue "democracy vouchers" to residents who can donate them to candidates. The candidates, in turn, cash them in for money taken from a city fund (Beekman, 2019). Voters approved the measure to raise and use additional property taxes to fund the program in 2015 and it went into effect in 2017. The idea is to get more people involved in the political process, to support grassroots candidates, and to encourage more interaction with voters and less time chasing wealthy donors. Each voter or eligible resident gets four $25 vouchers. They may donate them all to a single campaign, divide their donations, or decide not to use them. Candidates must abide by rules for using the vouchers. For the first city council election in which the program was in effect, there was a significant increase on the number of donors and more of them from within the city limits. Whether other municipalities or even states would want to consider this concept will be determined through the federal system where it may work better in some places than in others.

Mutual Disarmament Agreements

It appears that we are not going to see the Republican Party or Democratic Party and their closely related companion groups pledge to give up on campaign spending in the current political environment. It will require either a new law to force compliance, or groups and individual candidates mutually agreeing to limit or end campaign spending. Outside groups will want to influence campaigns by any means that they can. It is left to individual candidates to not accept support from outside groups as part of their own pledge.

One hope for containment is through private decisions to mutually decide to limit spending or discourage groups from spending on your benefit. The People's

Pledge was used by Massachusetts U.S. Senate candidates Elizabeth Warren and Scott Brown during the 2012 election. This was a formal agreement between the candidates and their campaigns to limit expenditures to candidates' campaigns and party committees. The candidates would discourage outside groups from spending on television, radio, or Internet on their behalf. If groups made outside expenditures that provided a benefit to a candidate, then the campaign of that candidate that had signed the pledge was subject to a fine. For example Warren and Brown agreed to pay a penalty by donating half of the value of the ad to a charity chosen by their opponent. Brown donated twice (McGrane, 2017).

The People's Pledge did reduce the amount of outside spending in their race compared to others in 2012, Common Cause Massachusetts found. This resulted in significantly less negative ads in Massachusetts than in other states with competitive U.S. Senate races that year. Virginia, Wisconsin, and Ohio, in particular, were hard-fought races full of outside spending and negative ads, something somewhat avoided in the Warren–Brown matchup due to the People's Pledge. The Pledge also reduced the amount of dark money, a large component of some other 2012 races, and increased the amount of small donors relative to corporate donors in that campaign (Creighton, 2013).

Warren proposed a People's Pledge to her opponent in her 2016 reelection. Her Republican opponent said he would not sign the pledge and noted that Warren had $4.8 million cash on hand in her campaign account at the time. Warren said, "I wish the system were different. I wish that we could take steps across the country to get money out of politics but the People's Pledge is a step in the right direction" (McGrane, 2017).

The pledge was used in a couple of primaries in Massachusetts and Rhode Island, suggested in a few other races, including mayoral races in Boston and Los Angeles, but not widely adopted. It was taken up by Common Cause and Public Citizen in the 2014 campaign cycle, but the idea has not caught steam. While it may not simply be "only a matter of time" before campaign finance reform is passed, candidates or even local governments themselves can make greater use of the pledge to "control their campaigns while (1) sparing citizens from overwhelming and negative advertising and (2) showing citizens that they are willing to go beyond the minimum requirements of campaign finance laws to prevent the appearance that special interests are trying to buy their support" (Wechsler, 2014).

Republican Dan Sullivan challenged Democrat Mark Begich to sign the pledge in their 2014 Alaska U.S. Senate race. Begich's campaign refused and pointed to Sullivan's support for the *Citizens United* decision and Begich's support for a constitutional amendment to replace the decision. "What worked for Brown and Warren has really been nothing more than fodder for political arguments in other Senate races" (Sullivan, 2014). Candidates are not willing to give up on outside aid that can come in great bundles if party interests sense they need the boost.

It appears that the pledge works best – and possibly even at all – when candidates suggest it themselves rather than citizen's groups, when it is proposed early enough in the campaign to be seen as a viable option rather than simply a public relations tool, and under circumstances where the impetus stems from the perspective that both (or all, if multiple) candidates can benefit from the pledge. The inability to meet all these conditions makes it difficult to implement the pledge.

Legislative Recusal Rules

Another way to possibly get around the Court's decisions is through legislative procedural rules. Congress could pass rules under which its members need to operate. They would need to be passed by both the House and Senate and would be internal to their workings. The aim would be to shape legislators' behavior.

This approach would be moving from a focus on "inputs" of campaign contributions and instead focus on legislators' "outputs." One scholar argues that "Legislative recusal rules, enacted separately in the House and Senate, could be used to preclude members of each chamber from voting on any legislation that presents a member of Congress with a significant conflict of interest. For example, if a Super PAC spends a large sum of money to run ads on behalf of a congressional candidate and that Super PAC's funders happened to have a strong interest in a specific piece of legislation, the congressional candidate, once elected to office, would be deemed to have a conflict of interest and would be precluded from voting on such legislation" (Mazo, 2018).

Legislators could enact such rules easily, without fear of unconstitutionality – it is merely a matter of having the will to do so.

Recusal rules have existed since the early days of the American republic. They are used in many state legislatures and by judges and justices (National Conference, 2019b). It is a basic ethical precept that if you have a conflict of interest or stand to benefit personally from a decision, then as a public official you should not vote on that matter. There are laws at the local level against graft, but in Congress there has been a wide latitude for private benefit permitted under the rules and laws. Recusals are more common at the state legislative level, but there are also more times than not that legislators do not opt to recuse, whether consciously or not, and may or may not benefit from their votes.

Conclusion

As Justices O'Connor and Stevens wrote in the McConnell decision, "money, like water, will always find an outlet." Each time that Congress puts regulations in place to attempt to limit the amount of money in campaigns, the Supreme Court has chipped away at the standards and the political marketplace drives even greater spending through multiple channels.

It appears that the current arms race playing field – where access to enormous campaign funds are a critical aspect of our democracy – will continue. Part of the problem is that the people needed to reform the system are the ones with the stranglehold on the system and are perpetuating the problem. There is not likely to be a major fix provided by Congress, and even if there were, it may not likely withstand Supreme Court muster. The President of the United States can do little about campaign funding; and while candidates for the position may speak about reforms, they cannot drive the policy, only the rhetoric, and must still play the game of raising and spending gobs of money if they want to secure a major party nomination or seriously compete for the office.

Since it does not appear likely that *Citizens United* will be overturned, it rests with Congress and state and local governments to find their own ways to attempt to limit the raising and spending of money, or reducing the impact of campaign funding on American democracy.

Notes

1 See http://united4thepeople.org/amendments/
2 See https://www.americanpromise.net/who-we -are/the-28th-amendment/
3 See http://united4thepeople.org/state-local/

References

Beekman, D., 2019. These Voters Are Using Democracy Vouchers to Influence Seattle's City Council Races. *Seattle Times*, 19 June. https://www.seattletimes.com/seattle-new s/politics/ candidates-for-seattle-city-council-have-collected-1-6-million-in-demo cracy-vouchers-so-far/.

Brunner, J., 2019. Retired Rep. Dave Reichert Joins Lobbying Firm, Will Work Initially on Anti-Human Trafficking Project. *The Seattle Times*, 14 January. https://www.seattletimes .com/seattle-news/politics/retired-rep-dave-reichert-joins-lobbying-firm-will-wo rk-initially-on-anti-human-trafficking-project/.

Bump, P., 2013. Unmasking Ryan Lizza's Mystery Fundraiser. *The Atlantic*, 25 June.

Center for Responsive Politics. Dark Money Basics. *Center for Responsive Politics*. https:// www. opensecrets.org/dark-money/basics.

Center for Responsive Politics. Excluding Party Committees. *Center for Responsive Politics*. https://www.opensecrets.org/outsidespending/disclosure.php.

Citizens United v. Federal Election Commission (Transcript), 557 U.S. 932, 129 S. Ct. 2893. 2009. https://www.supremecourt.gov/oral_arguments/argument_transcripts/2008/ 08-205.pdf.

Costa, J., 2013. What's the Cost of a Seat in Congress. *MapLight*, 10 March. https://maplight. org/story/whats-the-cost-of-a-seat-in-congress.

Creighton, T., 2013. A Plea for a Pledge: Outside Spending in Competitive 2012 US Senate Races. *Massachusetts Common Cause*, 12 April.

Davidson, R.H., Oleszek, W.J., Lee, F.E. and Schickler, E., 2013. *Congress and its Members*. Washington, D.C.: CQ Press.

Democratic Platform Committee, 2016. *2016 Democratic Party Platform*. Democratic National Committee.

Foreman, S.D., 2008. Bipartisan Campaign Finance Act. In: Warren, K.F. ed., *Encyclopedia of US Campaigns, Elections, and Electoral Behavior*. Los Angeles CA: Publications.

Gottlieb, S., 2015. *Red to Blue: Congressman Chris Van Hollen and Grassroots Politics*. London U.K.: Routledge.

Graham, D.A., 2013. The Humiliating Fund Raising Existence of a Member of Congress. *The Atlantic*, 25 June.

Gribbin, B. ed., 2016. *Republican Platform 2016*. Republican National Committee.

Mayersohn, A., 2018. Most Expensive Midterms in History Set Several Spending Records. Center for Responsive Politics, 8 November. https://www.opensecrets.org/news/20 18/11/2018 -midterm -records-shatter/.

Mazo, E.D., 2018. Reguating Campaign Finance through Legislative Recusal Rules. In: Mazo, E.D. and Kuhner, T.K. eds., *Democracy by the People: Reforming Campaign Finance in America*. Cambridge, UK: Cambridge University Press.

McGrane, V., 2017. Warren Wants Another 'People's Pledge' Barring outside Advertising. *Boston Globe*, 31 March. https://www.bostonglobe.com/news/politics/2017/03/31/ elizabeth- warren-wants-sign-another-people-pledge-barring-outside-advertising-fr om-senate-race/HrNpCv9p3xholKFWd9mKAL/story.html.

McKay, A.M., 2018. Fundraising for Favors? Linking Lobbyist-Hosted Fundraisers to Legislative Benefits. *Political Research Quarterly*, 71(4), pp. 869–880.

National Conference of State Legislatures, 2019a. Overview of State Laws on Public Financing. *National Conference of State Legislatures*. http://www.ncsl.org/research/electi ons-and- campaigns/public-financing-of- campaigns-overview.aspx.

National Conference of State Legislatures, 2019b. 50 State Table: Voting Recusal Provision, National Conference of State Legislatures 8 May. http://www.ncsl.org/research/ ethics/50- state-table-voting-recusal-provisions.aspx.

O'Donnell, N., 2016. Are Members of Congress Becoming Telemarketers: Stop Fundraising, Start Working, Says Fla. Rep. David Jolly, Who Is Seeking to Ban Federal-Elected Officials from Dialing for Dollars. *60 Minutes*, 24 April. https://www.cbsnews.com/ new`s/60- minutes-are-members-of-congress-becoming-telemarketers/.

Sullivan, S., 2014. The 'People's Pledge' Is Back in Alaska. Wait, What the Heck Is That? *The Washington Post*, 10 June. https://www.washingtonpost.com/news/post-politics /wp/2 014/06/10/the-peoples-pledge-is-back-in-alaska-wait-what-the-heck-is-that/?nored irect=on&utm_term=.4f5da7ecab4d.

The Center for Public Integrity, 2019. Center for Public Integrity/IPSOS Poll: How Should Presidential Campaigns be Regulated? *The Center for Public Integrity*. https:// publicintegrity.org/politics/elections/center-for-public-integrity-ipsos-poll-electio ns-2019/.

Theiss-Morse, E.A., Wagner, M.W., Flanigan, W.H. and Zingale, N.H., 2018. *Political Behavior of the American Electorate*. CQ Press.

Toner, M.E. and Trainer, K.E., 2019. The Money Wars: Emerging Campaign Finance Trends and Their Impact on 2018 and Beyond. In: Sabato, L. and Kondik, K. eds., *The Blue Wave: The 2018 Midterms and What They Mean for the 2020 Elections*. Rowman & Littlefield.

Uhlig, M.A., 1987. Jesse Unruh, A California Political Power, Dies. *New York Times*, 6 August.

Waldman, P., 2014. How Our Campaign Finance System Compares to Other Countries. *The American Prospect*, 4 April. https://prospect.org/article/how-our-campaign-fina nce- system-compares-other-countries.

Wechsler, R., 2014. The People's Pledge in Mayoral Races. *Cityethics*, 18 June. http://www. cityethics.org/content/peoples-pledge-mayoral-races.

6

THE STRUCTURE OF PRIMARIES

Steve Vancore, Glenn Burhans, Dario Moreno, Anthony Kusich, and Patrick J. Villalonga

Rep. David Jolly: Closed primaries produce intrinsically partisan candidates often with little cross-partisan appeal. And it makes sense. To win a primary among only those voters who identify with your party will naturally incentivize candidates to take a more partisan approach to victory.

The argument for closed primaries also makes sense. If a party is to choose its nominee to put before voters, why should it allow non-members of that party to participate in its nominating process? The courts have largely agreed and supported the notion that parties can operate under their own rules and with exclusivity.

But closed primaries raise two points to consider. First, in a world in which ballot access rules largely favor the two major parties and provide significant hurdles to smaller parties with fewer resources, are we truly getting a contest of meritocracy on our November ballots when voters are faced with a simple binary choice between a Republican and a Democrat? Also consider that in some states, registered independents, those with no party affiliation, outnumber Republicans and Democrats. Why then do we allow the process to produce a result where voters, even the large number of independents, are faced with voting only for a Republican or a Democrat?

Secondly, the process of a party nominating a candidate has a rich history that at one time included large party conventions and gatherings at local, state, and national levels. Today we see the national conventions of the major parties, but very few have state nominating conventions. Over generations, the parties have largely defaulted to using state election machinery to support their party's nominating process. Which raises a very simple question of fairness. If closed primaries make intuitive sense, and if the courts recognize a party's right to exclusivity, to shutting out any voters except their own party members, why then should all taxpayers have to underwrite a party's exclusive activity by paying for public nominating of strictly party candidates? That is, why should a state or county election office administer through public financing the nominating process of a political party that demands the right to exclude all voters but their own?

Rep. Patrick E. Murphy: Upon entering Congress, I quickly realized that the vast majority of elected officials are most loyal to those they are directly accountable to: the small sliver of voters in a primary. Whether it is a local, state, or federal election, the same basic problem exists – too few voters in a primary are determining the outcome in the broader election. As mentioned previously, around 90% of U.S. House districts are predetermined to be Republican or Democratic, so the only election that really matters is the primary. And with 12–15% of voters showing up in a primary, the candidates have almost no choice but to appeal to that small base of people. While I've heard arguments on all sides of this conversation, I believe our democracy is better served with more access to the polls and more people voting in all elections.

While California is still weighing the pros and cons of the top-two system, for instance, I hope more states begin experimenting with ideas to expand the electorate in the primary and allow independents to have a formal voice, hopefully leading to reforms that may be adopted at the federal level. Our founders were brilliant in having the states be testing grounds for democracy, and now we have to learn and evolve accordingly.

The problem with primaries was made crystal clear to me after an official trip to Afghanistan I took in 2014 with several other members of Congress, one of whom was an ardent Tea Party leader. Throughout the trip I was impressed with this particular member's leadership and poise. However, upon returning to the States, we had a small meeting with the press to discuss lessons learned – and the member immediately began blaming Democrats and President Obama for everything wrong with the war. This was the first time a partisan word had been uttered in a five-day period and I immediately realized that the comments had nothing to do with the truth or even this person's beliefs, but rather another appeal to the sliver of primary voters that would be casting a vote. Any wavering from the extreme position or anything less than outright hatred toward the Democratic president would have been viewed as caving and weak leadership – and could have led to this individual losing the next primary election. As frustrating as it is to admit, far too many members of Congress, on both sides of the aisle, are voting against their beliefs and putting their party and re-election above what's best for our country.

One of the bases for the contemporary study of campaigns, political parties, and elected officials derives from the process and structure of elections. The electoral system influences who gets elected and, more importantly, how we are governed. Apart from a federal law which mandates quadrennial presidential elections and biennial Congressional elections, the manner in which candidates for office are selected is as convoluted and diverse as the constituencies themselves. The constitution grants each state the right to develop its own election procedures, rules, and laws. Additionally, each state has its own unique voter registration, identification procedures, and rules for mail-in and early voting.

Both parties rely on direct primaries as an integral part of the current candidate selection process, yet many observers argue that the current structure of primaries has contributed to the polarization and gridlock that currently plagues government. They argue that primaries are simply low turnout elections dominated by the die-hard party members. Without moderates or centrist voters participating, primaries tend to select candidates on the ideological extremes. The importance of primary elections and their structure cannot be overstated because they often determine the outcome of legislative races in non-competitive districts – particularly given pervasive gerrymandering. Consequently, reforming the structure of primaries to increase voter participation would result in the elections of candidates more representative of their states or districts, rather than representing only the most committed and ideological extremes as they tend to do now. By exploring the current structures of primaries and alternative models for those key elections, state legislatures and voters can make more informed decisions on reforming, or not reforming, the direct primary.

Our federalist system has created a great deal of variety in the types of primary elections across states. Primary elections come in various forms. The most common are *closed* party primaries – in which only registered members of the party can vote – and *open* primaries – in which non-party members can vote in a party's primary. Each of these has modified variants, such as partially closed or partially open, which also have variations. The general characteristics of these modified primaries range from allowing the non-party-affiliated to participate, allowing party members to cross over from one party to the other, allowing voters to pick a party's ballot to vote in that election, or allowing (or requiring) same-day party registration. In this chapter, we will take a quick look at the three main primary systems. We discuss their histories, their technicalities, and arguments for and against each.

Closed Primaries

Twenty-eight states currently have closed or semi-closed primaries. In this system, people may vote in a party primary only if they were a registered member of that party 30–60 days prior to the election. Voters not affiliated with any political parties may not participate in party primaries. Thirteen states have a strict closed primary system.[1] Another fifteen states have semi-closed primaries.[2] These states allow voters to register or change party preference on election day. For example, Massachusetts allows unaffiliated voters or members of minor political parties to vote in the primary of either major political party.

Primary elections were a product of the electoral reforms that occurred in the United States during the first three decades of the twentieth century. These reforms

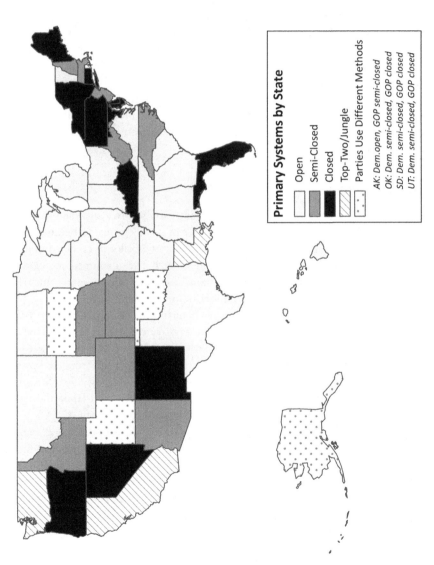

FIGURE 6.1   Primary System By State.

– along with direct elections of senators (the 17th Amendment), female suffrage (the 19th Amendment), and the adaptation of the Australian ballot (secret ballot) – were progressive efforts to expand and improve American democracy. Primary elections replaced caucuses and conventions as the primary method for selecting major party nominations. Primaries were viewed as a more democratic method of selecting the party's standard-bearer than selection by the party bosses. This is important because during the first three decades of the twentieth century, many states and most legislative districts were either solidly Democratic or solidly Republican. Having so many one-party constituencies meant that direct primary elections were, as Hirano and Snyder point out, "the only 'real' election for most offices" (2019).

Primary elections were kept closed because parties have a 1st Amendment right to determine who can select (or, more accurately, who cannot select) their respective nominees. Recently many states have abandoned closed primaries and instituted open primaries, primarily swayed by the argument that closed primaries give too much power to only a small sliver of registered voters, who tend to be the most active and most ideologically extreme. This in turn contributes to increased polarization and legislative gridlock. More and more states are adopting open primary systems in order to increase voter participation and mitigate party polarization.

Open Primaries

Open primaries allow voters to participate in any party primary regardless of party affiliation.[33] They are sometimes referred to as *pick-a-party* primaries because voters can select which party's primary they wish to cast a ballot in on election day. The evidence, however, suggests that the difference between an open and closed primary is quite small. Hirano and Snyder conclude that a shift to open primaries would not significantly increase the number of moderate nominees (2019).

The case of the 2014 election in Virginia confirms the limits of this reform. In 2014, few observers would question the conservative credentials of then-House Majority Leader Rep. Eric Cantor. His 100% rating by the National Right to Life Committee and 0% rating by NARAL Pro-Choice America stood as a clear testament to this fact. He was not only a true conservative earning a 96% lifetime rating from the American Conservative Union, he was also anti-labor and had earned the enmity of the nation's largest labor organization, the AFL-CIO.

Despite these top-notch GOP credentials, Cantor was soundly – and some would say "easily" – defeated in his primary in a near-landslide after outspending his opponent more than 10-1. He lost 55% to 45% to a college professor named Dave Brat in what was viewed as a stunning and altogether unexpected defeat. The *New York Times* quoted Mr. Brat as saying, "The American people want to pay attention to serious ideas again," and that "our founding was built by people who were political philosophers, and we need to get back to that, away from this kind of cheap political rhetoric of right and left" (Martin, 2014).

Dave Brat viewed himself as the voice of the American people. His sage reflection on the philosophies of our nation's founders claimed to eschew the rhetoric of the left and right. This was, according to Brat, a win for the hearts and minds of *all* Americans. Fox News' Laura Ingraham claimed he won because he had "a lot of heart." But more importantly, and perhaps more tellingly, she claimed this was something "really big" not for our country but for the Republican Party.

Attempting to explain his defeat, analysts cited Cantor's incumbency, lackluster campaign, and his losing touch with constituents by being rooted in Washington within House leadership. They pointed to Cantor's dispassionate campaign, poor polling analysis, and other seemingly thoughtful reasons why he lost. Some analysts like FiveThirtyEight.com pointed out that Cantor's loss could be attributed in part to a general decline in respect for incumbents across the board (Enten, 2014).

Yet the Congressman with a lifetime rating of 100% on pro-life issues and who earned a solid A-rating from one of the leading conservative institutions simply was not conservative enough for the small sliver of the electorate that actively participates in primaries. Indeed, Mr. Brat and conservative talk radio claimed that the Republican majority leader had softened his stance on issues like immigration and were aghast that he proffered regret over shutting down the government during budget negotiations. (This was a sentiment that was nonetheless shared by an overwhelming majority of Americans at the time.) But the reality remains that Cantor drifted to the center and was, as it is commonly known, "primaried" in his own district. In a constituency with nearly 780,000 residents and a voting-age population of 590,000, Brat secured a victory with just 36,105 votes – or 55% of those who took a Republican ballot that day.

Eric Cantor was not voted out of office by all of his constituents, or by voters who felt he had lost touch, or by those who saw his opponent as a college professor with heart. The fact of the matter is that only a tiny sliver of his constituents cast ballots: primary-voting Republicans. Virginia's primary election model is far from the most restrictive. Virginia has what is known as modified open primaries, where voters are not registered by party at all and can grab any party's ballot on primary day. But some voters not affiliated with a major party often see this for what it is – being invited to someone else's election. And while they are legally allowed to cast a ballot, they rarely do. Non-party affiliated voters are simply not inclined to go out and vote in these types of races.

Nonpartisan Blanket Primary

A more radical reform is the adaptation of a blanket primary system. In the blanket primary, all candidates for an office appear on the same ballot, with the top two highest vote-getters in the primary advancing to the general election, regardless of party. Unlike the closed, open, or modified primaries, blanket primaries do not determine a party's nominee. Rather, they serve as a broader winnowing process.

Supporters have claimed that a blanket primary system – one that lets all voters participate – ensures that lawmakers do not just have to answer to just a small fraction of voters, but must answer to everyone. Louisiana has famously operated under this system since 1975, which has been nicknamed the "jungle primary." California first used the blanket primary in 2012 after passing Proposition 14 in 2010, and the state of Washington has used a nonpartisan blanket primary since 2008.

Proponents reasoned that the current system of closed and semi-open primaries are disadvantageous for nonpartisans because most duly registered and qualified voters are excluded or discouraged by law from casting a ballot. They argued that the results of most contests in closed primary systems are statistically predetermined. In Florida, for example, more than four out of five legislative seats will be effectively selected in the primary due to statistical manipulation by the legislators who have drawn the legislative districts. In other words, voters only cast "meaningful" ballots in 20% of the contests. By the time most voters are allowed to vote in a general election, the outcome has already been determined by the thinnest slice of the majority party's voters.

If 80% of candidates know they only have to answer to a small sliver of the electorate – a shrinking electorate, by the way, as more and more voters chose "no party affiliation" – then they can easily disregard the will of the other voters. For Democrats, that means never saying no to unions, environmentalists, pro-choice activists, or gun control activists. For Republicans, it means always following dictates by the NRA, never considering tax raises, and opposing any measure that expands healthcare or resembles Obamacare.

This is not to pass judgment on the NRA or labor unions, but in virtually every case in virtually every district, most incumbents and candidates need only pay homage to their respective flanks: the Democrats to the left and the Republicans to the right. In the closed system there is virtually no room for working across the aisle, compromising, finding middle ground, or simply trying to solve real problems.

After the horrific shooting in Parkland, Florida at Marjorie Stoneman Douglas High School, Florida state lawmakers were under tremendous pressure to pass a comprehensive school safety bill. The shooting happened in the middle of the legislative session, meaning lawmakers had no chance to duck for cover. As the bill began to take shape, the impact of closed primaries began to appear. Most far-left Democrats opposed the bill, citing the expansion of some guns into schools and the fact that many of the measures did not go far enough. Conversely, the far-right expressed concern that any gun control was too much and stood with the NRA in opposing the bill. For exactly the opposite reasons, far-left and far-right members were united in opposition. Perhaps if more members represented swing districts where opinion was likely to be more measured and persuadable, this would not be the case. The national pressure – which was enormous – coupled with leadership from the Speaker of the House, the Speaker-designate, and the Senate President (all conservative Republicans) as well as the lawmakers who represented Parkland (all Democrats) led to the close passage of a comprehensive bill, aided by the passionate urging of the Parkland families. It got done, but it took all that just to hold the center.

Proponents of blanket primaries point to the example of California to illustrate how reforming the structures of primaries can empower voters. They argue that blanket primaries have had a substantial impact on California's system. In the early 2000s, shortly after the Enron scandal, the state was in the midst of a financial crisis. Due to government inflexibility and a persistent unwillingness for the parties to compromise in the legislature, Californians were forced to endure planned rolling blackouts. Republican lawmakers refused to accept any proposal that raised taxes, borrowed money, or expanded the role of unions. The Democrats, on the other hand, would not accept any changes that were not approved by the state's largest and most influential labor groups or in any way angered environmental activists. Crippling deadlock ensued.

Frustrated by a system where most lawmakers only had to answer to a small subset of the electorate, voters revolted by electing moderate Republican Arnold Schwarzenegger as governor in an unprecedented recall election. Still, nearly a decade after the Enron scandal, things were not much better and California lawmakers could not pass budgets on time. Gridlock intransigence was becoming the norm by now. After two tries, Schwarzenegger and his allies pushed a blanket primary system initiative through the legislature in order to secure votes for the budget. Under the system, all voters are allowed to vote in the first-round primary regardless of party affiliation. The top two vote-getters move to the general election where voters get a second look at the top two candidates, regardless of their party affiliation. The candidate who gets a majority from this run-off is the winner.

The key here is that candidates must face *all* voters in their respective districts and not just a small sliver of party activists. Indeed, the results were remarkable. In more open electoral systems, lawmakers are free to solve real problems even if on occasion they have to disagree with their party – and that's acceptable because a tiny slice of an electorate no longer can turn them out of office like the voters in Virginia's 7th Congressional district did to Eric Cantor. It is clear that the type of primary system used can have a profound effect on who governs, how they govern, and, most importantly, to whom they are answerable.

There are some other things we should note about this system. First – and this is vital – the balance of power did not change. California was and still is a Democratic state. Democratic districts still by-and-large remained in Democratic hands and Republican seats likewise remained in Republican hands. And the fear that parties would substitute shill candidates to dilute the other side's vote simply never materialized.

But what did happen was transformative. Today, one only needs to go to any major online search engine and enter "top economies in America" or "strongest economy by state" or "most business-friendly state" and California comes up in the top five of these kinds of rankings in publication after publication. Back in 2001 or 2006 or 2008, when California was embroiled in non-stop financial crises, the state government simply failed to work. The business climate was abysmal.

Changing how lawmakers get elected had a significant impact on the way California is governed. Lawmakers can no longer hide in the shadows of the extreme wings of their respective parties. They can – and must – answer to every voter in their districts and it makes a positive difference in how they govern. They must solve problems, they must act responsibly, and party allegiance is no longer a proxy for the principal. An unofficial caucus of moderate Democrats in the legislature – known in the Sacramento as "Mod Dems" – has significant sway on what bills get passed and which extreme legislation gets stalled in committee.

Conclusion

Having said all that, the jury on the blanket primaries is still out. There is not yet enough data to assess with confidence how the system performs in Washington and California. The existing evidence is modest, but encouraging. In the case of California, Hirano and Snyder found "a noticeable drop in the extremism scores in 2012 and 2014, especially relative to other states' congressional delegations." They concluded that "this is suggestive evidence that the top-two system may be having a moderating effect, or at least is not contributing to greater polarization" (2019).

The direct primary system was an important part of the progressive era's effort to improve and expand American democracy. These reforms were part of a movement that eventually broke the power of party bosses, corrupt big-city machines, and the polarization that had plagued U.S. politics since the Civil War. A hundred years later, reformers are looking to reduce ideological and cultural polarization, and the resulting gridlock, by again advocating structural reforms. Improving the direct primary system is critical and doable. A growing number of U.S. voters are choosing not to identify with a political party and are pressuring their state governments to do away with closed primaries either through legislative reforms or referenda. The U.S. federal system permits each state to adopt reforms best suited for its politics and traditions. There is no clear path that all 50 states should take. But what is clear is that the traditional closed primary that disenfranchises over a third of voters is very likely becoming a relic of the past.

Notes

1 Connecticut, Delaware, Florida, Kansas, Kentucky, Louisiana, Maine, Maryland, Nebraska, New Mexico, New York, Pennsylvania, and Wyoming
2 Alaska, Arizona, California, Colorado, Illinois, Iowa, Kansas, New Hampshire, New Jersey, North Carolina, Ohio, Oregon, Rhode Island, Utah, and West Virginia.
3 Fourteen states – Alabama, Arkansas, Georgia, Hawaii, Michigan, Minnesota, Missouri, Montana, North Dakota, South Carolina, Texas, Vermont, Virginia, and Wisconsin – have open primaries.

References

Ballotpedia, 2020. *Primary Election Types By State - Ballotpedia*. [online] Available at: https://
ballotpedia.org/Primary_election_types_by_state [Accessed 30 August 2020].

Enten, H., 2014. *The Eric Cantor Upset: What Happened?* FiveThirtyEight. Available at:
https://fivethirtyeight.com/features/the-eric-cantor-upset-what-happened/ [Accessed
May 14, 2020].

Hirano, S. and Snyder Jr, J.M., 2019. *Primary Elections in the United States*. Padstow:
Cambridge University Press.

Martin, J., 2014. Eric Cantor Defeated by David Brat, Tea Party Challenger, in GOP
Primary Upset. *New York Times*.

7

NO "REGULAR ORDER"

Nicol C. Rae

Rep. Patrick E. Murphy: Reading this chapter makes me jealous I didn't get to serve in Congress 60 years ago when expertise and committee involvement actually mattered. The reality is in today's Congress, a great deal of the legislation starts with a political incentive and is pushed down to members. If a poll shows that legislation on Medicare, gun rights, or choice could potentially help in the upcoming election – or contrarily could put the opposing party in a bad position – then you can bet you will see a vote on that topic. There are so many important issues to be addressed, it is as if the tail is wagging the dog. There is very little long-term planning or goals set out by committees on issues that must be addressed. As Nicol Rae points out, with more party unity and involvement, House and Senate leadership basically decide to move bills that are politically advantageous to them. The exceptions are topics that arise because of national emergencies or ones that a major lobbyist or donor is pushing.

This has a chilling effect for newer and often naive members of Congress who get elected with big dreams and goals to pass meaningful legislation, but quickly realize how hard it is to introduce a bill in a subcommittee, move it upward to the full committee, then get a vote on the House floor. Instead members are given floor cards with the votes of the day and how the party recommends you vote. While I was lucky enough to serve in a very competitive and tough district and therefore did not receive much political pressure from House leadership, most members of Congress are expected to vote a certain way. Once members realize they probably will not pass their intended legislation until they get to leadership, they realize they need to either become better fundraisers so they can support their friends in Congress and move up the ladder quicker, or become media stars and begin building their own unique coalitions, like Sen. Bernie Sanders or Rep. Alexandria Ocasio-Cortez have.

Rep. David Jolly: The saying used to go, "If you want to see Congress at work, study the committees." That is no longer the case. All major legislation is created and directed from the leadership level to ensure it reflects the partisan and ideological underpinnings of the majority party, sufficient to control the public narrative of the party's priorities, and sufficient to placate the massive special interests that financially underwrite the two major parties.

As a result, leadership in Congress suffocates any independent thought of rank and file members. Policy proposals of rank and file members are rarely given significant consideration. This reality is less a reflection of the spirit of those serving, but more a reflection of legislative processes largely abandoned by the modern Congress. Statistically very few bills ever get considered by a congressional committee, despite the hard work by a member to develop the idea and the work of legislative counsel to draft the bill to align with the federal code. As a result, my experience in Congress taught me that most members who introduce legislation do so never expecting it to be considered. Instead the culture of Congress has become in the modern era one in which a member gets defined not by what legislation they have successfully passed, but merely by what they've introduced – a much more superficial, and frankly easier, standard.

Additionally, for the member who is determined to advance his or her policy proposal by attaching it to legislation that might otherwise be considered within a committee of jurisdiction, the opportunity simply is not there like it used to be. Committees in today's climate generally don't move major legislation with any expectation of getting it all the way to the president's desk, and when legislation does move through a committee, it is rarely open for any amendment at all. Instead, the speaker often designates committee chairs or policy leaders to draft the core principles together, and upon sign-off from the speaker, the legislation is too often afforded only an up or down vote in committee, or even at times simply brought directly to the full House for consideration without any committee consideration.

Many colleagues that I served with found the lack of regular order, the quieting of independent thought, to be their greatest frustration, and for some it was the reason they retired from Congress. In the end, today's leadership-driven process arguably provides greater efficiency in moving major policy solutions through Congress more quickly, as we saw during the great recession of the 2000s and again during the 2020 pandemic crisis. But the streamlined process sacrifices the contributions of many important thought leaders, and too often the lack of legislative thoroughness leads to policy mistakes and public relations nightmares for Congress as major policy changes often end up incomplete in addressing our national priorities.

For the past quarter century American politics has been characterized by increasing partisanship and polarization. The impact of this development on America's governing institutions has been generally regarded as highly adverse, giving rise to concerns regarding the "dysfunction" of the American government at the federal level. The impact of increased partisanship and polarization had been particularly marked in Congress, with both House and Senate demonstrating dramatically increased levels of partisan polarization that has driven significant change in the operations of the legislative branch. Among congressional scholars and Washington observers this has often given rise to laments over the decline of "regular order" on Capitol Hill and how partisan polarization has undermined Congress's efficacy as a legislative body and a necessary check on the executive branch (Brownstein, 2008). "Regular order" refers to the federal legislative process as it operated from the New Deal era to the end of the 1980s characterized by relatively weak congressional political parties and party leaders, strong and independent congressional committees, and a high degree of bipartisanship on major issues. For most Americans born after 1940 these were the characteristics of the textbook legislative process that they learned in school and college introductory government and civics classes in the post-World War II era.

This chapter will argue, however, that "regular order" in the legislative process was in fact the product of the dominance of the bipartisan "conservative coalition" in Congress from the mid-1930s to the mid-1970s. The erosion of that coalition led to the emergence of much more coherent and cohesive American parties in both houses of Congress in the last decades of the 20th century, and as a consequence the regular order of the mid-late-20th century has been replaced by a 21st century Congress organized around partisan–majoritarian lines. This in turn led to a procedural revolution in Congress that we are now experiencing for better or worse. That said, vestiges of the era of bipartisanship and regular order persist on Capitol Hill, both in certain policy areas where congressional divisions do not fall along party lines, and in the yearning among many members of the House and Senate for a great degree of comity among members and a more positive public conception of the legislative branch.

Congressional Regimes

Beyond the constitutional stipulations as to the structure and powers of Congress in Article 1 of the Constitution, Congress's internal procedures and leadership structures have continued to evolve over the course of U.S. history. The development of national political parties in the Jacksonian era (1825–1840) had considerable impact on how Congress performed its legislative function, and changes in the party system have driven changes in Congress's organization and procedures (Binder, 1997). Changes in the party system have also led to changes in the balance between governing institutions, or the American political "regime," which has also had an impact on how Congress does its business. Changes in congressional organization and procedures or the "congressional regime" have tracked changes in the electoral balance between the parties and the nature of the party system (Shafer, 1991). When political parties are polarized and national and congressional elections are highly competitive between the parties, congressional party leaders and party caucuses control the business of the chambers, rates of party voting are high, and congressional committees and individual members play a generally subordinate role in the legislative process. The strong speakership regime and very high rates of partisan voting in the U.S. House in the late 19th century was the product of very strong political party organizations and very high rates of partisan adherence among the electorate (Peters, 1997). After the national political balance tilted decisively in favor of the Republican Party during the Progressive era (1900–1917), party organizations weakened due to – largely bipartisan – progressive reforms and political alignments on the most important issues of the day no longer fell along party lines (Burnham, 1982). Indeed the "House Revolt" of 1910 that ended the Strong Speaker System and fostered the rise of strong congressional committees was a consequence of the bipartisan coalition of progressive House members who saw Speaker Joseph Cannon as a major barrier to their reform objectives (Peters, 1997). Interestingly the weakening of congressional party leaders also occurred as the Presidency began to play the leading role in American politics during the Progressive era, and the executive branch began to grow in size and scope.

Whereas the U.S. House has always tended toward more formal rule and organization and been more responsive to partisanship, the U.S. Senate by contrast has tended to eschew partisanship and resist formal leadership structures. The smaller chamber has tended to operate more on an informal basis with rules and norms that empower individual senators. As with the House, progressive party reforms – and the introduction of direct election of senators in 1914 – had a decentralizing effect in the Senate and weakened party influence further, and a series of Senate norms empowering individual senators became even more entrenched (Koger, 2010).

The New Deal Regime and the Conservative Coalition

The New Deal era established the Democratic Party as the dominant party in American national elections for a generation, and the executive branch as the dominant branch in the federal government. The onset of World War II followed by the Cold War cemented and accelerated these developments. The long-term effects of the progressive reforms also continued to weaken political parties and mitigate against strong congressional leadership (Burnham, 1982). Ostensibly the Democratic party held a dominant position in Congress during this period, save for the two GOP Congresses of 1947–8 and 1953–4. In practice the dominant ideological bloc on Capitol Hill on most issues was a bipartisan bloc, the "conservative coalition" of most of the Republican members and Democrats elected from the southern states. While both Republicans and southern Democrats accepted some features of the New Deal, both were wary of further expansion of the domestic and national security state. The southern Democrats had been a key component of the Democrats' electoral and congressional coalition since the Civil War. After the end of reconstruction in the 1870s, the Republican Party gradually disappeared as a significant political force in the southern states (Key, 1949). But Democratic power in the former confederacy was entrenched by electoral reforms (sometimes passed in the guise of progressive reforms) that effectively disfranchised the largely Republican-supporting African American population of the region (and many poorer southern whites). By 1900 the "solid" Democratic South was firmly established with the GOP reduced to an electoral bystander, and the election of members of Congress taking place in "white only" Democratic Party primaries (Key, 1949). Those elected under this system understood that their continuation in office was contingent on defending southern white supremacy to the hilt and on using the power of seniority to defend the interests (as they perceived it) of their home region.

In the face of this powerful bloc the party caucuses became largely moribund and the power held by party leaders in both chambers was a result of their political skill rather than the inherent prerogatives of the party leadership positions, which became greatly eroded (Sundquist, 2002). Specialized committees became the key to legislative success during the New Deal era, and more often than not the committee chairs and ranking members were more powerful players in legislation than the party leaders (Fenno, 1973). In the Senate traditional "folkways" and procedural devices protecting the prerogatives of individual senators added additional barriers to the passage of legislation (Matthews, 1960). In this congressional regime the initiative on setting the policy agenda largely passed to the president and the executive branch, yet Congress retained formidable powers over the budget and the passage of legislation on domestic policy, while largely abrogating its powers on foreign policy to the president (particularly after Pearl Harbor and during the Cold War) (Sundquist, 2002). The norms of Congress during this period characterize what critics of the current Congress refer to as "regular order": bipartisanship, weak congressional leaders, and a strong congressional committee system.

In the initial years of the New Deal, FDR largely got his way in Congress in securing passage of New Deal measures due to the severity of the national economic crisis, although it became evident that there were some misgivings about the direction of this administration among the Republican minority and some southern Democratic conservatives (Patterson, 1967). In fact during FDR's first terms as president, the main roadblock to his legislative agenda was not Congress but the Supreme Court. FDR was emphatically reelected with a record electoral and popular vote majority in 1936, and with huge Democratic margins in Congress. In the wake of his electoral triumph, FDR proposed a reform of the composition of the Supreme Court that would have allowed him to appoint a new justice for every sitting justice over the age of 70. It was this measure, dubbed by its detractors as the "Court Packing" bill, that led to the formation of the conservative coalition of Republicans and southern Democrats that succeeded in successfully blocking the measure (Patterson, 1967). FDR's efforts to defeat recalcitrant southern Democrats in the 1938 primary elections failed (demonstrating the limited authority of national party leadership in an era of weak parties) and major Republican gains in the 1938 congressional elections entrenched the power of the coalition for the next three decades on Capitol Hill.

The Legislative Process: 1937–74

The dominance of the conservative coalition was manifested in congressional legislative procedures during the New Deal era. Much of the key to the coalition's power lay in the power of the committee system and the committee chairs who set the committees' agendas (Fenno, 1973). Members were ranked within committees according to their seniority in Congress, with the most senior member in the majority party (invariably the Democrats during this period) becoming chair. As southern Democrats enjoyed great electoral security with general elections in their state not being seriously contested by the Republicans, more often than not committee chairs during this period in both chambers tended to be southern conservative Democrats.

In both chambers the committees were critical to the passage of legislation with chairs having control over amendments, the texts of bills, and even whether legislation made it out of committee at all (Fenno, 1973). Committee members came to be seen specialists in the subject matter of their committee as the seniority rule meant that they tended to serve on committees for a long time, sometimes even for decades. Within committees there was a clear hierarchy with the Ways & Means (Revenues), Appropriations (Expenditures), and Rules Committees (see below) enjoying a privileged position in the House, and the Finance and Appropriations Committees enjoying pride of place in the Senate. Due to the Senate prerogatives on foreign policy and judicial confirmations, the Foreign Affairs, Armed Services, and Judiciary Committees also played a more prominent role in that chamber. With a significantly lower membership senators also tended to have far more committee assignments that House members (four to five compared to one to two) and therefore tended to be regarded as somewhat less "expert" than their House counterparts. Looser floor procedures in the Senate also meant that it was harder for committee chairs there to stall legislation than in the House.

In the House of Representatives there was an additional hurdle for non-budgetary legislation as the approval of the House Rules Committee was also required before bills could reach the House floor, since that committee wrote the procedures for debate of the bill or "rule" (Fenno, 1973). The Rules Committee also acted largely independently of the party leadership and for most of the postwar period was dominated by the conservative coalition rather than the ostensible Democratic majority. From 1955 to 1967 the committee was chaired by the very conservative, southern segregationist Democrat Rep. Howard W. Smith of

Virginia, who used his position to keep civil rights legislation from reaching the House floor.

In the Senate the rules operated theoretically in favor of the individual senator. Legislation bottled up in committee could be brought to the floor as amendments to completely different bills due to the Senate's lack of the House's "germaneness" rule (at least for non-budgetary legislation). Until 1917 the chamber had lacked any rule for ending debate beyond senators' sense of "fair play" (Koger, 2010). With direct election in 1914 and a less genteel era in the 20th century the Senate did introduce a rule for cloture or ending of debate in 1917, but this required a super, bipartisan, majority of two-thirds of senators to implement, meaning that with the support of one third of the body a minority of senators could essentially "talk legislation to death" on the Senate floor. While the "filibuster" was more threatened than actually employed it acted as an additional barrier to the passage of legislation in the decades after 1917 (Koger, 2010).

By contrast with the committees, congressional parties were weak during this period. The party caucuses barely met save for largely ceremonial purposes at the start of each Congress. Congress had some outstanding leaders during this period such as House Speakers Sam Rayburn and Joseph Martin and Lyndon Johnson in the Senate, but their power came more from their own political acumen and skills as consummate political brokers rather than the inherent power of the offices of Speaker or Senate Majority Leader. The system built by the conservative coalition achieved its objectives of slowing the expansion of the domestic state, constraining budgetary growth and keeping Civil Rights off the congressional agenda. The conservative coalition's "committee-seniority" system also led to a cadre of expert senior members of Congress who could challenge the executive in legislation and exercise their government oversight role. To this extent the committee-seniority system helped maintain the institutional power of Congress at a time of executive branch expansion, while partisan-dominated legislatures in other western democracies became wholly subservient to the executive and the party leaders who led it.

The Decline of the Conservative Coalition and the Erosion of Bipartisanship in Congress

The decline of the conservative coalition in the wake of the civil rights revolution of the 1960s would usher a new congressional regime and the erosion of bipartisanship and regular order on Capitol Hill. The end of racial segregation and black voter suppression in the South, as confirmed by the 1964 *Civil Rights Act* and the 1965 *Voting Rights Act*, led to a new two-party politics in the South between a very conservative new southern Republican party and a southern Democratic party that was much closer to the liberal ideology of the national Democratic party (Rae, 1994). The Vietnam War and the political upheaval of the 1960s coincided with the decline of traditional American party organization and the rise of more ideologically coherent parties from coast to coast. The impact of these changes was first felt in presidential elections which swung wildly between the national parties in the 1960s and 1970s before settling into a clear conservative Republican/liberal Democrat divide after Ronald Reagan's victory in 1980. Change in Congress moved more slowly as many former southern segregationist Democrats accommodated themselves to the changed electoral arena and successfully appealed to newly enfranchised black voters. During the 1970s and 1980s, however, the old congressional order built by the conservative coalition gradually eroded, and conservative southern white Democrats were more or less wiped off the political map in the elections of the 1990s.

Since the 1970s we have witnessed the erosion of the New Deal congressional order characterized by ideologically indistinct parties, strong specialized committees, and relatively weak party leadership based on the dominance of the bipartisan conservative coalition. This has been replaced by a new congressional order based on united and polarized parties. Another attribute of this new congressional order has been competitive congressional elections and alternation of power between parties (Fiorina, 2017). For all but four of the 40 years of the congressional coalition era, Democrats held a comfortable majority in both houses of Congress and that majority was not seriously under threat for most of that time. Since 1980 (for the Senate) and 1994 (for the House) partisan control of the Senate has changed seven times and control of the House four times. In the modern era no party has enjoyed the very large congressional majorities that the Democrats generally enjoyed from 1936 to 1980.

The onset of more unified and polarized parties began in the 1970s and has continued apace ever since, as demonstrated by congressional voting data. The post-civil rights revolution electoral realignment has led to a consistently liberal Democratic Party and a consistently conservative Republican Party in Congress as opposed to the era of the conservative coalition and the committee-seniority system when congressional party allegiances fell more along regional than ideological lines. During the 1980s astute political scientists like David Rhode were already noticing that southern Democratic and national Democrats were becoming more aligned on Capitol Hill (Rohde, 2010). On the Republican side the progressive Republicans who were formerly common in regions such as the Northeast and the Pacific Northwest had essentially disappeared and the numbers of relatively moderate Republicans being returned from those regions were also in gradual decline (Rae, 1989).

By the early 1970s we already begin to see the effect of this trend in the congressional Democratic Party. Younger more liberal northern Democrats revived the House Democratic Caucus and made it their instrument to mount a serious challenge to the committee-seniority system and the vestigial power of the conservative coalition. Committee chairs now had to be voted on by the party caucus as a whole and the seniority rule could be disregarded. The speaker and the party leadership also gained control of the referral of bills to committees and of the House Rules Committee which no longer acted as an independent power center in the chamber but reverted to leadership control. The caucus was not shy about exercising its new powers and at the start of the 94th Congress in 1975, three elderly southern conservative committee chairs were ousted and replaced (in one case by the 4th ranking Democrat on that particular committee). Seniority still generally prevailed but its power was seriously weakened by these changes (Sundquist, 2002).

With the gradual rise in levels of party voting came a decline in comity and an increasingly partisan tone. Democratic Speakers Thomas P. "Tip" O'Neill (1977–86) and Jim Wright (1987–90) were not shy about using the their new-found powers awarded by the caucus to direct control of the House's legislative agenda much more easily and effectively than their immediate predecessors (Peters, 1997). The election of conservative Republican President Ronald Reagan made these Democratic leaders even more determined to solidify their troops in opposition to the Reagan agenda at home and abroad. This in turn led to the increasing embitterment of the Republican minority. During the era of the conservative coalition, the minority Republicans had enjoyed a high degree of power and influence both in the committees and in the chamber as a whole. Under O'Neill and Wright the GOP House minority became increasingly marginalized with little control over legislation (Connelly and Pitney, 1994). By the mid-1980s the House Republican minority in response had adopted a strategy of total confrontation inside the chamber, utilizing every opportunity on the House floor to lambaste the majority for the benefit of the viewing audience of the newly televised chamber. The onset of a slew of scandals affecting senior Democratic House leaders such as Speaker Jim Wright (who was forced to resign his office) and Ways & Means Committee Chair Dan Rostenkowski paved the way in 1994 for the first Republican majority in 40 years under Speaker Newt Gingrich, the pioneer of the minority's confrontation strategy a decade earlier (Rae, 1998). As we shall see all the tendencies toward centralization and empowerment of the party caucuses (conference in the case of the Republicans) and the House leadership that were underway in the last decade and a half of Democratic rule would be reinforced during the 12 years of Republican rule that followed.

None of these changes occurred in a vacuum of course. The homogenization and polarization of the congressional parties reflected sea changes in the American electorate and conduct of congressional elections due to the transformation of the national political parties in the wake of the political upheaval of the 1960s. By the 1990s this had resulted in more polarized and more ideologically homogeneous national parties. With this "nationalization" of the parties members also had to be more responsive to primary electorates in their districts for whom adherence to ideology was the most important consideration. As an unintended effect of the *Voting Rights Act*'s strictures to enable proportionate representation of African Americans and other minorities, continuing control of the restricting process by state legislatures, and developments in mapping software, the districts themselves were invariably drawn to overwhelmingly favoring one party or the other thus enhancing the importance of the more ideological primary electorate (Oppenheimer, 2005). Changes in campaign finance laws also enhanced the influence of interest groups and associated single issue or ideological political action committees over the candidate selection process, thus reinforcing the trend for each party to select strongly liberal or conservative candidates (La Raja and Schaffner, 2015). All of these factors helped drive the Democratic reforms of the 1970s that ended the power of the southern Democrats and enhanced the power of the party caucus and party leadership. These changes were also reflected among the Republican minority and contributed to the rise of Newt Gingrich and the much more confrontational approach of the House minority in the 1980s.

In institutional terms the big losers from the resurgence of unified House parties and strong party leadership were the congressional committees: the pillars of the committee-seniority system (Sinclair, 2014). The revival of the caucus in the 1970s and increased power for the speaker and the party leadership over committee assignments put committee chairs and members on notice that committees were now expected to follow the line of the party leadership and no longer operate as independent power centers in the House. The removal of the four southern committee chairs in 1975 gave a powerful warning to the remaining committee chairs who either left Congress or accommodated themselves to the new political order. The erosion proceeded slowly during the remaining two decades of Democratic rule but really became apparent after the Republican takeover in 1994, when new Speaker Gingrich disregarded seniority and appointed committee chairs who were in alignment with his policy agenda as set out in the 1994 Republican campaign manifesto *The Contract with America*. Gingrich also disregarded the congressional committees in formulating policy proposals preferring to rely on party "task forces" with a membership selected by the majority party leadership. Gingrich had to trim his sails somewhat after his defeat in the 1996 budget showdown with Democratic President Bill Clinton, and his successor as speaker for the remainder of the 12-year period of Republican rule in the House (1999–2006), Dennis Hastert, was more respectful of committee prerogatives. Nevertheless the Gingrich era in the mid-1990s marked a permanent change to a much stronger party leadership and weaker congressional committees regardless of partisan control of Congress in the ensuing quarter century (Theriault, 2008).

The Senate Story

What of the notoriously individualistic U.S. Senate? William S. White's classic study of the Senate in the mid-1950s defined the institution for a generation of Americans but as with many great studies of a political regime at its zenith, White depicted the Senate just as it was about to undergo a transformation similar in many ways to that of the House (White, 1957). White's Senate was ruled by an "inner club" of largely southern conservatives who accumulated the necessary seniority to control the major levers of power in the chamber (including the committees) due to safe seats and largely Democratic majorities after 1932. More junior senators tended to defer to the "inner club" on arrival in the chamber serving an "apprenticeship" to hopefully gain admission. Unlike the House, Senate rules made restricting floor debate all but impossible (requiring a two-thirds majority of the chamber) and did not require amendments to be "germane" to the subject matter of the bill (with the exception of Appropriations bills). Advancing legislation in the Senate thus required a very high degree of bipartisan consensus with committee chairs in an even more powerful role and party leadership even weaker than in the House. The southern flavor of the 1950s Senate was not accidental of course. The procedures mentioned above made the Senate an almost insuperable barrier to the passage of Civil Rights legislation.

The Senate parties introduced leadership positions in the 1920s largely for housekeeping functions and more to serve senators than to actually lead them. Yet in doing so senators conceded a very useful power to party leaders: the right of first (majority leader) and second (minority leader) recognition in floor debate. What might have initially been seen as a chore would now allow enterprising Senate leaders often working in tandem to forge bipartisan agreements that would allow legislation to pass on the Senate floor (Sinclair, 1989). With the growing importance of national news media at mid-20th century, it also became increasingly important for Senate parties to have an articulate spokesperson to represent the position of the Senate parties on television news. The first Senate party leaders to really capitalize on these developments were Lyndon Johnson (D-TX), majority leader from 1955 to 1961 and his Republican counterpart Everett Dirksen (R-IL), minority leader from 1959 to 1969 (Caro, 2002). In 1964 and 1965, as president, Johnson worked with Dirksen to pass the landmark *Civil Rights Act* of 1964 and the *Voting Rights Act* of 1965 (Hulsey, 2000). After the passage of the *Voting Rights Act* the chamber became much less conservative as southern Democrats either came closer to national Democrats or left the Senate and were replaced by less conservative Democrats or Republicans. As the Senate became even more individualistic as White's norms of deference and apprenticeship eroded, senators made the filibuster easier to overcome by reducing the number of votes required to close debate from two thirds (67 senators) to three fifths (60 senators) in 1975. Bipartisan dominance by the conservative coalition was thus supplanted by a temporary, bipartisan, moderately liberal "reformist" majority for much of the 1970s.

By the 1980s, however, some of the same tendencies in train on the House side had begun to become apparent in the Senate as well (Sinclair, 1989). While filibustering might have become easier to overcome with 60 votes, it began to be utilized far more frequently as a partisan dilatory device. Other such devices such as "holds" (requests by individual senators for "additional information" before allowing debate to proceed) and non-germane amendments became more common. Like House members senators had to respond to more partisan and more ideologically polarized primary electorates, and party leaders were expected primarily to deliver a party agenda or thwart the agenda of a president of the opposite party, and score debating points against their partisan opponents in the news media. The post-civil rights era also brought a new breed of intensely ideological senators – such as Jesse Helms (R-NC) or Howard Metzenbaum (D-OH) who from the moment of their election were willing to use every procedural device open to them to advocate for their views or to block legislation. If the party leaders in the Senate were able to conclude bipartisan unanimous consent agreements (UCAs) legislation could still pass the Senate but these became harder and harder to achieve in a more partisan political environment.

As in the House increasing partisanship in the Senate became more evident after the election of Ronald Reagan with the first Republican Senate majority in a quarter century in 1980. While the chamber remained more bipartisan overall than the House during the 1980s and 1990s, the overall atmosphere became more rancorous – particularly on votes that were highly important to partisans on both sides of the aisle such as the highly contentious Supreme Court confirmation votes on Robert Bork (1987) and Clarence Thomas (1991). Astute party leaders such as Republican Trent Lott (1996–2002) and Democrat Thomas Daschle (1995–2004) were able to take advantage of windows of opportunity to forge UCAs and pass significant legislation through the Senate in the mid-1990s and after the 9/11 attacks in 2001–2, and both worked well to ensure that the highly charged impeachment trial of President Bill Clinton in early 1999 did not reflect badly on the Senate as an institution (Rae, 2018). But this became an increasingly uphill struggle and from 2005 onward the Senate has been more associated with partisan bitterness and legislative stasis than an effective lawmaking body proceeding according to regular order.

One final note on the Senate and regular order concerns the use of the budget process to drive or even change legislative outcomes. An attempt to streamline the federal budget process through the 1974 *Budget Control and Impoundment Act* created a new process called "reconciliation" that tethered congressional taxing, welfare, and appropriations bills to an overall Congressional Budget Resolution in terms of budgetary targets and outcomes. Astute congressional leaders increasingly perceived that this process could be used to short-circuit potential obstacles in the legislative process (particularly the filibuster in the Senate) as budget bills could not be filibustered or loaded up with non-germane amendments. Placing major policy changes into Omnibus Budget Bills would thus allow a majority party to achieve legislative objectives by short-circuiting the regular committee process in each chamber and marginalize the congressional committees. This device became an increasingly common resort for congressional party leaders and presidents in passing major components of their legislative programs, while reducing the effectiveness of congressional scrutiny and adding to the overall atmosphere of rancor in the Chamber (Sinclair, 2014).

The Shortcomings of the Contemporary Legislative Process: Can Bipartisanship Be Restored?

The current legislative process in Congress reflects growing party polarization over the past quarter century, combined with relatively narrow and tenuous partisan majorities in both House and Senate. In these circumstances the stakes involved in legislation seem much higher than during the long era of Democratic dominance from 1933 to 1980, where the ideological fault line in Congress fell within parties rather than between them and the bipartisan conservative coalition generally prevailed. In the modern era the leadership of both parties has bent over backward to find ways around dilatory congressional procedures so they can pass legislation or confirm federal judges and executive branch officers with small partisan majorities rather than supermajorities. Congressional scholar Barbara Sinclair noticed what was happening in the 1990s and referred to these revised procedures as "unorthodox lawmaking" (Sinclair, 2016). She particularly noted the practice of utilizing omnibus budget bills to drive policy change and avoid legislative hurdles in Congress, which has continued apace since the publication of her book. Twenty years later these procedures and practices have become the new orthodoxy.

In the one party-dominant/conservative coalition era, congressional committees reigned supreme on legislation in their bailiwicks, almost operating as independent power centers or fiefs within each chamber. In the current order the party leadership predominates and the committees serves the leadership's policy agenda. Key legislation is invariably written and amended by the party leadership in concert with the White House if the party happens to also control the presidency. Special committees and task forces have also occasionally been used to manage important initiatives and bills at the leadership's behest. In the House the Rules Committee sets the agenda for House floor debate according to the interest of the party leadership and no longer operates as an independent power center. Particularly in the House, legislation reflects the preferences of a majority of the majority party caucus/conference rather than the bipartisan majority of the chamber as whole (Theriault, 2008).

In the Senate we have seen escalating efforts by the leadership of each party to erode important Senate prerogatives that characterized the conservative coalition era also in pursuit of expediting the policy preferences and nominees of the majority party and that party's president. As the federal judiciary has played a larger and larger role in public policy issues and in highly contentious cultural issues such as abortion that also form the basis for party polarization, nominations to all federal courts, and especially the Supreme Court, have become especially contentious. Traditionally these were seen as so important that a consensus of 60 votes to invoke cloture (close debate) was felt to be necessary. On the other hand this gave the minority party in the Senate the opportunity to use the cloture requirement to delay and even kill judicial nominations. In response Senate Majority Leader Harry Reid obtained a rule change in 2013 to end the filibuster for executive branch and federal circuit and district court nominations in response to Republican obstruction of the confirmation of President Obama's judicial nominees. In similar fashion Republican Majority Leader McConnell jettisoned the filibuster for Supreme Court nominations in the confirmation process of President Donald Trump's nominee Neil Gorsuch in 2017. Part of the reason for the filibuster's likely demise (the 60-vote rule for cloture remains at present for non-budgetary legislation) has been its abuse. From a device of last resort the filibuster became almost routine on legislation from 1980 onward as partisanship increased (Sinclair, 1989). With several 2020 Democratic presidential candidates pledged to eliminate it, the filibuster in the Senate (probably the strongest incentive to bipartisanship in the Senate) is clearly on life support.

One consequence of increased partisanship has been the increasing marginalization of the minority party in both chambers, although the Senate minority still has prerogatives that provide more leverage for the minority than in the House. This atmosphere and non-stop battle to retain or achieve the critical majority has also raised the stakes inside Congress (Fiorina, 2017). Several promising congressional careers have been shortened by the grind of partisanship in recent decades, and the impression of unceasing partisanship leads to the Chamber being seen as ineffectual. If power is divided between the chambers or between a congress and presidency of different parties, the experience of recent presidencies is that an atmosphere of stasis prevails on Capitol Hill, and little gets accomplished legislatively because the incentives for bipartisan compromise are so weak on Capitol Hill. Periodic and largely manufactured crises over lack of funding for the federal government and raising of the national debt ceiling have become commonplace and in a ratchetlike effect the public reputation of Congress and the federal government continues to diminish further (Hibbing and Theiss-Morse, 1995).

Yet while partisan and majoritarian battles have often tended to predominate in Congress of late, we should not underestimate the degree of bipartisan consensus that persists in several important areas. Trade issues which often reflect powerful constituency concerns tend to unscramble partisanship with advocates of globalist free trade policies and their more protectionist opponents, each having influence in both parties. Acute crises that pose a threat to the economy – such as the banking crisis of fall 2008 and the 9/11 terrorist attacks – can still occasion an extraordinary degree of bipartisan unity of remedial actions such as the Troubled Assets Relief Program (or TARP), the Patriot Act, and the military interventions in Iraq and Afghanistan (for better or worse). The Trump administration has revealed a very high degree of bipartisan suspicion of the president's critiques of international organizations and norms, and the Trump administration's eagerness to pursue a less confrontational relationship with Russia's President Vladimir Putin.

Conclusion

Undoubtedly bipartisan consensus can work to stifle debate, delay necessary policy change (for example the need for civil and voting rights reform), and unconsciously lead the county in an adverse policy direction (the Gulf of Tonkin resolution). Yet the American constitutional order requires a large degree of consensus for a major change in policy direction to be seen as legitimate and congressional procedures that operate to preclude consensus may only create policy gridlock and undermine the public authority of the American system of government. The "regular" congressional order of the 1932–80 period was a product of the American New Deal Political regime and a bipartisan consensus on foreign and domestic policy during an era of Democratic Party dominance in the federal government. This order was largely based on a "conservative coalition" of southern Democratic and minority Republicans and it had several shortcomings including the delay of civil rights legislation and a deference to the presidency in foreign policy that contributed to the disaster of Vietnam. Yet it also legitimated federal government action to save the U.S. economy in the 1930s, did eventually lead to bipartisan compromise that broke the logjam on civil rights, and contributed to a postwar global order based on American dominance. And while there is much to condemn in several of the "conservative" approaches of the dominant bipartisan bloc in Congress, their relative fiscal conservatism contributed to the congressional budget process that seriously sought to restrain federal spending and avoid budget deficits, and which was generally seen a legitimate by both parties and the general public. Congressional committees did provide a platform for perhaps overly powerful committee chairs, but they also contributed to the development of expertise among committee members on specific policy areas and ensured that legislation would reach the floor with a good chance of significant support from both parties.

When that consensus eroded and was replaced by a more polarized and partisan regime on Capitol Hill, the congressional order changed. Now Congress is majoritarian and partisan with party leaders clearly in charge of the legislative agenda and the passage of legislation in both chambers, and the minority parties in the House and Senate marginalized and focused largely on winning back the majority in the next election so they too can exercise dominance (Fiorina, 2017). New congressional procedures work against consensus and bipartisanship and partisan outcomes reinforce partisanship. This also leads to congressional weakness *vis-à-vis* the executive (and courts) and loss of institutional power and legitimacy. The breakdown of the federal budget process and endemic deficits over a quarter century is illustrative of this. The new congressional order based on majority party rule will not disappear of itself unless there is a broader relaxation of the polarization in contemporary American electoral politics. We have seen instances where imminent national threat has led to a rapid bipartisan response even in our partisan era. This will only become institutionalized, however, if the incentives to bipartisanship and coalition building in the system increase.

The American separated system of government demands consensus and does not work well in the context of partisan polarization. The challenge is to find means by which the electoral and legislative process can operate in such as fashion as to incentivize these habits.

References

Binder, S.A., 1997. *Minority Rights, Majority Rule: Partisanship and the Development of Congress.* New York: Cambridge University Press.

Brownstein, R., 2008. *The Second Civil War: How Extreme Partisanship Has Paralyzed Washington and Polarized America.* New York: Penguin.

Burnham, W.D., 1982. *The Current Crisis in American Politics.* Oxford; New York: Oxford University Press.

Caro, R.A., 2002. *Master of the Senate: The Years of Lyndon Johnson.* New York: Vintage Books.

Connelly, W.F. and Pitney, J.J., 1994. *Congress' Permanent Minority?: Republicans in the US House.* New York: Rowman & Littlefield.

Fenno, R.F., 1973. *Congressmen in Committees.* Boston: Little, Brown.

Fiorina, M., 2017. *Unstable Majorities: Polarization, Party Sorting, and Political Stalemate.* Stanford: Hoover Press.

Hibbing, J.R. and Theiss-Morse, E., 1995. *Congress as Public Enemy: Public Attitudes Toward American Political Institutions.* Cambridge; New York: Cambridge University Press.

Hulsey, B.C., 2000. *Everett Dirksen and His Presidents: How a Senate Giant Shaped American Politics.* Lawrence: University Press of Kansas.

Key, V.O., 1949. *Southern Politics in State and Nation.* New York: AA Knopf.

Koger, G., 2010. *Filibustering: A Political History of Obstruction in the House and Senate.* Chicago: University of Chicago Press.

La Raja, R.J. and Schaffner, B.F., 2015. *Campaign Finance and Political Polarization: When Purists Prevail.* Ann Arbor: University of Michigan Press.

Matthews, D.R., 1960. *United States Senators and Their World.* Chapel Hill: University of North Carolina Press.

Oppenheimer, B.I., 2005. Deep Red and Blue Congressional Districts: The Causes and Consequences of Declining Party Competitiveness. In: *Congress Reconsidered* (Vol. *8*, pp. 135–57). Washington, DC: CQ Press.

Patterson, J.T., 1967. *Congressional Conservatism and the New Deal: The Growth of the Conservative Coalition in Congress, 1933–1934.* Lexington: University of Kentucky Press, for the Organization of American Historians.

Peters, R.M., 1997. *The American Speakership: The Office in Historical Perspective.* Baltimore; London: John Hopkinds University Press.

Rae, N.C., 1989. *The Decline and Fall of the Liberal Republicans: from 1952 to the Present* (p. 40ff). New York: Oxford University Press.

Rae, N.C., 1994. *Southern Democrats.* New York; Oxford: Oxford University Press.

Rae, N.C., 1998. *Conservative Reformers: The Republican Freshmen and the Lessons of the 104th Congress.* Armonk, New York; London: ME Sharpe.

Rae, N.C., 2018. Ambition and Achievement: The Senate Republican Leadership of Trent Lott. In: Campbell, C.C.(ed.) *Leadership in the US Senate* (pp. 214–234). New York: Routledge.

Rohde, D.W., 2010. *Parties and Leaders in the Postreform House.* Chicago: University of Chicago Press.

Shafer, B.E., 1991. The Notion of an Electoral Order: The Structure of Electoral Politics at the Accession of George Bush. In: Shafer, B.E. (ed.) *The End of Realignment?: Interpreting American Electoral Eras* (pp. 37–84). Madison, Wisconsin: University of Wisconsin Press.

Sinclair, B., 1989. *The Transformation of the US Senate.* Baltimore; London: Johns Hopkins University Press.

Sinclair, B., 2014. *Party Wars: Polarization and the Politics of National Policy Making* (Vol. *10*). Norman, Oklahoma: University of Oklahoma Press.

Sinclair, B., 2016. *Unorthodox Lawmaking: New Legislative Processes in the US Congress.* Thousand Oaks, California: Sage CQ Press.

Sundquist, J.L., 2002. *The Decline and Resurgence of Congress.* Washington D.C.: Brookings Institution Press.

Theriault, S.M., 2008. *Party Polarization in Congress.* Cambridge; New York: Cambridge University Press.

White, W.S., 1957. *Citadel: The Story of the US Senate.* New York: Harper.

8

CAMERAS AND LEGISLATIVE COMMITTEES

Kathryn DePalo-Gould

Rep. Patrick E. Murphy: Clinton campaign strategist Paul Begala is sometimes credited with coining the phrase "Washington is Hollywood for ugly people." A bit crude and distasteful, there is a kernel of truth in the remark: that, like movie stars and celebrities, those in the nation's capital have enormous power and sway over public opinion.

Historically I would have argued for more cameras and more transparency at all levels of government, but after seeing the grandstanding, I've revised my opinion. I had an opportunity to sit on two great committees and see the impact of cameras on the legislative process firsthand. One was the Financial Services Committee, which has numerous cameras on during hearings – and therefore members of Congress on both sides focused more on them than on the actual issues. I simply didn't understand why members would be so rude to those testifying or why ten representatives would ask the same exact question until I realized that it had nothing to do with the substance, but all to do with capturing a 30-second soundbite that could be played in their home district or even national TV if they were lucky enough.

Contrast this with the Intelligence Committee, on which I sat for a term and which did not have any cameras present due to the classified material we would discuss. The difference was profound. Members of Congress were respectful to each other and to those testifying and rarely was the same inquiry repeated. Members prepared questions themselves and were thoughtful in their debate and deliberation. After serving on Intel, I realized that without a C-SPAN audience of millions, members were taking their job seriously and acting like adults debating real issues and substance.

Based on the trajectory over the last 30 years, with more media outlets and partisan venues available, I don't see how we put this cat back in the bag. Interestingly, all of these structural issues work together as the problem snowballs because the incentive is to be more extreme

– with little-to-no upside for compromise. The more extreme a member is, the more media he or she gets, which leads to more money raised, more power within one's party, and a stronger desire to remain in a safe, gerrymandered seat. It doesn't matter the order in which one starts the cycle, because all the elements feed each other. As the conversation becomes more extreme, moderates become more disengaged and disenfranchised, thus leading to a larger impact of the partisans.

Rep. David Jolly: Many committee hearings are poorly attended by members. Often that may be a result of a scheduling conflict, with members routinely having hearings of different committees on which they serve simply conflict. Congress after all is typically in session only three full days a week, and hearings are typically scheduled mid-morning, with others mid-afternoon. Committees never coordinate on scheduling so members sometimes have to choose which is most important.

In my experience there are two exceptions to the pattern of sparse attendance. First, when a committee meets to "mark up" legislation, that is to vote on amendments and committee passage of legislation, as opposed to a routine hearing where testimony is taken from witnesses but no legislative action is taken. Members generally always attend mark-up.

The second is when it is a high-profile hearing that has caught the attention of the nation – i.e., caught the attention of the media. It happens periodically, in moments of scandal, national security, impeachment, or a pressing policy matter such as public health. Members know they will have at least five minutes of closely watched time to make an impact – and the impact of most concern to them is often their own political brand, not the policy question at hand.

I was on the House Veterans Affairs Committee during an era when veterans had died awaiting treatment at a Veterans Affairs medical facility. It became such a compelling national conversation that our committee chairman moved our hearings to the evening so they would be covered on prime-time television – and it worked. All major news networks covered some or all of the hearings.

I was well aware of the television presence and prepared for each night with the thoroughness that members should otherwise bring to every hearing. At one of the final hearings, I was able to secure a comment from a senior VA official – a confession no one in the administration had yet been willing to make – that the wait times at the VA had indeed "contributed" to the deaths of veterans. CNN broke in live and called it a "stunning admission" by the administration.

Would such an exchange have occurred without the intensity of so many cameras on the hearing? Perhaps. But would such a confession have immediately made it to national news? Probably not. It would have been days before a transcript had been circulated and a reporter picked it up.

Every member of that committee knew they were on camera. So did the witnesses. And while we each kept on eye on the policy conversation, we always had the other eye on the camera, and we knew whatever happened in that room was going to have a lasting effect on our careers, perhaps more so than the policy changes we were responsible for securing to address the scandal itself.

In the final scene of the Frank Capra classic *Mr. Smith Goes to Washington*, Jimmy Stewart as Sen. Smith whispers, "Somebody will listen to me," as he faints on the floor of the Senate after a 23-hour filibuster attempting to expose corruption in his state. In contrast, senators in recent memory read *Green Eggs and Ham* and proclaimed themselves Spartacus.

In what seems a bygone era, most policymaking took place behind the scenes, deals were negotiated in stereotypical smoke-filled rooms, and the media was needed to get their message out. Today, Congress rarely relies on private meetings to negotiate or on the media to communicate with constituents. All they need are some good props and a Twitter account. The advent of C-SPAN, 24-hour cable news, and social media have allowed members to grandstand by speaking directly to the people without a media filter. Whether it is Sen. Ted Cruz reading *Green Eggs and Ham* on the floor of the Senate to try to defund Obamacare, or Sen. Cory Booker's "Spartacus" moment during the Kavanaugh Supreme Court confirmation hearings, grandstanding has become a staple of C-SPAN, partisan cable news channels, and social media outlets, especially Twitter, making it increasingly difficult to bring both parties to the bargaining table. Policymaking is now media-centered and out of the backrooms.

What motivates individual members to "go public"? Members often want to increase their own bargaining power by seeking the attention of a subset of the public or even the general public more broadly. However, when the president goes public and directly to the people, it can damage the bargaining process with Congress, even making compromise more difficult (Kernell, 2006; Sinclair, 2014). Congressmembers themselves now "go public" in the policymaking process, largely bypassing backroom deal-making between the parties. Mayhew's seminal work (1974) finds members of Congress as "single-minded seekers of re-election" engaging in advertising, credit-claiming, and for the purposes of this chapter, position-taking, where the policy position becomes the "political commodity." Increasing partisanship and polarization leave little room for bargaining privately.

The ideological parsing of parties and gerrymandered districts have made Congress more acrimonious, and those moving from the House to the Senate brought those attitudes to the upper chamber. However, ideology alone does not explain increasing polarization because there is also conflict on non-ideological issues. The near parity in the chambers has created a constant battle for majority status resulting in the permanent campaign. The opposition party wants only to be in control after the next election. Both parties exploit those divisions and manufacture conflict when necessary, creating a sort of "tribal politics." Party messaging has become more important with the competitive nature of flip-flopping majority status. This reflexive partisanship is essentially propaganda that permeates everything members do today; their primary goal is now selling the party brand to voters (Mann and Ornstein, 2006; Lee, 2009; Lee, 2016).

Grandstanding on camera before a C-SPAN audience, appearances by extreme members of Congress on partisan cable news, and encouragement to go negative on Twitter have made it difficult for negotiating and deal-making in this hyperpartisan environment. This chapter looks at the history and impact of media – the influence of C-SPAN, the proliferation of cable news creating congressional celebrities, and the social media exchanges – on the lack of bipartisanship in Congress today.

C-SPAN Comes to Congress

Television coverage of "flashy" hearings – from the 1950s McCarthy hearings in the Senate to the House Judiciary Committee considering impeachment against Pres. Nixon during Watergate in the 1970s – provided the public with the first glimpses into the inner workings of Congress. But by the end of the 1970s, both parties were disgusted by how the broadcast networks covered their national conventions, focusing on someone "picking his nose or scratching his ass" (O'Neill, 1987). House Speaker Tip O'Neill installed closed-circuit television in 1977, which eventually led to C-SPAN operating cameras in 1979. O'Neill wanted cameras to combat the unfair coverage by the broadcast networks and endorsed Brian Lamb's vision of gavel-to-gavel coverage – unedited, unfiltered (Cook, 1998; Shirley, 2017).

C-SPAN (Cable-Satellite Public Affairs Network), created in 1979, opened the legislative process to public eyes and ears. Screenings of debate on the House and Senate floors were initially intended to be viewed by other members, although soon after the public at large began to tune into the broadcast. This changed the nature of how Congress operated. Instead of debate on the rules, speeches became "sharper thrusts meant to move the public" (Brownstein, 2008). Al Gore delivered the first speech on C-SPAN, on March 19, 1979, where he claimed that "The marriage of this medium and of our open debate have the potential, Mr. Speaker, to revitalize representative democracy" (Lamb, 1988).

Back in the 1950s, Speaker Sam Rayburn was vehement about not wanting cameras in the House. He particularly hated what television had done to the Senate committee process: "All they do there is preen and comb their hair and run for President. It's like a presidential primary over there." But what Speaker Rayburn, then a man in his seventies, feared more was that television would give junior members more influence and youth would overtake the elders in leadership (Halberstam, 2000). While it did not happen in his lifetime, no one knew how prescient he would be.

Mr. Gingrich Goes to Washington

In a speech to College Republicans in 1978, the year Newt Gingrich would finally win election to Congress after two losses, he said the following: "I think that one of the great problems we have in the Republican Party is that we don't encourage you to be nasty. We encourage you to be neat, obedient, and loyal and faithful and all those Boy Scout words, which would be great around the campfire, but are lousy in politics" (Frontline, 1978). Gingrich entered Congress in January 1979 when his Republican Party had been the minority in the House for close to 30 years. As members of the minority party, their best hope at getting any legislation passed was to rely on their long-term relationships with committee chairpersons. By the 1980s, the majority Democrats stripped even that ability away by removing seniority from chairpersons and becoming more invested in the policy priorities of the Democratic caucus. Gingrich disliked Republican leadership that went along with Democratic rule, seemingly satisfied with their minority status. His vision was to nationalize congressional elections and show how Democrats in power had become corrupt. Gingrich's election to Congress coincided with the creation of C-SPAN; Gingrich and his fellow Republicans now had direct access to a new media outlet through which to express their frustrations.

C-SPAN began broadcasting two months after Gingrich was first sworn into office. In order to galvanize support on conservative issues, Gingrich quickly assembled a core team of like-minded House Republicans consisting of Bob Walker (R-PA), Vin Weber (R-MN), and Connie Mack (R-FL), and created the COS (Conservative Opportunity Society) to master television from the floor. Gingrich and his cohorts in the COS believed that "confrontational activism" through the media was going to get them farther than trying to nickel and dime their way in legislation controlled by the Democrats. Walker realized that C-SPAN coverage could provide them with the platform they needed. The key was rhetoric so over the top, it was described as using "adjectives with rocks," something Gingrich was especially adept at (Brownstein, 2008). "We'd been getting on their nerves. They tried to debate us and we sent them away whimpering ... Tip [O'Neill] was using the rule against us to keep us from speaking during the regular session and this was our way of getting our message out ... getting it heard" (Steely, 2000).

The GOP Wednesday Team planned and coordinated messaging efforts, including the "special orders" on C-SPAN nightly after regular House business. These speeches gave members up to one hour to talk about anything they desired on a medium where people could see congressional business unfiltered. At 5:00

PM, every day, C-SPAN viewership numbered around 250,000 people with an estimated 17 million people tuning in monthly (Steely, 2000; Shirley, 2017). According to Gingrich, "We rapidly discovered that there was an audience that was eager to follow politics and government without editing or distortion … Members who would fly a thousand miles to talk to 250 people could not imagine that they could walk across the street to the House Chamber and address tens or hundreds of thousands of people at no cost" (Gingrich, 2019).

Gingrich and the so-called "Young Turks" took advantage of the national presence C-SPAN gave them, even if no one else was on the floor, speaking twice as much as Democrats (Frantzich, 1996). Gingrich would attack a Democratic member, step back, and pause like he was waiting for a member to answer despite knowing no one else was there. Gingrich was not concerned about the audience on the floor of the House – his only concern was the audience at home experiencing a fiery speech. When Democrats would not refute claims on C-SPAN because regular business had ceased for the day, the audience began to believe the charges. Under Gingrich's assessment, "In Special Orders, we reach the country, the reporters. In the fights on the floor in regular sessions, we create the drama that gets the press to watch, we create the votes that become decisive. In the Special Orders, we get the information out" (Lamb, 1988: 118).

The animosity had been building, especially over the Republicans' use of special orders and effectively not allowing Democrats time to defend themselves and their policy priorities. According to O'Neill, "What really infuriated me about these guys is that they had no real interest in legislation. As far as they were concerned, the House was no more than a pulpit, a sound stage from which to reach the people at home. If the TV cameras were facing the city dump, that's where they'd be speaking" (O'Neill, 1987: 353–4). O'Neill curbed their ability to speak on the floor during regular debate stating that only those in "legitimate leadership" positions (those on committees) could be recognized on the floor (Shirley, 2017: 99). That is when Gingrich and his cohort took their televised attacks to a whole new level.

For several days in May of 1984, the war raged on C-SPAN. On May 10, Speaker O'Neill, so incensed over the special orders speeches and the manipulation of national television time after regular session, ordered the camera to pan over the empty chamber of the House while Rep. Walker had the floor, violating House rules in the process. While still speaking, Rep. Walker was notified the cameras were capturing the empty House chambers. Walker remarked to the C-SPAN audience, "It is one more example of how this body is run: the kind of arrogance of power that the members are given that kind of change with absolutely no warning." The incident, which came to be known as CAMSCAM, ignited the furor of Republicans who thought Speaker O'Neill "manipulated and maneuvered the system to insure his iron-fisted control … to embarrass the Republicans" (Farrell, 2001: 633; Zelizer, 2007: 119). But it backfired on O'Neill.

Instead of exposing the Republicans for their dirty tactics, the Democrats came across as heavy-handed. Then Gingrich got personal.

Gingrich had ammunition against the House Democrats – including the caucus leadership, who had written a letter to Daniel Ortega in which the initial salutation read "Dear Commandante." The letter to Ortega, the Marxist leader of Nicaragua, offered peace negotiations in contrast to Reagan's combative policies. Gingrich accused Democrats on the floor of "being blind to Communism" and expressed just how cozy he thought they were with other Communist countries around the world. "The pattern for 1984 [Democratic] rhetoric was locked in long ago: give the benefit of every doubt to the communists and doubt every benefit of your own nation. Make mincemeat of any ally dumb enough, or imperfect enough, to fight on the side of the U.S. Trash America, indict the president and give the benefit of every doubt to Marxist regimes. That's the standard formula" (Johnson, 1984). He also accused Democrats in believing "America does nothing right and communism … rushes into vacuums caused by 'stupid' Americans and its 'rotten, corrupt' allies" (Reid, 1984). Gingrich's partisan attack on absent member Ed Boland (D-MA), described as the "bane of the Contra armies," was the last straw for the speaker (Farrell, 2001: 632).

Republican Rep. Trent Lott (R-MS) called Gingrich at his home in Georgia on May 14, 1984 and told him to get back to D.C. as Speaker O'Neill had been personally attacking him on the floor. Gingrich took the floor the following day. Because Gingrich called members by name in his speech, Democrats were livid claiming they were not informed ahead of time and were not given the opportunity to respond during special orders. Gingrich attempted to refute this allegation claiming he sent a letter to each member the day before. When Gingrich refused to yield the floor to Majority Leader Jim Wright (D-TX), O'Neill threw down his gavel and came down from the dais, asking if Gingrich would yield. The speaker, pointing his finger in Gingrich's direction, said, "My personal opinion is this. You deliberately stood in that well before an emptied House and challenged these people and you challenged their Americanism and it is the lowest thing that I've ever seen in my 32 years in Congress" (C-SPAN).

Rep. Lott immediately moved to have the speaker's words recorded in the *Congressional Record*. "Words taken down" often leads to the censure of a member on the floor for uncivil and inappropriate discourse and further prevents that member from speaking on the floor for another 24 hours. At the time, O'Neill and the Democrats were stunned that the Republicans would claim he broke the rules when the speaker admitted to having "much harsher thoughts" about the matter. But "lowest" was deemed "intemperate language" by the parliamentarian and against House rules, making O'Neill the first speaker to be censured on the floor of the House (New York Times, 1984). While he could have been prevented from speaking on the floor the rest of the day, Republicans relented on that point to prevent further embarrassment. The speaker had been officially rebuked and thoroughly beaten by Gingrich and his Young Turks.

Gingrich gleefully remembers, "That night, thanks to C-SPAN, for the first time in history an internal fight made all three national networks. Republican activists across the country saw a House GOP on offense for the first time in a generation. The seeds had been planted for what would (a decade later) become the House GOP majority" (Gingrich, 2019). Years later a retired O'Neill told Walker, "Until I attacked you, you were nothing but backbenchers. I made you into national figures" (Gingrich, 2019). O'Neill had no idea how right he was. He died in early 1994, before he would see a GOP majority in the House following the 1994 midterm elections, the first Republican majority in 40 years and largely of Gingrich's making with a little help from C-SPAN. What Speaker Rayburn feared all those years ago came to be: these Young Turks took over the Republican Party from their elders and turned it into the ruling majority party.

While some, even in Gingrich's own party, later expressed dissatisfaction with his hardball tactics, conflict and high drama made for great television, making C-SPAN an influential player in Washington politics from that day forward. The broadcast networks picked up the news and continued following and using C-SPAN footage. Gingrich said, "Television is the dominant medium in our society. The guys and gals in Congress who don't master it get killed" (Lamb, 1988: 117). Democratic Rep. Gephardt recalls, "We all came knowing the power of television, knowing the power of having messaging on television and believing that our leaders had to carry a message. So from that point on, the leadership in congress assumed more of a loyal opposition [role], or just an opposition persona in the country" (Brownstein, 2008: 123).

CAMSCAM was arguably the "seminal moment in a subsequent loss of 'civility' in Washington" (Farrell, 2001: 636). According to congressional scholar Thomas Mann, "Gradually, it went from legislating, to the weaponization of legislating, to the permanent campaign, to the permanent war … It's like [Gingrich] took a wrecking ball to the most powerful and influential legislature in the world" (Coppins, 2018).

The Senate Jumps Onboard C-SPAN

The Senate was not keen on allowing cameras in, especially after CAMSCAM. Sen. Russell Long (D-LA) opined, "When the Senate is on television, we will see a big increase in expediency and we will see a substantial decline and an erosion in statesmanship … I think that those of us who feel that statesmanship is altogether too scarce a commodity the way it is now will find that is going to be more scarce on television" (Broadcasting, 1986: 35–6). Susan Swain, co-chief executive at C-SPAN, said of that time, "The House was coming into people's living rooms via C-SPAN and then regularly on the nightly news because what we did could be picked up regularly for nightly stories about the House. Television loves pictures, so they would do more stories about the House. The Senate was becoming concerned that it was becoming the second-tier citizen of Congress" (Jacobs, 2019).

What really changed was the perspective of Democratic Sen. Minority Leader Robert Byrd. At the height of the debate over whether to allow cameras in the Senate, Byrd went home to West Virginia and was mistaken for Speaker Tip O'Neill. While the only thing they had in common was white hair, Byrd began to question whether the House was gaining the upper hand over the Senate because of the camera time and sincerely believed that more House visibility was a detriment to the Senate (Frantzich, 1996).

The Senate went live on C-SPAN March 3, 1986. Not everyone was as excited about this new intrusion. Sen. William Proxmire, a Democratic Senator from Wisconsin, warned, "television will make it easier for demagogues to win election to the Senate … Instead of an institution where sharp differences are ground down and compromised, this floor will become a place where they are sharpened." Sen. John Glenn (D-OH) spoofed with a mirror on the floor commenting that members had gotten dressed up for this moment in the spotlight (Lamb, 1988: 283; Frantzich, 1996).

By the early 1990s, C-SPAN was available in two-thirds of all U.S. households and surprisingly, viewers expressed greater dissatisfaction with Congress than the average person polled (Frantzich, 1996). In 1994, the House Democratic Caucus commissioned a study that predicted a wave of dissatisfaction and the loss of majority status which was to come. C-SPAN seemed to be to blame. "People see partisan debate and they confuse it with partisan bickering; they see the legislative process and confuse it with inaction" (Seelye, 1994). By the end of that year, the man who had built a political career and national following by grandstanding for a decade in the House successfully changed the landscape forever with the Republican Revolution. Newt Gingrich was dubbed "Speaker C-SPAN" and he relished the title.

C-SPAN's Impact

By the mid-1990s, congressional sessions in both chambers had gotten longer and "special order" speeches increased by 250% compared to the pre-C-SPAN era. Short one- and five-minute speeches that opened the House each morning and "special orders" that took place at the close of business were largely policy-based and employed mostly by minority party members and those on the ideological extremes. In a 1997 report on civility (or lack thereof) on the floor of the House, the Annenburg School found partisan rancor increased in part due to floor proceedings televised on C-SPAN, especially through "special order" speeches. The number of times "words taken down," challenging a member with uncivil discourse on the floor, increased to their highest point in 1995 in the House. Further, the increasing use of filibusters in the Senate is attributed to C-SPAN coverage (Frantzich, 1996; Jamieson, 1997; Jamieson and Falk, 2000; Mixon et al., 2003).

Richard Gephardt, a Democratic member of the House and former Democratic leader, claims, "the rhetoric on the floor became much more sharp and much more partisan, and much more [oriented toward] message making" (Brownstein, 2008: 121–2). For the first time in 1995, with the 104th congress, managing who and what the message would be on the floor through "special order" and one-minute speeches and on cable news and Sunday talk shows became a true party effort. Republicans created the GOP Theme Team and Democrats the Message Group to convey one cohesive message. The House and Senate employed "rapid response teams" to go to the floor immediately to refute what the opposition party was saying (Rothstein, 1999; Brand, 2002; Malecha and Reagan, 2012). In 2003, The House Republican Conference created the Message Action team that did not involve leadership. The object was to create a list of "people who are good on camera and good on their feet. We need to have a cadre of willing folks when the press calls" (Pershing, 2001).

Republican Rep. Don Young (R-AK), a member of the House for the first 40 years C-SPAN has been on the air, says the coverage "has contributed to the coarsening of debate and the polarization between the parties." When freshman Sen. Barack Obama (D-IL) entered office in 2005, he was not too keen on the way legislative business was conducted: "Each of us is speaking to an empty floor and to C-SPAN and giving stock speeches." In 2012, Democratic Sen. Saxby Chambliss (D-GA) blamed C-SPAN directly for increasing partisan rancor: "Partisanship has gotten worse and worse every year that I've been here. I think one thing that's made it that way is C-SPAN ... You know, being able to portray back home 'I'm fighting' is the kind of mantra that a lot of people carry here." Brian Lamb, founder of C-SPAN, shot back: "It's like blaming the Bureau of Printing and Engraving for our $15 trillion debt. Since the beginning of time, television has been criticized for everything possible. I mean, if you can't get your job done, you look around and try to blame it on somebody else. Television has nothing to do with the inability of this town to deal with the problems that are right in front of them" (Kiely, 2006; Mak, 2012; Davis, 2019).

This attention paid by television also changed the nature of deal-making. There were no longer private deals and arm-twisting by party leaders, the kind of in-your-face politics of decades past, but rather a "new era pressured them to deliver strong partisan messages that helped define the party to the public." The way to change minds was now "mobilizing opinion among the voters," instead of elected members of Congress (Brownstein, 2008: 122).

The media publicity strategy may set the agenda, but members still need to get work done. With increasing polarization many are just agitators in media using an issue to run on in the next election without coming to the table to compromise. Grandstanding takes place not only on the floor, but also in committees. Members of committees are "far more interested in speechifying than in asking substantive questions (much less listening to the answers)" (Graham, 2019). However, there is a difference between being a "show horse" and a "work horse." Those with national policy issues or who want to raise their profile to increase their influence within the chamber often go public – and straight to the media. Making news is now a "central focus of policy-making activity" (Cook, 1989: 152–3; Cook, 1998: 151–3).

Members became better-prepared on camera bringing graphics and visual aids which were then picked up by other networks. In a 1995 study, members had indeed become celebrities: 5% of House and Senate members received airtime on 50% of the news on broadcast networks (Frantzich, 271). But the national media landscape was changing: "as mass communications advanced, the showboating moved off the Senate floor. The sugar rush of instant gratification and slightly bolstered name recognition now comes from appearances on the ideologically driven cable shows – or from late night 'tweetstorms' on social media" (Kane, 2016).

Rise of Cable News

The 24-hour cable news concept began with Ted Turner's CNN in 1980. The mission was clear: to present continuous news and information around the clock, but unlike C-SPAN, CNN went into business to make money. Both MSNBC and Fox News were founded in 1996, but with very different purposes. MSNBC was originally a joint venture between NBC News and Microsoft with the idea of highlighting the high-tech industry. Fox News, run by Republican strategist Roger Ailes, took on the mainstream media "liberal bias" with a more right-leaning news channel. With all of these additional options available to viewers, cable news by the mid-1990s became the primary source of news for Americans (Sinclair, 2006; Dagnes, 2010).

Political pundits were used to fill air time and attract ratings in an increasingly competitive market. This encouraged conflict and outrageous behavior, not only on the part of the hosts, but with the guests as well. The more extreme members of Congress get more face-time on cable news. On left-leaning shows, the most liberal members participate most frequently and to a lesser extent the most conservative members. Moderates are glaringly absent (Mitchell et al., 2014).

During the George W. Bush era, cable news outlets began to cater to their fragmented audiences. A 2014 study of media habits by Pew showed that liberals watch CNN and MSNBC and conservatives watch Fox News (Frisch and Kelly, 2013). Ideological polarization of viewing audiences further encourages grandstanding. The public is now inundated with extremists on both C-SPAN (unbiased and unmediated) and cable news (with a definite ideological bias). In addition, the strongest partisans watch the largest number of political programs (Mutz, 2016).

Cable news and the media in general tend to focus on disagreement and scandal and not where the parties may agree on policy furthering this idea that everything is just a battle. Shows with high political content tend to display the most incivility. Interruptions and yelling violate social norms. When faced with conflict, people prefer to distance themselves leading to even more polarization and negativity towards those they dislike and vehemently disagree with. When it comes to ratings, however, the public loves conflict. This harkens back to our survival instincts forcing us to pay more attention to negativity as a threat to our well-being; hence, uncivil discourse draws the most attention. By separating into camps, incivility as portrayed through cable news makes compromise much more difficult (Mutz, 2013; Mutz, 2016). A liberal counter-argument made on Fox News, for example, can come across as less legitimate in viewers' estimation leading to increased polarization.

The plethora of talk radio, cable news networks, and comedy news shows give members ample opportunity to make that one pithy statement that goes viral. Communication has become deeply partisan and structured by the parties to "wage continual partisan public-relations warfare against one another." The caucuses have committees to handle media and technology. Members use the recording studio on the Hill to talk with cable channels and local television stations, and to produce content for their websites. The growth of staff dedicated to media has grown exponentially over the years from little to none in leadership office in the 1970s to 44% in the Senate and 30% in the House by 2015. The increase in communications staff is also related to the 24-hour news cycle where the media are constantly in need of material and members need to supply it and respond quickly. According to a staffer, "You stay silent on Twitter at your peril" (Lee, 2016: 114–5, 131–2, 138–9).

Social Media

Social media has upended the way members of Congress discuss policy and contributes to polarization. Platforms like Facebook and Twitter have largely taken this gatekeeping role out of the hands of the media, and many of these messages are deeply partisan and aggressive. Often the messages themselves become the news.

As seen in Figure 8.1, almost every single member of Congress uses Facebook and Twitter to communicate, as compared to only 68% of adults in the U.S. on Facebook and 24% on Twitter. Twitter is used more often by members of Congress than Facebook. Many on Twitter manage their accounts personally, such as Sen. Marco Rubio (R–FL) and Sen. Clair McCaskill (D-MO). Democratic members are more active on Twitter than Republican members with a Democratic average of 809 posts compared to 485 posts for Republicans. The most active Senator on Twitter was Marco Rubio and the most active Senator on Facebook was Bernie Sanders (I-VT) (Quorum, 2018). Members of Congress use Twitter to provide information and advertise their policy positions. Rep. Alexandria Ocasio-Cortez

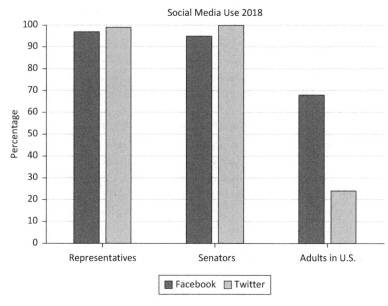

FIGURE 8.1 Social Media Use 2018. Sources: data for members of congress: Quorum Report: 2018 Congressional Social Media Report, https://www.quorum.us/resources/congressional-social-media-report-2018/413/; data for U.S. Adults: Aaron Smith and Monica Anderson, Pew Research, "Social Media Use in 2018," March 1, 2018, https://www.pewinternet.org/2018/03/01/social-media-use-in-2018/.

(D-NY) uses only Twitter for her "press releases" becoming the first member of Congress to not issue traditional press releases to the media (Panetta and Lee, 2019).

The more one-on-one combative exchanges and "You lie!" posts are most prominent on Twitter (Newhauser, 2010). These posts are not always based on the merits of policy, but personal and aggressive. Outrageous tweets, provocative language get mainstream media attention. The minority party, in particular, use this outside, outsized strategy. Republicans were more prevalent on Twitter in 2010, an election year in which they won the House back. Republicans used more negative attacks on Twitter than Democrats exploiting policy differences (Gainous and Wagner, 2013). Today, the Twitter user profile is younger and more Democratic, and more educated with a higher income (Wojcik and Hughes, 2019). Twitter is not used the same way by all who have accounts: 10% of tweeters make up 80% of all tweets. In 2018, those who use social media as primary news sources surpassed newspapers (Shearer, 2018). Now, nine in ten Americans get some news from online sources (Pew Research Center, 2018).

Twitter impacts major national newspaper agendas with such rapidity. One tweet can change what the news is and what members are focusing on in an instant (Conway-Silva et al., 2018). It is a symbiotic relationship with journalists just as likely to influence what members of Congress are posting as members are posting to make news. Journalists are, in fact, the most active group on Twitter (Kamps, 2015). People find same amount of political content on both Facebook and Twitter but from different sources. Facebook users often find political information from those they know personally, but on Twitter, they follow many more public figures and others in their political networks of interest (Duggan and Smith, 2016). For members of Congress, it is not so much about how many followers or friends they can boast, but about having followers who retweet and share their posts to thousands, extending the message perhaps even farther than traditional media. Hashtags get wider audiences and connect people with common interests or policy topics that are trending that the media may then pick up on.

Just like with speeches on the floor and cable news appearances, grandstanding via social media, especially Twitter, gets more notice by the media. "C-SPAN was a political ancestor of social media and the megaphone it has given to newcomers such as Rep. Alexandria Ocasio-Cortez. No longer did lawmakers have to spend decades working their way up the ranks before they had any real voice or influence" (Tumulty, 2015). The perfect example of polarization and grandstanding on all three mediums came in March 2019.

While Congress debated the controversial Green New Deal proposed by Democratic Rep. Ocasio-Cortez, she took to Twitter, mocking Republican Sen. Mike Lee, saying, "Like many other women + working people, I occasionally suffer from impostor syndrome: those small moments, especially on hard days, where you wonder if the haters are right. But then they do things like this to clear it right up. If this guy can be Senator, you can do anything" (See Figure 8.2).

Earlier that day on C-SPAN, Sen. Lee brought a series of props to the floor of the Senate during debate, including a photos of Pres. Reagan carrying both a machine gun and a rocket launcher while riding a dinosaur (a velociraptor, to be precise), Aquaman serving as transportation to Hawaii once airplanes were banned, and Luke Skywalker sitting on a tauntaun in *Star Wars* (see Figures 8.3, 8.4, 8.5).

Cable news covered the events. On CNN, Anderson Cooper on his eponymous show "360" mocked Sen. Lee in his "Ridiculist" segment; the "Fox and Friends" morning show on Fox News interviewed Sen. Lee for his reaction to Rep. Ocasio-Cortez's tweet; and MSNBC gave Ocasio-Cortez her own platform: an hour "Town Hall with Chris Hayes" to discuss her Green New Deal just three days later (CNN, 2019; FOX News, 2019; MSNBC, 2019).

Not every debate and negotiation begins and ends with a Twitter feud. The budget deal reached between Sen. Patty Murray (D-WA) and Rep. Paul Ryan (R-WI), both chairs of their respective chambers' Budget Committees in December 2013, is an example of how members of different political parties

Alexandria Ocasio-Cortez ✔
@AOC

(Follow) ⌄

Like many other women + working people, I
occasionally suffer from impostor syndrome:
those small moments, especially on hard
days, where you wonder if the haters are
right.

But then they do things like this to clear it
right up.

If this guy can be Senator, you can do
anything.

Waleed Shahid ✔ @_waleedshahid
"The solution to climate change is not this unserious resolution...the
solution to so many of our problems at all times and in all places is
to fall in love, get married, and have some kids." -@SenMikeLee on
@AOC and @SenMarkey's Green New Deal...

Show this thread

10:15 AM - 26 Mar 2019

37,835 Retweets **160,767** Likes

💬 15K   🔁 38K   ♡ 161K

FIGURE 8.2 Rep. Ocasio-Cortez Mocks Sen. Lee on Twitter. Source: Twitter, last
accessed May 31, 2019, https://twitter.com/aoc/status/111059121
9804049408?lang=en.

and different chambers can negotiate and compromise to get work done. They
began their negotiations in earnest as the government shut down for 16 days in
October. This was a politically charged time when many had given up hope of
any compromise on the draconian budget cuts looming with sequestration. Sen.
Murray said during a joint appearance on "Meet the Press," December 15, 2013:
"One of the things we had to learn to do was listen to each other and to respect
each other and to trust each other. A lot of discussions in this room, either one of

FIGURE 8.3 Sen. Mike Lee with a Photo of Ronald Reagan. Source: "Senators Durbin, Murkowski, Cantwell, Lee, and Murray on 'Green New Deal,'" March 26, 2019, https://www.c-span.org/video/?459016-8/senators-durbin-murkowski-cantwell-lee-murray-green-deal.

FIGURE 8.4 Sen. Mike Lee with a Photo of Aquaman. Source: "Senators Durbin, Murkowski, Cantwell, Lee, and Murray on 'Green New Deal,'" March 26, 2019, https://www.c-span.org/video/?459016-8/senators-durbin-murkowski-cantwell-lee-murray-green-deal.

FIGURE 8.5 Sen. Mike Lee with a Photo of Luke Skywalker. Source: "Senators Durbin, Murkowski, Cantwell, Lee, and Murray on 'Green New Deal,'" March 26, 2019, https://www.c-span.org/video/?459016-8/senators-durbin-murkowski-cantwell-lee-murray-green-deal.

us could have taken out and blown up and killed the other person on politically. We agreed from the start we wouldn't do that" (NBC News, 2013). The Murray–Ryan budget compromise took place largely in their respective home states over the phone, without their staff or other pressures in the room. The budget, while containing things both parties disliked, prevented yet another budget shutdown without the use of grandstanding on C-SPAN or cable news or Twitter.

The keys to successful negotiations include secrecy, deadlines, repeated interactions, and messaging that is not demonizing (Binder et al., 2015). With full transparency, people want to know what their government is doing, but if all phases of negotiation take place in public view, members may feel pressured to carry the party mantra. Negotiating involves compromise; no one is ever fully satisfied. To play out serious debate and deliberation in the public square involves differing motivations than in private. Public opinion, often fickle, can prevent compromise before it truly begins. Negotiating involves trust between the parties to come in good faith and not tweet about it afterward. Ideas need to be tested and teased out. Perhaps not every idea should first come before the court of public opinion.

Repeated interactions are important in this process. It involves more than just one speech on the floor on C-SPAN or a sound bite on cable news. Politics is built on relationships and trust. There should be a spirit of collaboration, not competition, at the negotiating table. While this may be almost impossible to expect in a highly polarized partisan environment, the Murray–Ryan budget deal serves as a template for success. The two built trust over time and found areas of agreement without sacrificing their core principles (Lawrence, 2015).

There is one more glimmer of hope. In May 2019, Rep. Ocasio-Cortez and Sen. Cruz made a pact on Twitter to pass a lifetime ban on former Congress members becoming lobbyists (see Figure 8.6). Ocasio-Cortez tweeted at Cruz: "if you're serious about a clean bill, then I'm down. Let's make a deal. If we can agree on a bill with no partisan snuck-in clauses, no poison pills, etc- just a straight, clean ban on members of Congress becoming paid lobbyists- then I'll co-lead the bill with you." Cruz responded, "Here's something I don't say often: on this point I AGREE with @AOC Indeed, I have long called for a LIFETIME BAN

Alexandria Ocasio-Cortez ✓
@AOC

(Follow) ⌄

.@tedcruz if you're serious about a clean bill, then I'm down.

Let's make a deal.

If we can agree on a bill with no partisan snuck-in clauses, no poison pills, etc - just a straight, clean ban on members of Congress becoming paid lobbyists - then I'll co-lead the bill with you.

Ted Cruz ✓ @tedcruz
Here's something I don't say often: on this point, I AGREE with @AOC Indeed, I have long called for a LIFETIME BAN on former Members of Congress becoming lobbyists. The Swamp would hate it, but perhaps a chance for some bipartisan cooperation? twitter.com/aoc/status/113...

1:46 PM - 30 May 2019

20,342 Retweets **158,614** Likes

FIGURE 8.6 Bipartisan Twitter Agreement between Rep. Alexandria Ocasio-Cortez and Sen. Ted Cruz. Source: Twitter, last accessed May 31, 2019, https://twitter.com/aoc/status/1134199323263209480.

on former Members of Congress becoming lobbyists. The Swamp would hate it, but perhaps a chance for some bipartisan cooperation?" Maybe those who are the media darlings of cable news and grandstand the most on C-SPAN will be the ones to find compromise through social media.

Conclusion

Is serious debate even possible these days given our media environment? It appears unlikely. Instead of deliberation and backroom dealing, going public has now become a governing tool. Public relations blitzes on cable news, vitriolic speeches on C-SPAN, and biting comments on social media have replaced the desire for interpersonal legislating from the past. Both congressional members and their parties have developed strategic public relations campaigns and members closely align with their party's goals.

You can no longer disagree without destroying. Position-taking often takes the form of speeches on the floor and outbursts in committees, cable news sound bite attacks, and negative tweets. Parties have switched majorities in both chambers so frequently since 1994 that stakes are constantly raised every two years. Through these devices, members attack the other party in an all-out war to gain votes and possibly majority status next election. The hyper-partisanship that exists does not promote compromise. Backroom deals are not so secret when everyone is tweeting about it in real time. Grandstanding can also advance political careers, not only increasing a member's standing within their chamber, but also getting them noticed by the national media to court an increasingly extreme wing of their party in a presidential or even their own house or senate primary.

However, we have examples such as Murray–Ryan where members pursue the goal of getting work done for the people that overrides purely partisan considerations. But there needs to be the will among at least a subset of members to find agreement and not exploit differences in governing for their benefit. A zero-sum game being fought out in the media is never a winning proposition.

References

Binder, S.A., Lee, F.E., Mansbridge, F.J. and Martin, C.J., 2015. Making Deals in Congress. In: Mansbridge, J.J. and Martin, C.J. (eds.) *Political Negotiation: A Handbook* (pp. 91–120). Washington D.C.: Brookings Institute Press.

Brand, P., 2002. House Democrats Create 'Message Teams'. *The Hill.*

Broadcasting, March 3, 1986. Senate Votes to 'Enter the Modern Age'. pp. 35–36.

Brownstein, R., 2008. *The Second Civil War: How Extreme Partisanship Has Paralyzed Washington and Polarized America.* New York: Penguin.

CNN, 2019. Cooper Mocks GOP Lawmaker's Use of Props on Senate Floor. https:// www.cnn.com /videos/politics/2019/03/27/ridiculist-anderson-cooper-mike-lee-p olitical-props-green-new-deal-sot-ac360-vpx.cnn.

Conway-Silva, B.A., Filer, C.R., Kenski, K. and Tsetsi, E., 2018. Reassessing Twitter's Agenda-Building Power: An Analysis of Intermedia Agenda-Setting Effects During the 2016 Presidential Primary Season. *Social Science Computer Review, 36*(4), pp. 469–483.

Cook, T.E., 1989. *Making Laws and Making News: Media Strategies in the US House of Representatives*. Washington D.C.: Brookings Institution Press.

Cook, T.E., 1998. *Governing with the News: The News Media as a Political Institution*. Chicago: University of Chicago Press.

Coppins, M., 2018. The Man Who Broke Politics. *The Atlantic*.

C-SPAN. 2019, May 15. C-SPAN-35 Years-1984. https://www.c-span.org/video/?318187-7/span-35-years-1984.

Dagnes, A., 2010. *Politics on Demand: The Effects of 24-Hour News on American Politics*. Santa Barbara, California: Praeger.

Davis, S., 2019. Not Everyone Is a Fan of C-SPAN Cameras in Congress. *USA Today*.

Duggan, M. and Smith, A., 2016. Political Content on Social Media. *Pew Research Center*. https://www.pewinternet.org/2016/10/25/political-content-on- social-media/.

Farrell, J.A., 2001. [BOOK REVIEW] Tip O'Neill and the Democratic Century. *American Prospect, 12*(7), pp. 42–44.

FOX News, 2019. Sen. Lee Uses 'Photo' of Reagan Riding Velociraptor, Giant Seahorses in Floor Speech Mocking Green New Deal. https://insider.foxnews.com/2019/03/26/green-new- deal-mike-lee-rips-climate-change-reagan-velociraptor-hoth-ice-planet-animal.

Frantzich, S.E., 1996. *The C-Span Revolution*. Norman, Oklahoma: University of Oklahoma Press.

Frisch, S. and Kelly, S. eds., 2013. *Politics to the Extreme: American Political Institutions in the Twenty-First Century*. New York: Springer.

FrontLine, 1978. *The Long March of Newt Gingrich*. [May 11, 2019]. https://www.pbs.org/wgbh/pages/frontline/newt/newt78speech.html.

Gainous, J. and Wagner, K.M., 2013. *Tweeting to Power: The Social Media Revolution in American Politics*. Oxford; New York: Oxford University Press.

Gingrich, N., 2019. C-Span's 40-Year Mark on Our Republic. *Newsweek*.

Graham, D.A., 2019. C-SPAN Isn't All Good. *The Atlantic*.

Halberstam, D., 2000. *The Powers That Be*. Urbana, Illinois: University of Illinois Press.

Jacobs, J., 2019. As C-SPAN Turns 40, A Top Executive Reflects on Bringing Cameras to Congress. *New York Times*.

Jamieson, K.H., 1997. Civility in the House of Representatives. *APPC Report #10*.

Jamieson, K.H. and Falk, E., 2000. Continuity and Change in Civility in the House. In: Bond, J.R. and Fleisher, R. (eds.) *Polarized Politics: Congress and the President in a Partisan Era* (pp. 96–108). Washington, DC: CQ Press.

Johnson, H., 1984. Charade: Small Band of Republican Zealots Evokes Tactics from the Past. *Washington Post*.

Kamps, H.J., 2015. Who Are Twitter's Verified Users? *Medium*. https://medium.com/@Haje.who-are-twitter-s-verified-users-af976fc1b032.

Kane, P., 2016. What 30 Years of C-SPAN's Senate Broadcasts Have Taught the American Public. *Washington Post*.

Kernell, S., 2006. *Going Public: New Strategies of Presidential Leadership*. Washington D.C.: CQ Press.

Kiely, K., 2006. Fresh Faces in Congress Stress Cooperation. *USA Today*.

Lamb, B., 1988. *C-Span: American's Town Hall*. Washington D.C.: Acropolis Books.

Lawrence, J., 2015. Profiles in Negotiation; the Murray-Ryan Budget Deal. *Brookings*. https ://www.brookings.edu/research/profiles-in-negotiation-the-murray-ryan-budget-deal/.

Lee, F.E., 2009. *Beyond Ideology: Politics, Principles, and Partisanship in the US Senate*. Chicago: University of Chicago Press.

Lee, F.E., 2016. *Insecure Majorities: Congress and the Perpetual Campaign*. Chicago: University of Chicago Press.

Mak, T., 2012. C-SPAN Hammers Sen. Chambliss. *Politico*.

Malecha, G.L. and Reagan, D.J., 2012. *The Public Congress: Congressional Deliberation in a New Media age*. London: Routledge.

Mann, T.E. and Ornstein, N.J., 2006. *The Broken Branch: How Congress Is Failing America and How to Get It Back on Track*. Oxford; New York: Oxford University Press.

Mayhew, D.R., 1974. *Congress: The Electoral Connection* (Vol. *26*). New Haven, Connecticut; London: Yale University Press.

Mitchell, A., Kiley, K., Gottfried, J. and Matsa, K.E., 2014. Political Polarization and Media Habits. *Pew Research Center*. https://www.journalism.org/2014/10/21/political-polariz ation- media-habits/.

Mixon, F.G., Gibson, M.T. and Upadhyaya, K.P., 2003. Has Legislative Television Changed Legislator Behavior?: C-SPAN2 and the Frequency of Senate Filibustering. *Public Choice*, *115*(1–2), pp. 139–162.

MSNBC, 2019. Full Alexandria Ocasio-Cortez Town Hall, Unedited. https://ww w.msnbc.com/all-in/watch/full-alexandria-ocasio-cortez-town-hall-unedi ted- 1470189123632.

Mutz, D.C., 2013. Television and Uncivil Political Discourse. In: *Can We Talk?: The Rise of Rude, Nasty, Stubborn Politics*, pp. 67–81.

Mutz, D.C., 2016. *In-Your-Face Politics: The Consequences of Uncivil Media*. Princeton: Princeton University Press.

NBC News, 2013. Ryan, Murray Tout Bipartisan Budget Deal as Step in Right Direction. http://www.nbcnews.com/video/meet-the-press/53837045.

Newhauser, D., 2010. Congress is all Atwitter. *Roll Call*.

New York Times, 1984. O'Neill Assails a Republican and Is Rebuked by the Chair.

O'Neill, T., 1987. *Man of the House: The Life and Political Memoirs of Speaker Tip O'Neil with Wm. Novak*. New York: Random House.

Panetta, G. and Lee, S., 2019. Twitter Is the Most Popular Social Media Platform for Members of Congress — But Prominent Democrats Tweet More often and Have Larger Followings than Republicans. *Business Insider*.

Pershing, B., 2001. House GOP Conference Forms Message Action. *Roll Call*.

Pew Research Center, 2018. Digital News Fact Sheet. https://www.journalism.org/fact-sheet /digital-news/.

Quorum, 2018. 2018 Congressional Social Media Report. [May 31, 2019]. https://www. quorum.us/ resources/congressional-social-media-report-2018/413/.

Reid, T.R., 1984. Outburst: Speaker O'Neill and Republicans Clash Fiercely In House Debate. *Washington Post*.

Rothstein, B., 1999. House GOP Theme Team vs. Democrats' Message Group. *The Hill*.

Seelye, K.Q., 1994. Gingrich First Mastered the Media and the Rose to Be King of the Hill. *New York Times*.

Shearer, E., 2018. Social Media Outpaces Print Newspapers in the U.S. as a News Source. *Pew Research Center*. https://www.pewresearch.org/fact-tank/2018/12/10/social -media-outpaces -print-newspapers-in-the-u-s-as-a-news-source/.

Shirley, C., 2017. *Citizen Newt: The Making of a Reagan Conservative*. New York: Harper Collins.

Sinclair, B., 2014. *Party Wars: Polarization and the Politics of National Policy Making* (Vol. *10*). Norman, Oklahoma: University of Oklahoma Press.

Steely, M., 2000. *The Gentleman from Georgia: The Biography of Newt Gingrich*. Macon, Georgia: Mercer University Press.

Tumulty, K., 2015. Happy Birthday, C-SPAN. We Need You More than Ever. *The Washington Post*.

Wojcik, S. and Hughes, A., 2019. Sizing up Twitter Users. *Pew Research Center*. https://www.pewinternet.org/2019/04/24/sizing-up-twitter-users/.

Zelizer, J., 2007. Seizing Power: Conservatives and Congress since the 1970s. In: Pierson, P. and Skocpol, T. (eds.) *The Transformation of American Politics: Activist Government and the Rise of Conservatism* (pp. 105–134). Princeton: Princeton University Press.

9

THE DEMISE OF RELATIONSHIPS IN WASHINGTON, D.C.

Thomas B. Langhorne

Rep. David Jolly: As a student of government, I always presumed the House and Senate worked seamlessly together and that all those members of Congress walking back and forth on the House floor during votes televised on C-SPAN must mean the lower chamber in fact operated as a body. Then I got elected to Congress.

The House and Senate rarely if ever interact, and when they do it is primarily at the leadership level only. And within the House, you quickly learn that the institution does not operate as a singular legislative body, but instead operates as two partisan organizations rarely conferring with each other on the right direction for the nation. In some ways it is reflective of today's coarse politics, reflective of the electoral success and media reward that is often found in demonizing the other side of the aisle. Consensus and bipartisanship are rarely celebrated.

But it is also a function of today's congressional calendar. It has been said that bipartisanship ended with the jet airplane. Advances in transportation were followed by information age advances and then new media advances. Taken together, the modern Congress looks very different than it did generations ago when members of Congress would often live in the Washington area and report back to their constituents periodically through typed letters and occasional trips back home. Members forged relationships with their colleagues in Congress and often found bipartisan legislative success as a result of those relationships and their time focused on policymaking.

Today's Congress, conversely, routinely meets three full days a week, roughly three weeks a month, with long breaks in the summer and over the holidays. Members typically fly in immediately before the first vote and rush to the airport immediately after the last vote. Their time in Washington is distracted by the constant demands of fundraising and by satisfying an increasingly divided media environment.

The result is a striking lack of relationships among colleagues. And a resulting inability to trust each other when trust is required most. There are many strangers in Congress, and many opportunities for bipartisanship therefore missed.

But importantly, this division can also be seen within the parties themselves. As Democrats wrestle with balancing progressive ideas with their less progressive members, and as Republicans wrestle with balancing more conservative ideas with their less conservative members, the lack of relationships appears as well even within the major parties themselves.

Whether more time in Washington would create better public policy or allow for greater consensus is a fair question, just as is the question of whether members of Congress should spend more time in their home districts with their constituencies. But what is certain is the opportunity to build bipartisan relationships, to foster inter-partisan relationships, and to work on policy making together simply won't exist if Congress limits the time they spend together in Washington. The modern congressional schedule inhibits consensus, marginalizes rank and file members, and empowers party leadership to make the majority of all policy decisions, even the most detailed work that in the past would be done by committees. The result is not the mere sidelining of members of Congress hoping to advance policy deserving of a diverse nation; the result is the sidelining of their constituencies whose wish for an attentive Congress is left wanting.

Rep. Patrick E. Murphy: There is undoubtedly more division between voters and elected officials, but the lack of relationships between members of Congress has certainly made the problem worse. After being elected by campaigning on bipartisanship and reaching across the aisle, one of the first actions I took was to form a broad coalition of freshman members from both parties willing to find compromise on a handful of issues we could agree on – addressing our national debt, fixing our broken tax code, and preserving Social Security and Medicare. After making progress on legislation to cut wasteful government spending, I was notified by my Republican counterpart in the deal that the bill would no longer move forward because I was in a tough district for re-election, and the number one focus for Republicans would be defeating me … in an election two years later! Imagine how difficult it is to continue working on macro issues with your friends on the other side of the aisle when they are bashing you on TV, raising millions to spend against you, or simply can't even cosponsor a bill with you.

Unfortunately this behavior occurs on both sides of the aisle and was an early wake-up call that politics was superseding policy. Historically, members of Congress were able to forge real friendships and trust and actually learn about what is driving their way of thinking. With the expectation that every member will be home every weekend to campaign and be present to raise money, the opportunity to make these relationships simply doesn't exist.

What I was especially surprised to discover is the increased divisions within the parties themselves – moderate Republicans rarely socialize with Tea Party Republicans and ultra-liberal progressives don't spend much time with moderate Democrats. So we're dealing with almost four parties in Washington, none of which trust each other or have any incentive to compromise. Each group's respective base does not want to see its team compromise or give in, and even being seen socializing with the other side could lead to problems. Again, it's clear to see the connection between all these structural issues: the more pressure to raise money and get re-elected, the less likely members will become friends, and the more likely they will bash each other on TV, making it less likely they will work on legislation together and the more likely voters will dig in to support their "team."

The U.S. House of Representatives is a 435-member body. Spending just a few days a week in Washington when they do come here, members hurtle through a whirlwind of meetings, committee hearings, floor votes, and fundraising calls and events that keeps them dashing all over the Capitol complex.

It takes time and effort for House members to nurture more than a handful of close working relationships among colleagues – time and effort many of them can't or don't make. Relationships that cross party lines are especially challenging.

"Most of their life when they're in Washington is blocked into 15- and 30-minute segments," notes Brad Fitch, head of the non-partisan, D.C.-based Congressional Management Foundation, which works with members and their staffs to improve the way congressional offices operate. "It's very rare for a member of Congress to spend 30 minutes in one place before they move on."[1]

Confusion clouded the face of Rep. Emanuel Cleaver II when Indiana Congressman Larry Bucshon's name came up. Who?

"Larry Bucshon," Cleaver repeated, pausing as if to rack his brain. "Did he just get, uh …" he said, leaving the word "elected" unsaid. "I just don't know who he is."[2]

That's not necessarily surprising – unless you consider the fact that Cleaver, a Missouri Democrat, had served in Congress with Republican Bucshon for nearly eight years at the time.

Several other House Democrats said they've heard of Republican Bucshon, but they don't know him. Cleaver's face lit up when he was asked if he knew Bucshon's predecessor, Brad Ellsworth – a Democrat who last walked the halls of Congress in 2010.

"Yes, of course!" Cleaver said.

When he was in Congress, Ellsworth admitted he did not know many of the House's other 434 members and sometimes did not realize they were members until he saw them on C-SPAN. He said he had formed some close working relationships – mostly with other members of the "Blue Dog" caucus of moderate Democrats.

And Ellsworth's predecessor, Republican John Hostettler? His closest relationships in Congress were among a group arguably composed of the House's half-dozen most conservative members – a group to which Hostettler himself belonged.

The pace of congressional life doesn't help. When the work week whirlwind ends – usually at about noon on a Thursday or Friday – it ends fast. Most members return to their districts in a mass exodus. Some are in a hurry to make their planes.

"You can smell the jet fuel," one House staffer quipped.

The Good Old Days

There is a stately hallway just outside the House Chamber, behind the doors flanking the rostrum of the Speaker of the House, that members and staff call the Speaker's Lobby. Reporters linger there hoping to catch House members on their way in and out, but no cameras are allowed. Male visitors must wear neckties.

There's another rule too, this one unwritten – Republicans and Democrats in the Speaker's Lobby enter the chamber through different doors. To understand how the House became so insular, you have to go back decades – to a day when members of Congress actually lived in Washington with their families.

Standing at the bottom of the steps at the U.S. Capitol Building at the end of a long day, Cleaver, the former Kansas City mayor and previous chairman of the Congressional Black Caucus, blames hyper-partisanship in both parties and the legislative dysfunction that results.

"Republicans sit on one side of the floor, we sit on one," he said. "The only time I see a Republican is when I come up here (to the Capitol) to vote. Or go to a committee hearing. That's probably the biggest reason things have turned nasty. All of the incivility, all of the difficulty working together."

He has long been a voice for comity and conciliation in Washington. He pointedly refused to join the roughly 40 House Democrats who boycotted President Donald Trump's inauguration in 2017, attending "out of respect for the peaceful transfer of power." Washington used to be a parochial town, and living here helped members of Congress build the kinds of relationships that helped them govern. They played golf and went out to dinner together with their families on weekends. In this bipartisan bonhomie, everybody knew everybody.

"It's difficult to call somebody a nasty name when your kid and their kid are in the Cub Scouts together," Cleaver said.

An indelible legend has grown up in this place about those days. It was just the latest iteration of a clubby congressional culture that had held sway for decades. In the 1980s, Democratic House Speaker Tip O'Neill and Republican Minority Leader Bob Michel were thick as thieves. Contemporaries of the two men said they traveled together, played cards and golf, shared drinks in the evenings, and even bet on sports events. O'Neill urged members to move their families to Washington. It wasn't unusual for them to visit each other's homes here.

The burly old-school Boston politician set the culture in the House, holding court over regular Wednesday night poker sessions at the University Club. There, members and former members of both chambers swapped stories, played cards, and roared with laughter.

Debbie Dingell was in the thick of it all – married for nearly four decades to longtime House Energy and Commerce Committee Chairman John D. Dingell Jr., who retired after 59 years in Congress in 2015. She succeeded her husband in his Michigan House seat that year.

"When I married John, Tipper Gore took me under her wing," Dingell said, referring to the wife of then-Congressman Al Gore. "We all got involved in issues and projects and got together on a regular basis."[3]

John Dingell died in February 2019 as the longest-serving member of Congress in U.S. history.

When she thinks of those early days in Washington, Debbie Dingell recalls a committed Democratic spouses group and friendships among the men that transcended party lines. Those days are gone.

"It was a different day. Before our marriage, my husband played paddle ball with George Bush, Don Rumsfeld, and Sonny Montgomery," she said. "It was a different time, a different place."

Rich Cohen, chief author of the Almanac of American Politics, saw it all from his seat in press row. He has been covering Congress since 1977, has written for the National Journal, POLITICO, and Congressional Quarterly, and has authored several books. Like Dingell, he's still here.

"It used to be said by the leaders of the House that the other party was the opposition and the Senate was the enemy," Cohen said. "Now the other party in the House really is the enemy."

Even for members who hold safe seats, Cohen said, "there are really strong disincentives for cooperating with the other party."[4]

"If [Republicans] were to spend a lot of time trying to legislate or socialize or work with Democrats, it would be noticed and it would be frowned on," he said. "It would be talked about. There are limits to how far bipartisanship can go."

Cohen authored the 1999 book "Rostenkowski: The Pursuit of Power and the End of the Old Politics," a biography of legendary former House Ways and Means Committee Chairman Dan Rostenkowski.

"[Rostenkowski, a Democrat] talked to and worked with, was friendly with, and legislated with Republicans to the point that a lot of Democrats frowned on it," Cohen said. "Well, he was very effective and productive. He got a lot of legislation. But that style of Rostenkowski – working across the aisle – that's gone. That doesn't happen anymore."

Like everything else in politics, explaining why is a matter of who you ask.

"Potomac Fever"

Sometime in the 1980s and 1990s, gentleman politics gave way to populist zeal. Newer, younger representatives with anti-elitist sensibilities began nudging the

House into permanent campaign mode. Cleaver, a Democrat, blames Republicans, who took control of the lower chamber in the 1994 mid-term election. Democrats until then had been in the majority for all but four of the preceding 72 years.

The new House Speaker, Newt Gingrich, encouraged members to spend more time back home and accused those who didn't of having "Potomac fever" – shorthand for falling out of touch with constituents. Several high-profile members of Congress did subsequently lose their seats amid criticism that they lived in Washington instead of the places they represented.

Gingrich's ascension to leadership after the 1994 elections would become a watershed event in American politics, a fulcrum in time whose effects are still being felt. It shocked the senses, to begin with. Democrats had held the majority so long – 40 years – that a sense of inevitability had crept in. Republicans were the Washington Generals to the Democrats' Harlem Globetrotters. They never won, until they did.

"It was just kind of assumed that the Democrats would control forever," Cohen said. Republican leaders and campaigners and pollsters, political strategists, would say, 'Of course we're going to try to win back control' – but in their heart of hearts, it just wasn't there."

To Democrats and supporters of a vigorous congressional influence in American life, the elevation of Gingrich wrought a dark age from which the institution still hasn't recovered. But to Gingrich and the House Republicans under his charge, it marked a bracing reversal of their own party's passive acceptance of permanent minority status.

Girded by his conviction that Washington is not the repository of all wisdom, the reform-minded Gingrich made sweeping changes. He slashed legislative support jobs – analysts, auditors, subject matter experts – in congressional service agencies. He eliminated the Office of Technology Assessment (OTA) entirely. The Government Accountability Office and the Congressional Research Service, which served both houses of Congress, also were among the losers.

According to the Brookings Institution's Vital Statistics of Congress, the GAO lost nearly 1,500 staff positions – from 4,958 in 1993 to 3,500 in 1997. But then, the agency continued to suffer cuts for years after Gingrich resigned as speaker after the 1998 mid-term election. CRS went from 835 to 726 staffers, also suffering further losses post-Gingrich. House standing committees lost staffers under Gingrich – attorneys, investigators, economists. Power and jobs flowed away from committees and to House leadership offices. Committees lost some of their autonomy.

Brookings reports that House committees employed 2,147 professional staffers in 1993 – and 1,266 in 1995, the first year of Gingrich's speakership. But subsequent House leadership teams didn't bulk up committee staff after Gingrich resigned in 1998. Professional committee staff stayed in the same range at least through 2015, the most recent year for which Brookings offers data.

Staffers working directly for House members in Washington did not see their ranks substantially thinned, as critics have charged. Personal staff went from 7,400 in 1993 – the year before Gingrich's ascension – to 7,186 in 1995. Large cutbacks didn't begin to happen until Gingrich was long gone. The number was 6,030 in 2015. Gingrich may have assumed some of the committees' power, but leadership staff itself did not rise by more than a few positions – from 132 in 1993 to 179 – until 1999, the year after he resigned. The number has grown in subsequent years.

"When Democrats took control of the House (in 2007 and 2019), they didn't go back to the past," Cohen said. "Because you can't go back to the past. Congress, like any institution, is always changing. It's never static."

Some of Gingrich's changes pre-dated his speakership. "They were changes that Democrats were already making. Gingrich went much farther in weakening the committees and strengthening the party leaders to run things, but that change was already taking place among the Democrats before Gingrich, and after Gingrich – and when the Democrats regained control in 2007 and this year, they're not returning control to the committees. They're not going back to the way it was. I think, frankly, [Democratic Speaker Nancy] Pelosi saw some benefits to the way Gingrich was running that House."

Pelosi hasn't cut leadership staff positions either, Cohen said. "She liked having a lot of staff around her. There's an old saying: 'There's only one job of the minority – which is to become the majority.'"

But critics said Gingrich's service agency and committee staff cuts deprived Congress of much-needed policy expertise, legislative know-how, and institutional knowledge of agencies and programs. It still stings Lorelei Kelly that Gingrich cut the pooled funding that paid for congressional staffers who worked for Congress itself. Hundreds of them – steeped in policy and intimately familiar with the way Congress works – were laid off.[5]

Eliminating the technology office was a particularly shortsighted move, according to Kelly, former leader of the Smart Congress initiative with the Open Technology Institute at New America. Congress suffered a collective brain drain under Gingrich, Kelly insisted.

"It was easy to chalk it up as sort of eliminating overhead, but it really lobotomized the legislative branch," she said. "I mean, it just wiped out its synapses. When you think about how policy is made, it's so much based on timing and trust and who's in the building with you and who can you ask for help?" OTA "brought expert judgment into the room" with 120 science advisors who worked within the workflow of Capitol Hill.

Kelly, who led Security for a New Century, a bipartisan House–Senate study group, is among more than 50 individuals and 40 organizations who signed a letter to senators in May 2019 seeking funding to revive OTA. The letter expressed concern that Congress "does not have sufficient capacity to tackle 21st century science and technology policy challenges." Kelly can't fathom was Gingrich was thinking in 1995. She said he "completely chose politics over his institution."

"I often want to get stuck in an elevator with him so I can ask him this question – did you mean to do this?" she said. "He's a smart guy. He gets systems, right? He's not a dummy. But I do think it was a really intentional consolidation of power to himself, and then it's just damaged the whole system of government terribly because that space was not just filled by lobbyists. It was filled by the executive branch."

David Skaggs, a former Democratic House member from Colorado, was there to see Gingrich and his allies take control in 1995. He had a front row seat – it was just on the other side of the aisle. What stings him are a series of petty reprisals he says Gingrich engineered – reduced funding for Democratic staff, rules that reduced Democratic members' ability to offer amendments and to debate. It was "payback time," he said – "an upheaval of the institution."[6]

But Skaggs admits the atmosphere in Congress was toxic before Gingrich took the speakership. He recalls a day before the 1994 election when he and a klatch of Democratic colleagues were discussing their party's prospects. Skaggs had been a minority member of the Colorado House of Representatives before his election to Congress in 1986. But by 1994, the House hadn't been controlled by Republicans in four decades. He was the only one at the table who had any experience in a minority.

"I said, 'You know, the Republicans actually do have some legitimate gripes about the way we run the place,'" he said. "That led to a discussion with some agreement and dissent at the table.

"But I think we need to take some responsibility for having fed to Newt Gingrich and his leadership allies some ammunition with which to, as was his intention, to take the place down." Like Kelly, Skaggs still grieves the loss of the OTA – Gingrich's "most foolish" mistake, he said.

"Here we were, in the mid-90s, looking at issues coming before Congress that are ever more technologically complicated and scientifically complicated, and we're disarming the institution of the capability of getting good, non-partisan advice about those kinds of issues," he said.

In that next Congress in 1995, Skaggs was elected chair of the Democratic Study Group, the party caucus's policy and reform organization. But that went badly.

"The Speaker decided that the mechanisms for funding those operations would be basically removed, so it made it very difficult for a lot of these caucuses and member organizations to function," Skaggs said. "The overarching, theory, I think, that animated Newt's approach to these things was that knowledge is power and – to the extent that knowledge can be monopolized by the majority party – it makes it much harder for the minority to function and much easier for the major-ity to determine how things turn out."

Always interested in improving relationships among members, Skaggs in 1997 teamed up with Illinois Republican Congressman Ray LaHood to organize the House Bipartisan Retreat, a series of weekend getaways for members and their families. The biennial events were funded by the Pew Charitable Trust and then the Annenberg Foundation.

"A bunch of us recognized that the place was much more fractious and unpleasant, and we theorized, I think correctly, that one of the most important reasons for that was that members simply didn't know each other very well personally except as political adversaries," Skaggs said.

"That impedes what is the fundamental business of the Congress, which is working out deals and compromises, as much as that is now held in lower regard. And you can't do that with people you don't know and don't trust."

The initiative started out gangbusters, attracting what Skaggs called the largest-ever gathering of members of Congress outside Washington. Hundreds of members. But there were troubling signs even then. "A lot of people who needed to be there didn't attend," he said.

Political developments outside Congress – the bitterly contested 2000 presidential election and cut-throat redistricting battles – eroded the desire for civility. The biennial churn of new members in, old members out didn't help. Skaggs himself left Congress in 1999. By the time of the final retreat in 2003, enthusiasm for the endeavor had waned. Slightly more than 100 members showed up – and sponsors pulled out.

Gingrich was long gone by then – but all these years later, Skaggs's distrust is so strong that he thinks partisan gamesmanship might have aided the death of the House Bipartisan Retreat. He said he heard rumors that Republican leadership advised its rank-and-file to stop attending.

"Passive Patsies"

To the man so often cited as the progenitor of congressional discord, these complaints are sour grapes by people who lost power and influence in an election. Gingrich said he didn't invent partisanship – but he did show House Republicans how to fight back.

"The bias of the news media has always been that Democrats can be vicious, dishonest and ruthlessly pursue power because they are liberals while Republicans are supposed to be passive patsies who do not fight back," Gingrich wrote. "Most of what I did I learned by studying [Democratic] President Franklin Roosevelt, President John Kennedy and other great partisans."[7]

On the subject of whether Gingrich told freshman Republicans not to live in Washington, he says that his party "wanted congressmen re-elected and wanted them to spend time home with their families and constituents."

And eliminating OTA? Congress could engage directly with learned people without needing OTA, Gingrich declared. "OTA was a bureaucratic layer between congressmen and scientists. You can reach Nobel Prize winners and learn from the best," he said. "You get much more sophisticated information by going directly to the best."

Like Skaggs, former Sen. Rick Santorum was there to witness Gingrich's rise – but Santorum had a better seat. He was a 30-something Republican House member from Pennsylvania who had been elected four years earlier.

Eliminating OTA didn't dumb down Congress, Santorum said.

"The reality is, over the past 30 or 40 years, we've seen an explosion of government involvement in all aspects of life and the ability through technology to have people from the outside influence what's going on in government," he said. "It's almost Neanderthal to suggest that in an age of technology development that we've seen in the last 30 years, that you were going to keep a small handful of government employees being the drivers of innovation and support."[8]

OTA wasn't needed in the same way that the National Endowment for the Arts isn't necessary to support the arts and National Public Radio isn't essential to disseminate the news, Santorum believes.

"As a result of technology and the communications that are now allowed – there's no shortage of ideas that are coming into the halls of Congress from all over the country, from constituents and from thinktanks, from businesses – the reality is, we're overwhelmed," he said. "The ability for a single staffer to be able to gather information and get it to a senator or member of Congress is 100 times greater than it was 25 or 30 years ago simply because of the technology."

Elected to the Senate in 2000, Santorum eyed another way for congressional Republicans to break out of their assigned role as "passive patsies."

He spearheaded the K Street Project, a campaign to get Republican congressional staffers, White House aides, or sympathetic lobbyists into key positions in high-powered industry trade associations and corporate offices. The effort owed its name to the confluence of such offices around D.C.'s K Street, a few blocks north of the White House.

Critics – namely Democrats – pounced. Here was an organized effort to give GOP congressional leaders a partisan substitute for the nonpartisan in-house legislative expertise that Gingrich wiped out, they said. The outsourcing of policy development at the city's most important and influential lobbying shops would bolster corporate interests at the expense of institutional integrity. Thus the K Street Project would become just another battleground for partisan war-making in Washington.

Santorum argues the K Street Project was an effort to level an "incredibly frustrating" uneven playing field created over four decades of Democratic House control.

"Washington was a Democratic town," he said. "All of the offices – whether they were the big companies or the lobbying firms – they had a very, very heavy Democratic bench in them because that's who you had to get if you wanted to get anything done. You had to go through a Democratic Congress. I would find myself in situations where I'm sitting here advocating for policies that I know that the companies that are affected would be supportive of – but everybody in charge of their federal affairs was a Democrat. If we were going to have any success in getting support for the ideas that we were trying to put forward, we had to get some people in these offices who actually told the truth to their leadership."

If corporate offices and industry trade associations felt they had to hire Democrats in their federal affairs offices, Santorum said, they also knew where the money had to go. Business PAC money – hundreds of millions of dollars – went to Democratic congressional candidates.

No one dictated hiring practices to K Street, Santorum said. "I wanted to make sure that when there were openings available, that good Republicans were aware of those openings – because the other thing that was happening was very incestuous. There was an informal network of people who made sure that quote, the 'right people' got slotted for openings in companies as they came up. It was so one-sided dominated. The fact that it's now more balanced is a problem for folks who were used to being the only game in town."

Goin' Home

The notion of a permanent political class entrenched in Washington had already begun to smell to many voters by the time Gingrich came to power. In a widely publicized 1990 House campaign in Pennsylvania, Santorum defeated six-term incumbent Democrat Doug Walgren by casting him as a creature of Washington. Santorum told voters Walgren lived with his family in D.C., claimed his parents' house as his residence in the district, and rarely showed up back home.

Two years later, headlines screamed that hundreds of House members had overdrawn their checking accounts at the legislative body's members-only bank without penalty. No taxpayer money was involved, but the free overdraft protection for roughly 20,000 bad checks – some of them for very large amounts – amounted to secret, interest-free, personal loans. It was the kind of perk most mere mortals couldn't dream of, and with the news came righteous anger. Dozens of House members linked to the scandal retired, lost their re-election bids, or failed in campaigns for other offices in 1992 elections.

The changes in the culture of Congress made living full-time in Washington a political liability for House members who must seek re-election every two years. It's not the 20th century anymore, for one thing. Control of the House does change hands. And for the most part, Congress doesn't live here anymore.

"Twenty to 30 years ago, most members of Congress would move their families here and go back home 20–30 times a year," said Fitch, who worked as an aide to four members of Congress in the late 1980s and '90s. "Now, 80 percent of members go back 40–50 times a year because their families are there." In the good old days, members would drive back to their districts together, building relationships on the long drives to such cities as Boston, Philadelphia, Chicago.

"Members now fly home. The schedule of the House has changed. Airplanes make travel easier, and it's less expensive. Very few families move to Washington,"

Debbie Dingell said. "As soon as the last vote is over, they're racing to an airplane to get home." Travel is just easier now.

"People need to go home, or they're going to lose their elections," said Dingell, who said she returns to her Detroit–Ann Arbor-area district nearly every week.

In 1990 Santorum was a 32-year-old lawyer short on cash. He'd maxed out all his credit cards and spend down his savings to support his young family while campaigning full-time. The Santorums had student debt to worry about, too.

"When I won, I was broke. I was worse than broke – I was in serious debt, and so I had to keep my expenses really low," he said.

The young lawyer's firm wasn't interested in having him come back for just a few weeks before his swearing-in. Santorum had already foregone seven months of income by taking a leave of absence to focus on his campaign.

Amid the pandemonium and delirium of his election night celebration, he remembers an unsettling thought popping into his head: It was early November, and he wasn't going to get his first paycheck until February. Santorum tried to keep an apartment in Washington his first year, but he ultimately became a member of "Club Fed," sleeping in his office for the two nights a week that he was in town and returning to Pittsburgh on the weekends.

"It used to be that travel was so hard, you went to Washington and you stayed there for a long time only because getting back and forth to, say, California was just untenable," he said.

But transportation options for members improved – and it wasn't an accident.

"There's a lot of political pressure that was put on the airlines to make sure that they had good service to all parts of the country – to take care of members' travel needs," Santorum said. "Let me assure you that members of Congress complained a lot when there weren't flights to, you know, Boise or Spokane. That's more changed Congress and the schedules than really any kind of political agenda – and the ability to be able to get home to your family on a regular basis has made it more doable for a congressman to keep their family at home, as opposed to the old days where it was just too hard to get home."

Debbie Dingell's upbringing in the old ways makes her a throwback of sorts in the modern fly-away congressional culture. Decades as the spouse of a powerful member taught her a few things.

"I call the airline and make sure they're taking care of all of us that are on that airplane," she said. "Sometimes we're cutting it – there's a 12:45 [p.m. flight] that many of us take. About a month ago, they left three members on the outside door while the rest of us are in, and we didn't pull away. So if we're out on close votes, I call Delta and say, 'This is who's on it, make sure they don't close the door until they absolutely have to close the door.'"

Dingell doesn't know any other way. Republican Congressman Fred Upton, a colleague in Michigan's delegation, is one of her best friends. Upton spoke at John Dingell's funeral. "I just watch out for everybody. I just think it's really important to be bipartisan, so I am," Debbie Dingell said.

How Close Your Election Is

The transition from a collegial stay-at-home Congress to a fly-away Congress hasn't significantly affected how much of the actual work gets done in Washington.

Even Gingrich's ascension to power didn't have much impact on the number of days House members worked in the Capitol. In 1994, the year before the Georgia Republican became speaker, the House recorded 123 days in session. The number rose to 167 in 1995, but it went right back down to 122 the following year.

Stiff-armed and stonewalled by a Republican-controlled House and Senate in election year 1948, Democratic President Harry Truman famously railed against the "Do-Nothing Congress" for meeting for just 108 days. But as recently as 2006, the House recorded just 101 days in session. 2018's number was 190 days – easily the highest in two decades, according to the days-in-session calendar hosted by the Library of Congress. But even that is still just more than half of a calendar year.

What has changed is how members spend all that off time they used to consume in D.C., playing golf and going out to dinner together on weekends. They spend it building their political profiles in their districts by making themselves available to constituents and raising campaign cash to keep challengers at bay.

Those activities help members promote their brands – just 3 percent of incumbents lost their re-election bids in 2016 and 9 percent in 2018 – but do little to build relationships with colleagues in Washington. Visualizing how it all works means understanding the typical Washington "session week" for House members. There are two models – Monday–Thursday and Tuesday–Friday. Only some of those days are full days.

In the Monday–Thursday model, the first roll call votes often come at 6:30 p.m. Monday. Some members roll into town from their districts later than others. Tuesdays and Wednesdays are full days.

If the House is in session on Thursday, it's typically in the morning or early afternoon. Votes are held no later than 3:00 p.m., and usually earlier. That accommodates members who are looking to get out of town. It works about the same for Tuesday–Friday.

Members and staff have a nickname for the weeks that begin on Tuesdays and end Fridays – "Friday fly-aways," because they're back in their districts from Friday to sometime on Monday night or Tuesday morning. Occasionally, some members do go back to D.C. on Sunday night, largely for fundraisers that depend on how close their race is or how much money they need.

A member locked in a tight re-election race likely would want to leave Washington as early as possible on a Thursday or Friday, because he or she might have a fundraiser back home that very night – and other political events over the weekend. The member probably would want to spend as much time as possible in his or her district before returning to Washington.

During these off periods, there are no more clusters of House members in the Capitol rushing to and fro, no stragglers wearing the lapel pin that marks one as a member of Congress. There would be little of the weekend socializing among House members that Cleaver described.

Debbie Dingell – insider witness to decades of congressional history as a spouse and a member herself – said fundraising demands have encroached on time that should be spent legislating and building relationships.

"The fact of the matter is, [members] come in on Monday night, do their votes at 6:30 [p.m.]," she said. "The two nights you have here are when you're doing fundraising, and then you're gone. It's not built around fundraising – but people are only here two nights, and everything that people are doing is thrown into those two nights."

In politics, like business, a big part of success is just showing up. The conscientious House member also holds district office hours to meet with constituents, gives speeches, holds town hall meetings, tours businesses and workplaces around the district, and performs innumerable other "official" tasks while away from Washington.

The official House calendar is dotted with them – "district work weeks" in congressional parlance. The traditional August recess – actually July 30 through Labor Day, September 3, in 2019 – accounted for five weeks in one fell swoop. The 435 House members used that time in 435 different ways, most leavening it with festivals, fairs, town halls, and other public appearances.

"It's All About Relationships"

None of it – not the breakneck pace of work on Capitol Hill, the desire of many members to fly away quickly, or even the fact that Congress isn't here for much of the year – has to prevent members from cultivating working relationships, Minnesota Republican Tom Emmer says.[9]

Elected in 2014, Emmer is an evangelist for the notion that congressional relationships must improve. He appreciates how hard that is. On top of all the existing obstacles, Emmer names another: The biennial churning of House ranks as dozens of members retire or lose their seats in even-year elections. There's a whole new class every other year.

"I know this is all about the relationships," said Emmer, who frequently introduces himself to colleagues he doesn't know. "So when I came to Congress, my staff set up 15-minute meetings with everyone on my subcommittees, everyone on my full committee, and then we just branched it off from there. Republicans and Democrats alike."

Emmer recalled a get-acquainted meeting in the office of David Cicilline, a Democratic member from Rhode Island.

"I told him I've found if I know why you're here and what you're looking to accomplish, there's going to be a point in time where we're either working on something together or we're on opposite sides of an issue," Emmer said. "And it's always better if I understand who it is that I'm working with and what they're trying to accomplish. Because we have different perspectives on how to get somewhere, but we generally want the same things."

Sitting in his own office on Capitol Hill, Emmer vividly recalled his colleague's reaction. Cicilline smacked his forehead, rocked back in his chair, and exclaimed, "I've wanted to do this for the last six years!" Cleaver, the Missouri Democrat who lamented the lack of collegiality in Congress, "could do the same thing," Emmer said.

James Comer, a Republican from Kentucky, said he too has made a concerted effort to know colleagues. It's a daunting task. Like many other House members, Comer is a former state legislator. But the Kentucky House of Representatives has just 100 members. That's a lot fewer than the 434 colleagues Comer has now. "It takes a while to learn everyone," Comer said.[10]

Comer got started even before he was sworn in to office. The 2016 House freshman class had 54 members – 27 Democrats and 27 Republicans. Many of those members have spoken publicly about the bonding that occurred between them during a freshman orientation program at Harvard University.

"We spent three nights together at a retreat to get to know each other, and we've tried to stay in touch – because we've heard that there are a lot of members in each party that never met each other that have served a decade in Congress," he said. "But I think that from my fellow freshman class standpoint, I think we have a close relationship."

The freshman class of 2010, by contrast, had 94 members – but 85 of them were Republicans. They didn't have the same opportunity to make friends in the opposition party from the start.

Comer started with his fellow freshman class members, branched out to members from Kentucky and surrounding states Tennessee and Indiana with whom he must work on regional issues, and then concentrated on the other 45 members of the House Agriculture Committee.

"And now it's through the [Republican] conference. We meet once a week, and I try to sit by somebody different in conference and on the House floor to try to get to know people," Comer said. "It's all about relationships, and that's what I'm focused on – trying to meet as many members of Congress as possible." It's possible to overcome the many obstacles to good working relationships in Congress, but members must learn to think anew.

"I would tell you the big problem in Washington, D.C. today – and I would suggest perhaps in most elected bodies in this country – is that somewhere, someone decided politics was a zero-sum game. Which means, in order for one person to win, another one has to lose. And that is simply not true," Emmer said. "We both generally want the same things, whether those are good schools, a great education, good roads, good transportation, clean air, clean water, whatever."

Republicans and Democrats must accept that those with opposing views are sincere instead of questioning their motives, as if to suggest no one could possibly have an opposing viewpoint without an ulterior motive or the desire to wreak havoc.

"You've got to be able to talk to people that disagree with you on how you take that journey and get there, because that's the way you solve it," Comer believes. But it's easy to speak in such high-minded ideals when your party has the thing that matters most in Congress – control.

Emmer made those remarks in the summer of 2018, when Republicans still had a majority in the lower chamber. A year later, as chairman of the House GOP's campaign arm, he proclaimed he would be "ruthless" in seeking a new Republican majority. Emmer was defending a National Republican Congressional Committee attack on Democratic Congressman Max Rose that was so hard-nosed POLITICO reported even some Republicans were offended by it.

"Our communications team has a direct mandate from me and [House GOP] Leader [Kevin] McCarthy to be ruthless," Emmer told POLITICO. That meant calling Rose, who stands 5'6", "little" in an NRCC press release. "Little Max Rose is content passing socialist bills," the June 2019 statement declared.

Dave Brat, a former Republican congressman from Virginia, came to his Richmond-area House seat in 2015 with a reputation as a giant-killer and a maverick. Brat staged a shocking low-dollar GOP primary upset of then-Rep. Eric Cantor, No. 2 Republican in the House and a major party fundraiser.[11]

But when Brat got to Washington, he found that cultivating good relationships with Democratic colleagues did him absolutely no good when the currency that matters most – his House seat – was at stake. He lasted just two terms, losing a sharply contested re-election bid in 2018. The bitterness in Brat's voice is unmistakable.

"So, you make friends with Democrats, you play golf, you play bridge – and then you run for election and in the election cycle, the Democrats call you every name under the sun," he said.

"Where are your friends on the Democratic side to say, 'Of course that's false. I know Dave. I've known Dave for years. This is absurd.' Where are your friends – your bipartisan golfing and bridge partners – when it counts?" There was a day when it happened, hard to believe as it may be now.

In his 2010 essay for The New York Times, "Why I'm Leaving the Senate," then-Indiana Democratic Sen. Evan Bayh lamented "dwindling social interaction between senators of opposing parties" and other changes that had made Congress more hyper-partisan. Bayh's father, Birch Bayh, also served in the Senate, from 1963 until 1981.

"One incident from his career vividly demonstrates how times have changed," Evan Bayh wrote. "In 1968, when my father was running for re-election, Everett Dirksen, the Republican leader, approached him on the Senate floor, put his arm around my dad's shoulder, and asked what he could do to help. This is unimaginable today."

Brat knows it too. That's why he didn't bother to ask any of his Democratic colleagues to speak out on his behalf. They would have had to jeopardize their own positions in Congress and their party.

Even at just 55, Dave Brat is certain he would never run again for Congress: "The politics up there are broken."

"A Representative Institution"

The impulse to blame members of Congress for the institution's hyper-partisan, cut-throat culture is understandable but wrongheaded, said David Skaggs.

"What we need to realize is that Congress is a representative institution, and if there is animus between members of the two parties, it is merely reflective of the animus between points of view among the citizens of the country," he said.

It's a more tribal country – and Skaggs thinks he knows why. "We no longer teach civics in our schools, so we have an electorate that is now largely unschooled in the complicated nature of American representative democracy. They are easy prey to the pandering and cheap shots and all the rest, sadly."

The fact that Republicans are no longer playing the role of the Washington Generals to the Democrats' Harlem Globetrotters has made all the difference, said Cohen.

Control of the House is legitimately up for grabs – arguably every two years. It's not like the old days, when Democratic control was perceived by both sides as a fact of American political life.

Seats are at stake, with dozens of the most competitive ones hotly contested. Power is at stake, perpetually. Millions and millions of dollars spent. In 2020, a gaggle of some 40 freshmen House Democrats have targets on their backs.

"Republicans are going to be cautious about cooperating with those Democrats or even socializing with them," Cohen said. "It's one thing to say hello politely, but it's something else to really get to know somebody and cooperate with them. With those 40 freshmen, there's disincentives for Republicans to be cooperative with them."

And if one does, there will be consequences.

"At first the [Republican] party leaders or the colleagues would be polite in saying, 'You know, maybe you don't want to cooperate with those Democrats,'" Cohen said. "But then if the Republican were to keep doing it, to become more obvious about it – there's lots of forms of punishment."

The offending member could be denied favors by GOP leaders that could help enhance his or her profile back home. In more extreme cases, he or she could even attract opposition in a party primary election.

Santorum said it's about where we are as a people right now: "The country is really divided. We have a huge cultural divide and increasingly economic divide as to what people think America should be," he said. "And I can tell you that 30 years ago, that divide was not nearly as wide – and 50 years ago it wasn't wide at all. But over the last 50, 60 years, we've seen a real separation between people in this country as to what America should be. That's the principal reason [members of Congress] don't associate with each other – because they have less and less in common with them."

Congressional leaders in the good old days of Congress sprang from a generation of Americans who wouldn't recognize today's perpetually steaming national political cauldron.

"We're not the same people," Santorum said. "Remember, those are people who came from World War II. There was a sense that everybody was together on our values and principles, and we just had a little different way of doing things. It's not true anymore. We don't have the same values. There's just big differences – and those differences make it very, very hard to find common ground, even personally."

Conclusion

It's not unusual for members of the United States House of Representatives to be unfamiliar with one another. But how could one member serve with another for eight years and never have even heard of him? After speaking with House members and former members – people on both sides of the aisle and with varying levels of experience – it's clear that the culture of Congress has radically changed. The collegial, stay-at-home Congress that relied on personal relationships to get things done is long gone. In its place is a fly-away Congress whose members work fast and leave town nearly as fast. Personal relationships – especially those that reach across party lines – are much fewer in number.

One of the major causes of this breakdown is that the 435-member House is no longer dominated by one party, as it was for decades before 1994. Control of the lower chamber is legitimately in play every two years. That instantly raises the stakes on each and every interaction between members. When winning elections is the business of Congress, there are powerful political disincentives to conducting business the old way. It has become a hyper-partisan Congress that relies on superior numbers to overwhelm the opposition. It reflects the nation's tribal divisions. Winning, not legislating, is what matters now.

A portion of this piece appeared in the Evansville Courier & Press *on October 14, 2018; reprinted by permission.*

Notes

1 Fitch, B. (June 2018) Phone interview
2 Cleaver, E. (July 2018) Personal interview
3 Dingell, D. (May 2019) Phone interview
4 Cohen, R. (April 2019) Phone interview
5 Kelly, L. (April 2019) Phone interview

6   Skaggs, D. (April 2019) Phone interview
7   Gingrich, N. (June 2019) Personal interview by email
8   Santorum, R. (April 2019) Phone interview
9   Emmer, T. (July 2018) Personal interview
10 Comer, J. (August 2019) Personal interview
11 Brat, D. (May 2019) Phone interview

10

THE DISAPPEARANCE OF BIPARTISAN REPRESENTATION

Todd Makse

Rep. David Jolly: Cross-partisan representation, whereby a community may have elected officials from different parties, is a welcome occurrence by many in the democracy reform movement, arguably ensuring the most voices among a diverse constituency are heard at some level of governing. But relying on cross-partisan representation to create greater consensus among elected officials is a uniquely American hope.

The United States' two-party democracy is largely an outlier among developed democracies, where we otherwise find multi-party democracies and coalition governing. Studies suggest the latter provides greater voter engagement, greater voter satisfaction, more diverse representation, and greater consensus around policy solutions.

But political leaders in the United States today have little incentive to advance greater competition within our democracy or to encourage the emergence of more diverse voices. For many of the reasons covered by this text, the very leaders that could effectuate change and usher in greater cross-partisan representation, or even cross-partisan cooperation, have very little reason to do so.

Most Americans in any line of work do the things that allow them to keep their jobs and to advance in their careers. The same is true of politicians. Through big data partisan gerrymandering, closed partisan primaries, a campaign finance and media culture that rewards partisanship over bipartisanship, our politicians are simply protecting and strengthening the incentives that keep them employed and allow them to advance. It is largely unrealistic to expect them to do otherwise.

Rather, the solution for those who believe the cure to our divided union is to unrig the rules of our current democracy, to increase competition and accountability, is likely not to put our hope in cross-partisan representation or the good character of our elected officials, but instead to work to change the system that rewards partisan behavior. Democracy reform solutions are just within reach in many states. Whether we choose to support them or not as voters is the contribution we make to today's democracy.

Rep. Patrick E. Murphy: Unfortunately, the current trend of increased polarization in Congress doesn't stop there, and as evidenced in this chapter, has extended to state legislatures. This is a 30-plus-year trend affecting all regions of the country. The same underlying foundational problems exist at the local, state, and federal levels – historic amounts of money being spent, egregious gerrymandering, polarized media, a lack of relationships, demographic changes, and primaries geared toward the extremes. As these structural problems become worse, we will continue to see more polarization at all levels of government and less real debate or conversation about the actual substantive issues like immigration, health care, employment, the national debt, and climate change.

There is a lot to be said for finding common ground in politics. This chapter notes the improved policymaking when literal common ground exists and representatives overlap a constituency. The same effect occurs in Congress when members have things in common like birthplace or work background or that they are from the same state or went to the same college or played the same sport in high school. More often than not, when faced with a similar set of facts and circumstances, people can agree on a reasonable solution.

I was personally able to push legislation and advocate for local issues with some very conservative members of Congress because we shared non-ideological common ground and could all identify rational solutions. As we look forward toward potential improvements, independently drawn districts that overlap between chambers will undoubtedly help move sensible legislation forward.

Amidst very high levels of polarization in Washington, many citizens enjoy representation from both parties, either from having Democratic representation in one chamber of Congress and Republican representation in the other, or from having a split Senate delegation. The existence of these patterns offers a welcome, albeit modest, counterbalance to polarization: not only does this mean that more citizens have at least some representation from their preferred party, but states and local regions often have bipartisan delegations in Congress to advocate on behalf of shared interests.

These patterns of bipartisan representation are somewhat novel as a subject of study per se, but closely relate to several other strands of the political science literature. For example, scholars of voting behavior have studied the causes of, and trends in, split-ticket voting (Burden and Kimball, 1998; Davis and Mason, 2016) and some have asked whether voters deliberately and strategically vote with the intent of producing divided government (Fiorina, 1988; Lacy et al., 2019). Even voters who do not split their tickets can surely appreciate when being on the losing side in one contest does not automatically equate to being on the losing side in others. This sentiment is likely to be especially true in a period of rampant polarization.

Beyond offering more citizens the opportunity to be on the winning side, bipartisan representation has other implications in terms of voter psychology. Having representation from both parties allows voters to hear competing perspectives *from their own representatives*, and thus, not just in the campaign context, but in the governing context. Voters with bipartisan representation can hear credit-claiming from both parties, experience casework through Democratic and Republican offices, and ultimately, can hold members of both parties accountable in the next election. This ability to hear competing perspectives cuts against many of the trends political scientists have linked with polarization, including homophily in social networks, residential sorting, and selective exposure in media consumption.

Given these potential benefits of bipartisan representation, we can take some comfort from the fact that bipartisan representation has hardly disappeared from Congress, even as polarization has soared. Over the past two decades, the percentage of Americans that have enjoyed bipartisan representation from Congress has fluctuated between 45% and 58%. This is hardly paradoxical; it can easily be understood as a product of the incumbency advantage, the Senate having two staggered seats per state, and the discrepancies between the constituencies of House members and senators.

In the state legislatures, however, far fewer citizens – less than one in five – enjoy bipartisan representation. The prevalence of bipartisan representation across states has ebbed and flowed over the past two decades in response to redistricting and other contours of American politics, varying the extent to which citizens enjoy representation from ideologically diverse legislators.

Research has found that legislators who share constituents are more likely to collaborate, even when they are members of different parties, and moreover, that they collaborate more than legislators of the same party who do not share constituents. The lack of bipartisan representation in many state legislatures, therefore, limits one of the major avenues to cross-party cooperation and increases the likelihood that polarization will result in legislative divisiveness or gridlock.

Patterns of Bipartisan Representation

In the state legislatures, there are several ways a citizen can have bipartisan representation. Some states allow voters to select multiple representatives in the lower chamber, either through a bloc vote, post system, or floterial districts, allowing for a bipartisan pair of representatives in the lower chamber alone. Two states have a form of multimember districts in the upper chamber as well. In most states, however, a citizen has one representative in each chamber; in these states, then, the only path to bipartisan representation is to have a Democratic representative in one chamber and a Republican in the other.

To identify the number of citizens who enjoy bipartisan representation, I begin by dividing a state into what I refer to as *district segments*. A district segment is a combination of a lower chamber district and an upper chamber district that has nonzero population in common. In a state with identical districts for the upper and lower chambers (e.g. Arizona), the number of segments will merely be the number of districts.[1] In a state with nested districts (i.e. when an upper chamber is exactly composed of two or three lower chamber districts), the number of segments will be equal to the number of lower chamber districts. But in most states, where maps for the two chambers are drawn independently, there may be several times more district segments than lower chamber districts. For example, California has 80 lower chamber districts and 185 district segments.

For each district segment, I then identify the party of all lower and upper chamber members who represent that segment.[2] This allows me to identify all district segments with at least one representative from each major party. The total population for all such district segments is then summed and divided by the state's total population, yielding the proportion of citizens who have bipartisan representation. This score is calculated separately for each state for each year from 2003–2004 to 2017–2018 (2002–2003 to 2016–2017 for states with odd-year elections).[3] I also calculate equivalent scores for Congress. As previously noted, bipartisan representation in Congress has fluctuated between 45% and 58% over the past two decades. In state legislatures collectively, that number is only 19%. The average score in each state is shown in Figure 10.1.

We can see immediately that very few states have levels of bipartisan representation comparable to the levels found in Congress. Vermont (64%), New Hampshire (59%), and West Virginia (57%) have slightly higher levels than Congress, while South Dakota's (42%) is slightly lower. All four of these states have some form of multimember districting in one or both chambers, meaning that every person in these states has at least three representatives in the legislature. (In Vermont and West Virginia, that number is as high as eight or nine). Naturally, having more representatives makes it easier to have bipartisan representation.

Among states with single-member districts in both chambers, the highest levels of bipartisan representation can be found in Mississippi and Louisiana (36%). These and several other states (West Virginia, Kentucky, Oklahoma, and Alabama) with higher scores are southern and border states whose transition from Democratic dominance to Republican dominance was still ongoing during part of the period of this study. States with many lower chamber seats and few upper chamber seats also tend to have higher rates of bipartisan representation; the ratio

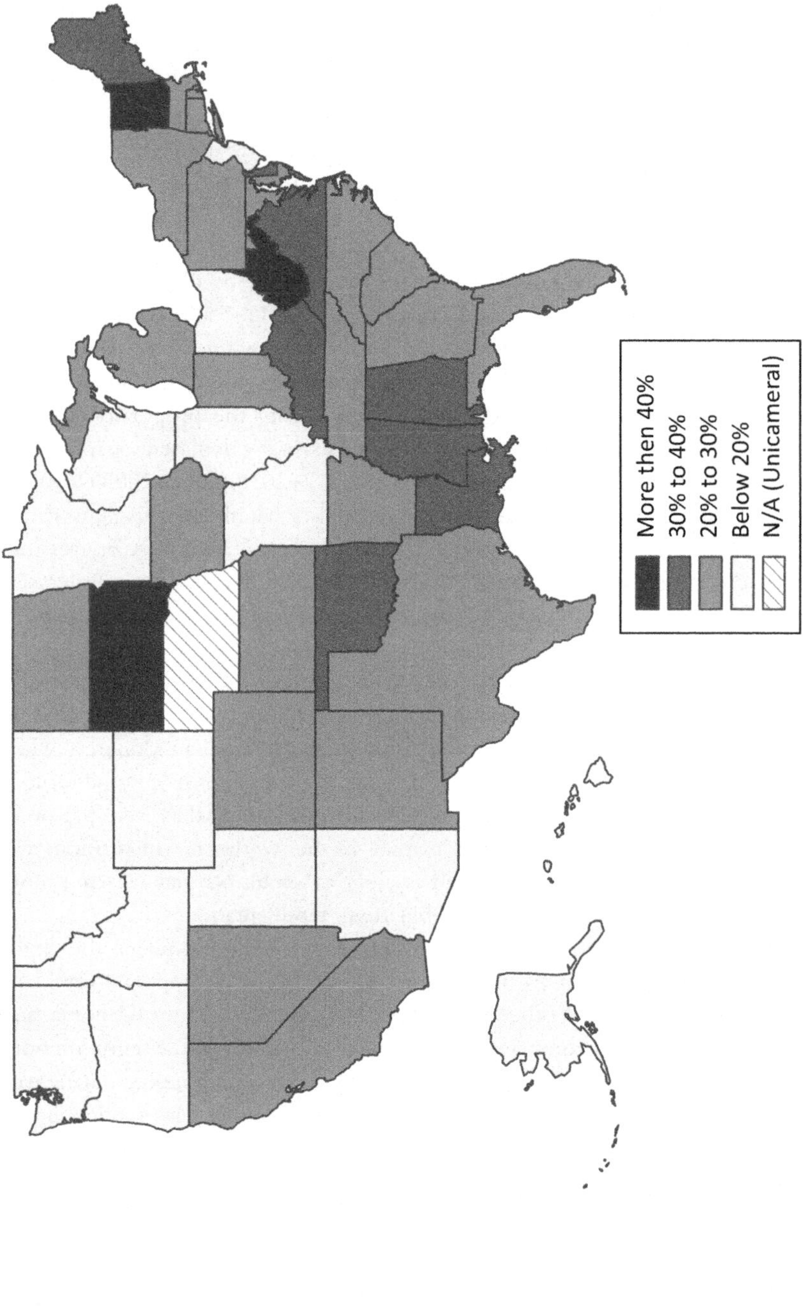

FIGURE 10.1 Bipartisan Representation by State

of upper chamber and lower chamber seats is correlated with bipartisan representation (r = -0.47).

At the other end of the spectrum, the lowest levels of bipartisan representation
can be found in Idaho (10%), New Jersey (11%), and Arizona (13%). These states
have multimember districts, but in these states, lower chamber and upper chamber districts are identical (the lower chamber elects two members). States with
nested districts also dominate the list of states with lower scores, including five
states below 16%: Alaska, Illinois, Ohio, Alaska, and Wyoming. The most extreme
observation in the dataset is the 2017–2018 legislative session in Idaho: only 3%
of citizens (i.e. districts) enjoyed bipartisan representation.

Over the period of this study, there is some evidence that this already low level
of bipartisan representation is declining, from around 20% in 2003–2004 to 17%
in 2017–2018. Figure 10.2 illustrates the patterns over time for the entire country,
as well for distinct regions of the country.

Given that many studies of state legislative polarization identify an earlier starting point (e.g. Masket, 2019), we might suspect that this timeframe captures only
part of a longer decline in bipartisan representation. For instance, the level of
bipartisan representation can be easily calculated for the 1993–1994 session for
the 15 states with nested districts or coterminous districts. In that biennium, 26%
of the lower chamber districts in those states had bipartisan representation, while
in this same subset of states, those numbers are 18% for 2003–2004 and 15% for
2017–2018. That suggests a longer-term (and perhaps steeper) decline over three
decades.

Looking at the impact of individual election cycles, there is only weak evidence that specific elections were especially impactful. As implied by the differing

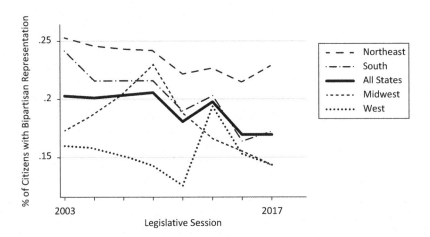

FIGURE 10.2 Trends in Bipartisan Representation, 2003-2017.

regional patterns, rates of bipartisanship fluctuated across years in different ways in different states. This makes sense, as states vary in myriad relevant traits, including long-term historical patterns (e.g. southern realignment), short-term determinants of party success (e.g. gubernatorial popularity), and micro-level factors (e.g. which staggered Senate seats are up for election in a given year). However, to the extent that any individual elections accelerated the downward trends, two stand out: 2010 and 2014. These elections could be distinctive due to the dynamics of the Obama presidency and the Tea Party movement, or this could be a more general characteristic of wave elections or midterm elections, but drawing these inferences based on these data would be premature.

Levels of bipartisan representation were also affected by the 2010s round of redistricting. In fact, the only meaningful uptick (from 18% to 20%) in the overall time series is between the 2011–2012 and 2013–2014 sessions, when most states completed their redistricting processes.

Who Enjoys Bipartisan Representation?

If less than one in five Americans has bipartisan representation, a natural question is whether bipartisan representation is enjoyed equally across the population or concentrated in the hands of some types of voters. We can examine whether voters in some types of districts (politically or demographically) are more likely to have bipartisan representation, and if differences exist, what are the magnitude of those differences?

It seems intuitive, for example, that lower-chamber districts that vote overwhelmingly for one party will be less likely to overlap with an upper chamber district that might plausibly vote for a legislator for the other party. However, does that mean the individuals in such districts have virtually no chance of enjoying bipartisan representation, or are the differences more subtle? Figure 10.3 answers this and other questions by comparing the levels of bipartisan representation across districts with high, moderate, and low levels of six traits: presidential voting, the presence of black and Hispanic voters, urbanity, educational attainment, and median income.[4,5]

Beginning with voting patterns, we can see that bipartisan representation approaches 30% in the most competitive districts and is considerably lower in districts where one party has a clear advantage. There is, however, some asymmetry in the patterns, especially if we look at the most politically one-sided districts in the data. For example, in very heavily Republican lower chamber districts (voted more than 75% for Bush in 2004), the chance of bipartisan representation does not decline too severely (14%). However, residents in heavily Democratic districts (voted less than 25% for Bush) have virtually no chance of having bipartisan representation (4%). As can be seen in Figure 10.4, most district segments with bipartisan representation can be found in the middle of the political spectrum, although a reasonable number of people live in a politically one-sided lower

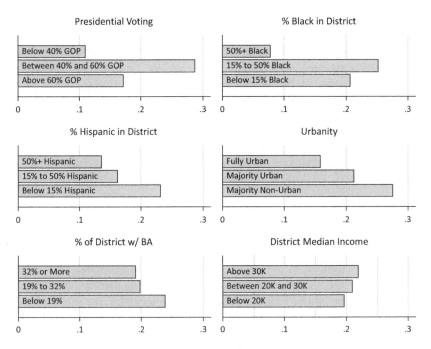

FIGURE 10.3 Bipartisan Representation by District Traits.

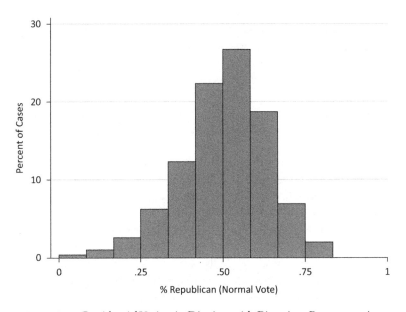

FIGURE 10.4 Presidential Voting in Districts with Bipartisan Representation.

district and still enjoy bipartisan representation – presumably because the upper chamber district they live in is more politically balanced.

Turning to demographics, strong patterns emerge for three of the five traits. Residents of majority-minority districts and urban districts are less likely to have bipartisan representation, although with respect to black voters, the relationship is somewhat nonlinear. This is almost certainly a consequence of partisan voting patterns and regional factors and not due to race, ethnicity, or urbanity themselves. However, it nonetheless indicates that black and Hispanic voters and urban residents are less likely to enjoy bipartisan representation. Patterns with respect to education and income are weaker. Districts with the lowest levels of education and the highest levels of income are more likely to enjoy bipartisan representation, but these differences are only a few percentage points.

Even in the absence of bipartisan representation, it is possible that citizens receive some modicum of ideological diversity in representation. It is possible, for example, that many lower-chamber districts elect more extreme legislators but overlap upper-chamber districts which, due to their larger size and constituent diversity, elect more moderate legislators. Although having ideologically diverse representation does not provide the same benefits described in the introduction, it may still provide some value in an era of polarization.

To explore whether ideologically diverse representation exists even in places where bipartisan representation is lacking, I use ideology scores from Shor and McCarty (2011) from the 2009–2010 biennium[6] to calculate the maximum ideological distance between any two legislators in each district segment. For states with only single-member districts, this is merely the distance between the lower and upper chamber representatives; for district segments in multimember states, it is the distance between the segment's most liberal and conservative members, regardless of chamber. I then divide this absolute ideological distance by the standard deviation for all members of the legislature and identify those district segments which have a ratio greater than one. I treat this trait – whether a district segment's legislators' ideologies are at least one standard deviation apart – to represent an ideological analog of bipartisan representation.[7]

As it turns out, the number of citizens who enjoy ideological heterogeneous representation (22%) is not dissimilar to the number who have bipartisan representation. (The similarity between the two metrics also holds true in Congress: both numbers are 53% for 2009–2010.) Moreover, it is mostly the *same* citizens who experience each: 87% of the citizens who have bipartisan representation also have ideologically heterogenous representation, and only 4.5% of those who lack bipartisan representation have ideologically heterogenous representation. Finally, as can be seen in Figure 10.5, these two metrics correlate very closely (r = 0.79) at the state level. There is little evidence, then, that the absence of bipartisan representation is compensated for by ideological diversity.

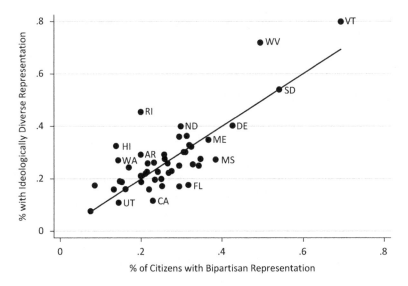

FIGURE 10.5   Bipartisan and Ideologically Diverse Representation.

The Impact of Bipartisan Representation in the Legislative Arena

The concept of bipartisan representation also has meaningful implications for elite cooperation. Even in this era of heightened polarization, studies of Congress (Harbridge, 2015) and state legislatures (Kirkland, 2014) have found healthy levels of bipartisan collaboration, and these collaborations can be fueled, in part, by bipartisan representation.

For every citizen who enjoys bipartisan representation, it means there is a pair of legislators who share some common interests despite belonging to different parties. Existing research on networks in legislatures indicates that these shared constituencies[8] can foster bipartisan collaboration. In studies of both multimember districts within chambers (Kirkland, 2012) and overlapping constituencies across chambers (Kirkland and Williams, 2014), these pairs of legislators (dyads) are more likely to collaborate. Similarly, studies of Congress find that collaboration occurs more often between members from the same state (Fowler, 2006; Kirkland and Kroeger, 2018).

The problem is that these overlapping dyads are not especially prevalent in legislatures. In a legislature with single-member districts, there are no same-chamber members who share a constituency, and even in states with multimember districts, most districts elect a cadre of legislators from the same party. For this reason, I focus on collaborations across chambers in this section. If we consider all pairs of legislators across the two chambers of a legislature, they can be divided into four

TABLE 10.1 Classification of Legislator Dyads

	Constituencies Overlap	No Overlap
Same Party	OSP (4%)	NSP (53%)
Opposite Party	OCP (1%)	NCP (42%)

Note: Percentages indicate prevalence of these dyad types across all states in dataset.

categories (see Table 10.1), depending on whether they are from the same party and whether they share constituents. I refer to the dyad types as OSP (overlapping same-party), OCP (overlapping cross-party), NSP (non-overlapping same-party), and NCP (non-overlapping cross-party), respectively.

Bipartisan representation, by definition, results in the existence of OCP dyads. The relationship between the proportion of citizens with bipartisan representation and the absolute number of OCP dyads is not purely linear, as it depends on the number of district splits, but the relationship between the two quantities is quite strong ($r = 0.60$). In the aggregate, however, these OCP dyads are the least prevalent of the four types, not only because levels of bipartisan representation are low (19%, as noted earlier), but because overlapping dyads make up only a small percentage of all dyads (5%). When bipartisan representation is at its lowest levels, these dyads are even rarer.

These OCP dyads, however, are crucial to maintaining a healthy level of bipartisan collaboration. To illustrate this, I draw on data from the website Legiscan for the 25 states[9] where at least 5% of all bills have at least one sponsor in the opposite chamber. Limiting the analysis to bills that have at least one cross-chamber sponsor, I examine those sponsorships for more than 33,000 bills introduced during the 2013–2014 and 2015–2016 sessions, excluding symbolic legislation, resolutions, and amendments. I limit the analysis to legislation with ten or fewer total authors and cosponsors, as legislation with many cosponsors might indicate a bandwagon effect rather than genuine collaboration. However, the patterns are very similar if I include bills with many cosponsors as well.

I consider two legislators to have collaborated during a legislative session if one member of the dyad cosponsored a bill authored by the other member of the dyad, regardless of which chamber the author belongs to. After identifying all such collaborations, I count the number of collaborations per dyad. Across all states, the mean number of collaborations is 0.29 per dyad, with 14% of dyads collaborating at least once. Less than 0.2% of dyads have more than ten collaborations.

A clear pattern emerges in the data, as can be seen in Table 10.2: OCP dyads are a strong source of collaboration. Although they do not collaborate as frequently as OSP dyads, they collaborate far more often than NSP dyads, which might be mildly surprising. Put another way, in non-overlapping dyads, same-party dyads

TABLE 10.2 Number of Collaborations per Dyad, by Dyad Type

State	OSP	OCP	NSP	NCP
All States	1.72	0.96	0.31	0.13
Alaska	0.16	0.00	0.10	0.06
Arkansas	0.72	0.35	0.12	0.07
Arizona	2.33	0.88	0.43	0.10
California	1.60	0.99	0.35	0.12
Colorado	1.64	0.82	0.58	0.41
Connecticut	1.64	0.40	0.07	0.01
Delaware	2.60	1.60	1.41	0.47
Georgia	0.31	0.16	0.06	0.01
Illinois	2.37	3.19	0.35	0.14
Indiana	0.72	0.57	0.18	0.17
Louisiana	0.32	0.21	0.04	0.04
Maine	2.92	1.54	0.53	0.30
Massachusetts	4.26	3.19	0.35	0.14
Nevada	1.46	0.10	0.35	0.07
New Jersey	0.61	0.63	0.23	0.08
New Mexico	0.16	0.18	0.03	0.05
North Dakota	1.30	0.64	0.23	0.12
Oklahoma	2.18	0.90	0.68	0.20
Oregon	2.67	0.73	0.43	0.21
South Dakota	0.87	0.55	0.23	0.15
Tennessee	3.85	2.13	0.60	0.10
Texas	2.36	1.01	0.32	0.21
Utah	1.90	0.91	0.60	0.16
Wisconsin	2.28	1.18	0.56	0.09
Wyoming	1.26	0.18	0.21	0.19

Note: Combined data from 2013–2014 and 2015–2016 legislative sessions.

are twice as likely to collaborate than cross-party dyads, but in overlapping dyads, same-party dyads are only 42% more likely to collaborate.

Moreover, these patterns hold in nearly every state. In Illinois, New Jersey, and New Mexico, OCP dyads collaborate even more often than OSP dyads. The only states where OCP dyads are not strong sources of collaboration are Alaska, Nevada, and Wyoming and these deviations may be due to small sample size: these states each have 16 or fewer OCP dyads over the two legislative sessions. The consistency of this pattern is especially impressive given the variety of differing rules and conventions states have on obtaining and recording sponsorships across chambers. For example, the data include some states which have limits on introducing or sponsoring bills, states where companion bills are more common, and states where the second chamber must have a lead sponsor to consider a bill coming from the first chamber. The patterns are also consistent across states that have dramatically different *rates* of cross-chamber collaboration (from 0.05 collaborations per dyad in Georgia to 1.10 per dyad in Delaware).

Although previous studies have identified constituency overlap and shared partisanship as crucial predictors of collaboration, these patterns clarify the interactive relationship between these two factors and highlights the power of bipartisan representation. In a state with little bipartisan representation, few OCP dyads exist, meaning that cross-party collaboration stems almost entirely from NCP dyads, which produce very little of it. In a state with higher levels of bipartisan representation, a sizable proportion of cross-chamber, cross-party collaboration can be attributed to OCS dyads, even if they are still a small proportion of dyads overall.

Within these crucial OCP dyads, I next examine how ideological distance influences patterns of collaboration. One might suspect, for example, that cross-party dyads only collaborate when their ideologies are reasonably proximate, while ideologically distant legislators will not collaborate even if they share constituents (Bratton and Rouse, 2011; Clark and Caro, 2013). But this is not the case, as Figure 10.6 shows. While collaboration does decrease as ideological distance increases, these dyads *do* collaborate even in the face of large distances. Even among dyads with the largest ideological distances, these dyads collaborate more frequently (0.51 collaborations per dyad) than NSP dyads *with the smallest ideological discrepancies* (0.31 collaborations).

Finally, we can evaluate the importance of these OCP dyads by examining how they continue to collaborate over future sessions. Reciprocity is an important feature of collaboration patterns (Kirkland and Williams, 2014) and there is

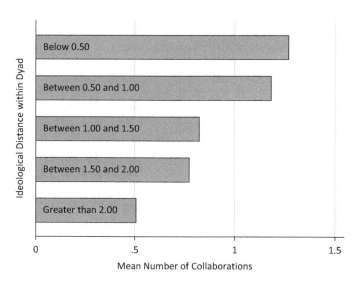

FIGURE 10.6 Ideology and Collaboration in OCP Dyads.

no reason to believe that such reciprocity necessarily ceases or resets between legislative sessions. At the same time, collaboration in some dyads may die out over longer periods of time, because one or both members may switch legislative priorities or because previous collaborations did not lead to success.

Because two legislative sessions of data in every state were analyzed, I can examine the extent to which patterns of collaboration are stable from the 2013–2014 session to the 2015–2016 session. Among dyads where both legislators continued to serve in the same position from one session to the next, only 36% of dyads who collaborated in one session also did so in the next session. Of the four types of dyads, OCP dyads exhibited the highest levels of stability: the correlation between the number of collaborations in 2013–2014 and 2015–2016 was r = 0.49. Those correlations were considerably lower in OSP (r = 0.39), NSP (r = 0.17), and NCP (r = 0.20) dyads. OCP dyads, then, not only represent an abundant source of cross-party collaboration, they also offer a *stable* source of it.

Political polarization does not stifle collaboration, but it does narrow the conditions under which collaboration thrives (Holman and Mahoney, 2018), so OCP dyads play a crucial role in generating cross-party collaboration. In general, the evidence suggests that in the states, there is still a strong link between bipartisan collaboration and legislative success (Clark, 2015). But even if that pattern were to dissipate, as has happened in Congress (Harbridge, 2015), bipartisan collaboration can be valuable in and of itself. Although most of our measures of legislative polarization are rooted in voting patterns, a lack of collaboration is indicative of another dimension of polarization in and of itself (Kirkland, 2012). Having a higher level of bipartisan representation is not a panacea for legislative polarization, but it at least establishes a floor on the level of cross-party collaboration.

Conclusion

Polarization has not touched the state legislatures in precisely the same way it has touched Congress, nor have its effects been uniform across state legislatures. While trends in the ideologies of voters and elected officials have been given a great deal of attention, political scientists have just scratched the surface in exploring polarization's effects on legislatures and representation. This chapter contributes to our understanding of polarization by exploring a characteristic of legislatures, bipartisan representation, which at once can be viewed as a casualty of the era of polarization and a tonic to some of polarization's effects.

Our understanding of both bipartisan representation and legislative polarization must be rooted in the study of party competition. Bipartisan representation, by its nature, emerges from political geographies that feature at least some two-party competition. Meanwhile, evidence shows that party competition at both the macro-level (Hinchliffe and Lee, 2016) and micro-level (McCarty et al., 2019) leads to higher legislative polarization.

One takeaway from this paper, then, is that we should consider not only the traits of districting plans for single chambers of the legislature, but the interplay between plans for the two chambers. The way that lower chamber and upper chamber districts map onto one another matters greatly in determining the degree of bipartisan representation. Drawing nested districts seems to inhibit bipartisan representation, while having multimember districts with independent maps for each chamber seems conducive to producing bipartisan representation. Future work should explore the ways that micro-level districting features, including compactness (Bowen, 2014) and respect for communities of interest (Makse, 2012), might also influence the level of bipartisan representation in legislatures.

Finally, bipartisan representation in state legislatures and the patterns of collaboration it produces may have upstream consequences in Congress. Over the period of this study, 51% of U.S. House members and 42% of U.S. senators previously served in state legislatures (Volden and Wiseman, 2014). Patterns of legislative collaboration, once learned, may become engrained, even when those legislators move to different institutions. The low and declining level of bipartisan representation in state legislatures, then, threatens to stifle collaboration not only in those legislatures, but perhaps in Congress as well.

Notes

1 A list of all district segments is generated using the Geographic Correspondence Engine from the Missouri Census Data Center. Nebraska is excluded from analyses in this chapter since every citizen has only one legislator.

2 For the purposes of this paper, I use Shor-McCarty ideology scores to allocate independent and third-party members: those with scores below zero are treated as Democrats, those with scores above zero as treated as Republicans. This avoids the problem of treating all citizens in SMDs with an independent/third-party legislator as not having bipartisan representation.

3 These scores are based on members serving at the start of the session. Members selected mid-session (special elections and appointments) are not counted. I also don't treat as separate observations the second biennium of states who elect the full membership every four years.

4 This analysis only compares the election prior to redistricting and the first election conducted under the new plan. Subsequent revisions to districting plans are not considered. Alaska and Texas are excluded because different plans were used in the 2010, 2012, and 2014 elections.

5 Presidential voting data is taken from Wright (2004). The remaining five variables are based on five-year averages from the 2010 American Community Survey. New Hampshire is not included in the presidential voting analysis due to missing data.

6 For less than 2% of the legislators in the dataset, no ideology score is available. In these cases, I interpolate a Shor-McCarty score in the following manner, First, if a member of the same party held the seat in the same decade, that member's ideology score was substituted. Second, if no such member existed, I estimated ideology with fitted values from a regression that predicted ideology as a function of district presidential vote, separately by state and political party.

7 I also tested a cutpoint of two standard deviations, but fewer than 5% citizens had legislators whose ideologies were that distinct.

8 The mere proximity of constituencies may increase collaboration also, even if the constituencies do not overlap (Fowler 2006; Bratton and Rouse 2011).
9 Although these states are slightly unrepresentative (Western states and states with larger Hispanic populations are somewhat overrepresented), there are no significant differences between these states and the remaining states in terms of size, partisanship, ideology, per capita income, professionalism, turnover, or Speaker power.

References

Bowen, Daniel C. 2014. "Boundaries, Redistricting Criteria, and Representation in the U.S. House of Representatives." *American Politics Research 42*(5): 856–95.

Bratton, Kathleen A. and Stella M. Rouse. 2011. "Networks in the Legislative Arena: How Group Dynamics Affect Cosponsorship." *Legislative Studies Quarterly 36*(3): 423–60.

Burden, Barry C. and David C. Kimball. 1998. "A New Approach to the Study of Ticket Splitting." *American Political Science Review 92*(3): 533–44.

Clark, Jennifer Hayes. 2015. *Minority Parties in U.S. Legislatures: Conditions of Influence.* Ann Arbor, Michigan: University of Michigan Press.

Clark, Jennifer Hayes and Veronica Caro. 2013. "Multimember Districts and the Substantive Representation of Women: An Analysis of Legislative Cosponsorship Networks." *Politics and Gender 9*(1): 1–30.

Davis, Nicholas T. and Lilliana Mason. 2016. "Sorting and the Split-Ticket: Evidence from Presidential and Subpresidential Elections." *Political Behavior 38*(2): 337–54.

Fiorina, Morris. 1988. "The Reagan Years: Turning Toward the Right or Groping Toward the Middle." In: Barry Cooper et al., eds., *The Resurgence of Conservatism in Anglo-American Democracies.* Durham, North Carolina: Duke University Press.

Fowler, James H. 2006. "Connecting the Congress: A Study of Cosponsorship Networks." *Political Analysis 14*(4): 456–87.

Harbridge, Laurel. 2015. *Is Bipartisanship Dead? Policy Agreement and Agenda-Setting in the House of Representatives.* New York: Cambridge University Press.

Hinchliffe, Kelsey L. and Frances E. Lee. 2016. "Party Competition and Conflict in State Legislatures." *State Politics and Policy Quarterly 16*(2): 172–97.

Holman, Mirya R. and Anna Mahoney. 2018. "Stop, Collaborate, and Listen: Women's Collaboration in US State Legislatures." *Legislative Studies Quarterly 43*(2): 179–206.

Kirkland, Justin H. 2012. "Multimember Districts' Effect on Collaboration between US State Legislators." *Legislative Studies Quarterly 37*(3): 329–53.

Kirkland, Justin. 2014. "Chamber Size Effects on the Collaborative Structure of Legislatures." *Legislative Studies Quarterly 39*(2): 169–98.

Kirkland, Justin H. and R. Lucas Williams. 2014. "Partisanship and Reciprocity in Cross-Chamber Legislative Interactions." *Journal of Politics 76*(3): 754–69.

Kirkland, Justin and Mary Kroeger. 2018. "Companion Bills and Cross-Chamber Collaboration in the U.S. Congress." *American Politics Research 46*(4): 629–70.

Lacy, Dean, Emerson M. S. Niou, Philip Paolino, and Robert A. Rein. 2019. "Measuring Preferences for Divided Government: Some Americans Want Divided Government and Vote to Create It.. " *Political Behavior 41*(1): 79–103.

Makse, Todd. 2012. "Strategic Constituency Manipulation in State Legislative Redistricting." *Legislative Studies Quarterly 37*(2): 225–50.

Masket, Seth. 2019. "What Is, and Isn't, Causing Polarization in Modern State Legislatures?. " *PS: Political Science and Politics 52*(3): 430–35.

McCarty, Nolan, Jonathan Rodden, Boris Shor, Chris Tausanovitch, and Christopher Warshaw. 2019. "Geography, Uncertainty, and Polarization." *Political Science Research and Methods* 7(4): 775–94.

Shor, Boris and Nolan McCarty. 2011. "The Ideological Mapping of American Legislatures." *American Political Science Review 105*(3): 530–51.

Volden, Craig and Alan Wiseman. 2014. *Legislative Effectiveness in the United States Congress: The Lawmakers.* New York: Cambridge University Press.

Wright, Gerald. 2004. *Representation in America's Legislatures.* Bloomington, IN: Indiana University and Arlington, Virginia: National Science Foundation.

CONCLUSION

Rep. Patrick E. Murphy, Rep. David Jolly, Dario Moreno, Eduardo Gamarra, and Anthony Kusich

The cause of so much dysfunction in our democracy appears to be obvious, staring us right in the face: the dominance of parties in our political system. Or rather, the dominance of partisanship – dividing the electorate into camps of which side is winning and which side is losing. The news is partisan. The drawing of districts is partisan. The structure of Congress is partisan. Donald Trump has rewritten longtime Republican orthodoxy on issues like trade and foreign intervention, but the policies on their own clearly aren't keeping voters in the party. It's the sense of belonging to the team and relishing the fight. Fans don't switch allegiance from one NFL team to another if a different city's team adopts their style of offense; they root for the team they grew up with, or the one with the best players, or the one that keeps on winning.

This broad generalization obviously doesn't describe the reason for everyone's allegiance to a party – nor the tens of millions voters who are simply independent or don't belong to a party at all. But in the two-party system we live in, it goes a long way toward explaining where the fault lines are and why it's so difficult to cross them. The concept of "political parties" was left out of the Constitution, but not because it was forgotten.

Through a negative lens, one may think of political parties as living organisms, perhaps extraterrestrial creatures from an *Avengers* movie. They live and breathe and consume. Their sole desire is to stay in power. They can perhaps be reasoned with, but there is nothing you can offer that they would accept if it involves giving up power. What incentive does a majority party have to make the political playing field more even – say, by drawing fair legislative districts or reforming campaign finance laws – if the party has the opportunity to consolidate even more power instead? The two parties' goals are at opposite ends, and any abdication of power in a zero-sum game gives it to the other.

But viewed through a positive lens, parties serve a crucial role in our democracy. They guide candidate recruitment and organize voters; they develop policy goals and push social change; they foster a sense of community and encourage civic engagement in all elements of daily life. Parties can bring those with different backgrounds together via shared beliefs and a common purpose to improve society for all. It is when the "winners and losers" view supersedes the "improve society for all" view that we as a nation lose our focus.

But extreme partisanship within our two-party system is where we are, and the institutions that have been erected over the ensuing decades to preserve it have made compromise exceedingly difficult – ironically, even for partisans who now wish to bring more fairness and equity into the broader body politic. This is why voter frustration rises while voter turnout and engagement head downward. It appears more often than not that there is simply no way to unrig the system for those in the middle.

Further, the levers of accountability have been moved further and further from voters. In past eras, politicians had more direct accountability to the voters sending them to office, but now redistricting, the enormous sums of money in politics, and other factors have made that divide more "efficient," so to speak. As it becomes easier to consolidate power within the parties, the will of individual voters can be eliminated with technical proficiency.

Optimistically, voters themselves have begun to take matters into their own hands to address the numerous structural challenges covered in the preceding chapters.

In 2010, California voters followed in the steps of reformers in other states by making the primary process more inclusive via a "blanket primary." In this system, candidates from all parties appear on the same primary ballot, and the top two vote-getters in the primary move on to the general election, regardless of which party they belong to. Advocates believe the process forces candidates to appeal to a wide swath of voters in the primary in order to advance to the next round, not just voters on the extremes. Indeed, when voters are faced with a palette of choices from across the ideological spectrum to choose from, logic might dictate that the most support gravitates toward those in the middle. A side consequence of the blanket primary is that it has sometimes allowed two members of the same party – in this state, Democrats – to continue to November without a Republican on the ballot. But advocates view this, too, as an upside: in a state as lopsidedly Democratic as California – where few Republicans would ever win a statewide election anyway – isn't it better that GOP voters have a say in *which* Democrat ends up representing them?

In Maine, after decades of elections where candidates for governor often won with less than 50% of the vote, voters approved a ranked-choice system in 2016. In this process, voters rank all candidates on the ballot in order of preference, and if no one receives a 50% majority in the first round of counting, the ballots of losing candidates get their runner-up choices redistributed until someone reaches a mathematical majority. After numerous court challenges, the process was upheld in time for the 2018 midterm elections, where a Democratic challenger, Jared Golden, narrowly ousted a Republican incumbent, Bruce Poliquin, after multiple rounds of counting. On election day, Poliquin ended up narrowly ahead of Golden by a plurality of 46.3% to 45.6%. But as neither hit the required 50%, the second-choice votes of minor candidates were distributed to the two leaders, and Golden ended up prevailing 50.6% to 49.4% to win the seat. Supporters of the change argue that rather than have candidates squeak by with plurality victories as ideologically similar – but minor – candidates draw away a few precious percentage points, voters can feel free to choose with their conscience without "spoiling" their vote. Another benefit for advocates of this system is that it doesn't always favor one of the two major parties. If ranked-choice had been in place for the 2010 gubernatorial race, it is likely that an Independent, Eliot Cutler, would've prevailed over Republican Paul LePage. While LePage eked ahead 37.6% to 35.6% on election day to win the race, a quarter of the remaining vote was divided between a Democrat and another left-leaning Independent – votes that presumably would've shifted to Cutler if second-place preferences were counted and redistributed.

Gerrymandering is another area where reform advocates have made progress despite frustration at the federal level. As the Supreme Court ruled that the politically biased drawing of district lines was – in Chief Justice John Roberts's words – "non-justiciable," voters have moved to state courts to make their arguments under the auspices of state constitutions. In Pennsylvania and North Carolina, state judges have firmly sided with reformers, putting in place far more neutral maps that clearly represent the swingy nature of those states' electorates. As a result, Pennsylvania's Congressional delegation moved from a 12–6 Republican advantage prior to the 2018 midterms to a more representative 9–9 split. North Carolina's maps – widely recognized as the most partisan and unrepresentative gerrymanders in the entire nation – will likely move from a 10–3 Republican advantage to a fairer 8–5 split. The Supreme Court narrowly ruled in favor of non-partisan redistricting commissions in 2015, allowing – for now – equitable programs in Arizona, New Jersey, California, and elsewhere to remain in place.

Campaign finance law is another area where states may be able to take the lead in accountability, although, as with any system, current rules vary widely by locality. On the one hand, states like Florida and Virginia allow unlimited donations from individuals and corporations into state-level races, whereas in Colorado and Montana, the donation limit is set much, much tighter – about $200 per person for legislative races. One presumes it's hard to buy favors from a politician for such a relatively low investment. Other states such as Connecticut and New Jersey use some form of public financing or "matching donation" system to keep the playing field level when it comes to campaign spending. Imagine how races for the U.S. House and Senate might turn out if both candidates were required to spend equal amounts of money. Would supposedly "safe" seats suddenly turn competitive as voters become aware of a different choice? Would Americans see more "wave" elections without the advantages of incumbency?

These measures are just the cusp of what voters may be able to achieve when the normal levers of government are not responsive. There may not be enough data to measure whether some of these reforms are working as intended, but the efforts do look promising.

The Founding Fathers – perhaps unwisely, without being able to predict the electoral paralysis we'd find ourselves in 230 years later – made it a herculean task to alter many of the institutions responsible for holding progress back. How can we get money out of politics or end gerrymandering if we need three-fourths of the states to pass a constitutional amendment, but half of the nation's population lives in just nine states? Any sort of reform on guns or taxes or climate change or immigration is subject to the will of a smaller population against the wishes of the larger population. (This same principle has permitted the winner of two of the last five presidential elections to take office despite receiving far fewer actual votes.)

For instance, of the 21 states with fewer than five electoral votes – what most people would characterize as "small states" – Donald Trump won 13, or nearly two-thirds. These states (with a combined population of 36 million) are represented in the U.S. Senate by 25 Republicans and 17 Democrats, who sit alongside the two Democrats from the single state of California, which has a slightly larger population of 40 million. No doubt, the inimitable character of the individual states is what makes this nation unlike any other on the planet. But it points to the structural issues that are so difficult to overcome. Our diversity, which is a strength of this character, is a weakness when it comes to affecting change on a grand scale.

The question must be asked, however, if bipartisanship is something we've ever really had in this country. Has it ever really worked, or is it just nostalgia? Political dysfunction over the past five decades has largely been accompanied by split control of the White House and Congress, but for the century prior to that, one party has typically ruled an era. The Republicans were dominant during the Civil War and the early part of the 20th century, while Democrats ruled Washington for the better part of twenty years through the Franklin Roosevelt and Harry Truman presidencies. Some of our nation's most consequential achievements were made during these periods: the end of slavery, the western expansion of the nation, surviving the Great Depression, victory in World War II. Would the historical outcomes have veered differently if the White House and Congress were acrimoniously split between the parties during these periods? Divided government is now the norm, so perhaps we yearn for bipartisanship in a way we simply didn't in the past.

Renowned political scientist Clinton Rossiter once wrote that there was "no America without democracy, no democracy without politics, no politics without parties, no parties without compromise and moderation. So runs the string of assumptions on which hangs this exposition of the politics of American democracy." All elements of this chain are vital, in other words, and we must maintain "compromise and moderation" alongside the rest. Structural domination by one party over another – whether at the municipal level or national level – is antithetical to the process of today's democracy.

The issues this nation needs to address are stacking up like old books on a desk. You intend to read them this weekend ... next month ... over the summer ... by the end of the year. But they remain there, dusty and unread, in plain view but always behind a distraction keeping you from picking one up and finally getting started. As Americans of all parties – and no parties – it is up to us to implement the reforms necessary to move our political debates forward, ensure our partisan fights remain honest, and keep this democracy as representative of its ideals as possible.

INDEX

Page numbers in **bold** denote tables, those in *italic* denote figures.

Abrams, S.J. 13–15
activists 108–109, 136
advertising 92, 131; negative 98; political 91; targeted 7; TV 84, 97
Affordable Care Act (ACA) 36
Amendment: Constitutional 95; Fair District 72; First 86, 89–93, 106; Fourteenth 68, 77, 79, 90; Nineteenth 106; Seventeenth 3, 106; Twenty-Eighth 95
American National Election Survey 19
American Promise 95
analysis 4, 8, 14–17, 19–20, 180; basic trend 6; comprehensive 17; detailed 86; geographic 19; multilevel 16–17; nuanced 10; of political segregation 16; poor polling 107
anxiety 19, 59; increasing 8; sense of 8
Arceneaux, K. 55
Asian 27–28, 32, 35, 40–41, **41**, 42, **43**; adults 32; American 27, 35; East 40
association 90; business 90; political 90; trade 160–161
Azavea 71, 75, 80

Baby Boomers 28, **37**, 42
Baker v. Carr 68, 77
Biden, J. 93
bipartisan 115, 118, 122–123, 162, 166, 172; agreements 122; bloc 115, 126; bonhomie 154; Campaign Finance Reform Act (BCRA) (2002) 90–192; coalition 115; collaboration 179, 183; compromise 125–126; consensus 122, 125–126; conservative coalition 114, 119, 124; cooperation 146; delegation 171; disdain 60; dominance 122; group 33; House 90, 157; legislative success 151; majority 124; relationship 152; Report 54; representation 171–173, *174–175*, 175–176, *177*, 178–179, *179*, 180, 182–184; response 126; Retreat 158–159; Senate sponsors 90; solutions 36; suspicion 125; Twitter Agreement *146*; unity 125
bipartisanship 5, 25, 33, 35–36, 40, 114, 116, 124–126, 132, 151–152, 155, 170, 176, 190; agreement 33; erosion of 118
Bishop, B. 10–11, 14, 17, 39
Border Security, Economic Opportunity, and Immigration Modernization Act (2013) 33
Brat, D. 106–107, 166–167
Bush, G. H. W. **37**
Bush, G. W. 2, 37, 90–91, 96, 139, 155, 176

CAMSCAM 134, 136
Capitol 3, 84, 154, 163–164; Building 154; complex 153; Hill 87, 114–115, 117–119, 125–126, 157, 164–165
Center for Responsive Politics 89

*Citizens United v. Federal Election
  Commission* 86, 92–96, 98, 100
civil rights 118, 126; Act (1964) 118, 122;
  Era 67, 123; legislation 118, 122, 126;
  Movement **37**; revolution 118–119
Civil War 14, 21, 30, 110, 116, 190
climate change 2, 4, 56–58, 60, 171, 190
Clinton, B. 37, 121, 123, 129
Clinton, H. 3, 38, 92
CNN 38, 130, 139, 142
Cohen, R. 155–157, 167
Cold War 115–116
community 11, 15, 65, 73, 170;
  competitive 65; LGBT 35; local 16, 65;
  minority 73; sense of 188
compromise 2, 33, 35–36, 38, 79, 109,
  130–131, 137–138, 140, 143, 145,
  147, 152–153, 159, 188, 190–191;
  intergenerational 38; meaningful 50;
  see also bipartisan
Congressional; Black Caucus 154; Budget
  Office 36; Management Foundation 153
conservatism 7, 9, 19–20, 126
Conservative Opportunity Society
  (COS) 153
coronavirus (COVID-19) 39–40
Cruz, T. 85, 131, 146
C-SPAN 129, 131–139, 142, 145, 147,
  151, 153
culture 6, 10, 19–21, 24, 35, 113, 154, 161,
  168; congressional 154, 162; cut-throat
  167; media 170; political 3; unknown 19

Davis v. Bandemer 77
Deferred Action for Childhood Arrivals
  (DACA) 33–34
DeGrandy v. Wetherell 74
Democratic: Congressional Committee
  (DCCC) 87; National Committee 93
Democrats 1, 6–7, 17–18, 25, 33–36, 38,
  42, *42*, 44, 50, 66, 71, 73, 75–76, 79, 80,
  88, 93–95, 102–103, 108–110, 115–117,
  119, 133–135, 138, 141, 152–157, 159–
  161, 164–167, 188, 190; conservative
  122; moderate 153; national 119, 122;
  northern 119; partisan 20; southern 25,
  115–117, 119, 121–122
demographic 6, 24–26, 32, 34, 44, 178;
  changes 13, 24–25, 32, 35, 44, 171;
  composition 42; differences 39; districts
  176; makeup 11; shifting 24, 33;
  transformations 39; trends 25, 44
diversity 6–7, 18–19, 25, 27, 33, 40, **41**, 190;
  constituent 178; cultural 24; ethnic

26–27, 32; geographic 8; ideological 9,
  178; intellectual 18–19; political 17; racial
  11, 24, 26–27, 32; sexual 6; vibrant 25
donations 85, 89–90, 97; political 89;
  private 96; soft money 90; timing of 89;
  unlimited 189
dyads 179–183; cross-party 181–182;
  legislator **180**; overlapping 179–181;
  same-party 180–181
dysfunction 114, 187; legislative 154;
  political 190

elections 4, 6, 52, 66, 69, 72–73, 78–79,
  90–91, 95, 103–104, 106, 119,
  161–162, 164, 168, 173, 175–176, 188;
  competitive 86; congressional 24, 50,
  85, 103, 115, 117, 119–120, 133; cycle
  of 2; federal 89; free and equal 78; free
  and open 78; general 117; gubernatorial
  40; integrity of 89; key 104; local 8; low
  turnout 104; midterm 36, 38, 136, 176,
  189; national 6, 115; presidential 8, 19,
  40, 85, 96, 103, 119, 190; primary 4,
  50, 96, 104, 106, 117; state 8, 79; UK
  parliamentary 60; U.S. House 8, 85; U.S.
  Senate 3; wave 176, 190
elite 56: cooperation 179; party 55;
  polarization 56; political 55–56;
  politicians 54
Equal Protection Clause 68, 77
Era of Conformity 36
ethnic: changes 44; composition 28, 33,
  40, 43; differences 32; diversity 26–27,
  32, 44; group 26–28, 34, 40, 42; identity
  44; issue 33; minorities 32, 41, 44, 73;
  population changes 35
ethnicity 25, 28, 31, 35, 178

Facebook 53, 55, 140, *141*, 142
fake news 50, 55, 58, 61
FEC v. Wisconsin Right to Life, Inc 92
Federal Election Campaign Acts 88
Federal Election Commission (FEC)
  89, 92
Ferber, D. 61
fertility rates 28, 30
Fortson v. Dorsey 77
FOX News 18
Frey, W.H. 28
fundraising 2–3, 7, 50, 83–84, 86–88, 90,
  93–94, 151, 153, 164

Gaetz, D. 72
Gallup 33

geographic 6, 10; analysis 19; areas
28, 73; category 38; chess board
12; consequences 20; context 18;
data 68; differences 7; divide 6, 38;
information systems (GIS) 69; mobility
32; movements 31; polarization 6;
redistribution 25; region 65; segregation
7; self-segregation 39; sorting 25;
space 9, 18, 20–21; units 8, 16; *see also*
diversity
gerrymandering 4, 7, 12, 24, 50, 64–66,
69–71, 76–80, 189–190; anti- 67;
egregious 171; partisan 77–80, 170;
pervasive 104
Gill v. Whitford 71
Gingrich, N. 120–121, 133–137,
156–161, 163
grandstanding 50, 129, 131–132, 137–139,
142, 145, 147
Great Migration 30
Great Recession 31, 37, 113

hate speech 40
health care 2, 24–25, 35–36, 108, 171; costs
36; expanding 36; policy 36; programs
36; spending 36
Heffley, R. 73
Hirano, S. 106, 110

identity 1, 35; candidate 14; cultural
19; ethnic 44; group 57; human 18;
movements 35; political 10, 13–14, 19,
35, 57; symbolic 57
ideologues 13, 20
ideology 3, 19, 120, 131, 178; liberal 118;
political 10, 12, 19; voter's 14
immigration 2, 20, 24–28, 33–34, 56, 58,
60, 107, 171, 190; foreign 17; illegal 58;
law 33; patterns 26–27; rates 43; reform
33; system 26
Immigration and Naturalization Act
(1965) 26
Industrial Revolution 30

Jim Crow 25, 30
Johnson, L. 26, **37**, 118, 122
Jolly, D. 6, 24, 51, 65, 84, 87–88, 102, 113,
130, 151, 170

Kennedy, J. **37**, 77, 159

Lamb, B. 132, 134, 136–138
Lamone v. Benisek 76
landslide 71, 106; counties 10, 14

League of Women Voters of Fla. v. Detzner
72–73, 75
League of Women Voters of Pennsylvania
et al. v. Commonwealth of Pennsylvania
et al., Pa. 78
Lee, M. 142, *143–145*
legislative 125; action 93, 130; agenda
116, 120, 126; arena 179; background
88; body 114, 151; branch 114, 157;
business 138; chambers 71; collaboration
184; counsel 113; districts 2, 66–67, 106,
108, 187; divisiveness 172; dysfunction
154; expertise 160; framework 89;
function 114; gridlock 106; hurdles
124; know-how 157; leaders 79; level
99; lines 68; majority 77; objectives
123; outcomes 123; polarization 175,
183; priorities 183; procedural rules 99;
process 69, 79, 113–115, 117, 123–124,
126, 129, 132, 137; programs 123; races
71, 104, 189; recusal rules 99; reforms
110; results 88; seats 108; session 108,
175, 180–181, 183; staff 72; stasis 123;
success 116, 151, 183; support 156;
thoroughness 113
Lewis, T. 72–73
Lizza, R. 87

Mann, T.E. 132, 136
Martin, J. 118
Mayhew, D.R. 131
McCain, J. 90, 96
McCain–Feingold Act 90
McCutcheon v. FEC 93
media: consumption 172; culture 170;
-driven solutions 62; environment 54,
147, 151; far-left 54; filter 131; free 96;
habits 139; hyperpartisan 54; impact of
50, 132; landscape 4, 139; loyalty 53;
mainstream 52, 54, 139, 141; national
147; network 51; news 52, 122–123,
159; outlet 51, 53, 56, 129, 133; partisan
54, 56–57, 64; personalities 1, 50;
platforms 51; polarization of 4, 50,
54, 59–60, 171; power of 18; publicity
strategy 138; reports 56; small 56; social
7, 21, **37**, 51–54, 56–57, 59–60, 72,
131–132, 139–142, 147; sources 54; stars
112; traditional 52, 60, 142
Medicare 36, 51, 112, 152
messages 59–60, 140; counter-attitudinal
57; extreme 64; moral 60; partisan 138,
140; pro-attitudinal 57
Michigan Campaign Finance Act 90

migration 12–13, 17–18, 28, 40
Millennials 36–39, 42
Miller, M. 76
Mitchell, A. 52–56, 58–60, 139
MSNBC 1, 139, 142
Murphy, P. E. 3, 7, 25, 50, 64, 85, 103, 112, 129, 152, 171

National Conference of State Legislatures 97, 99
National Council of State Legislatures 33
National Democratic Redistricting Commitee 71
National Immigration Law Center 34
National Republican Congressional Committee (NRCC) 87, 166
NBC News 33, 139, 145
Nelson, B. 85
New York Times 106, 135, 166
No Party Affiliation (NPA) 25, 40–42, 102, 108

O'Rourke, B. 85
Obama, B. 33, 37, 71, 73, 75, 92, 94, 96, 103, 108, 125, 138, 176
Obamacare 36, 131
Office of Technology Assessment (OTA) 156–160
O'Neill, T. 120, 132–137, 154
openness 18–20

partisanship 1, 19, 58, 64, 69, 72–73, 75, 115, 125, 138, 159, 170; blind 2; dominance of 187; extreme 188; hyper- 147, 154; increasing 44, 113–114, 123, 125, 131; influence of 2; reflexive 132; reinforce 126; shared 182; unceasing 125
Passive Patsies 159
Pepper, K. 73
Pew Research Center 8, 11, 26–27, 32, 34–35, **37**, 38, 141
polarization 6–10, 13, 18, 20–21, 25, 33, 35, 38–39, 44, 50, 52, 54–57, 59–60, 62, 71, 104, 110, 113–114, 120, 126, 131, 138, 140, 142, 171–172, 178, 183; actual 56; affective 52, 60; cultural 110; dimension of 183; geographic 6; group 39; growing 80; heightened 179; ideological 139; increasing 7, 57, 106, 131, 138, 171; legislative 175, 183; non- 55; partisan 44, 66, 71, 114, 126; party 106, 124; perception of 56; political 13, 15, 20–21, 33, 39, 54, 183; problem 52; reducing 55, 57; see also elite; media

POLITICO 155, 166
primaries 50, 64, 98, 103–104, 106–107, 116, 171; blanket 107, 109–110; closed 24, 102, 104, 106, 108, 110; direct 104; modified 104, 107; open 104, 106–108; partisan 170; party 104; pick-a-party 106; semi-closed 104; structure of 104, 109
Public Mapping Project 80

Quorum 140, *141*

racial: changes 44; composition 28, 33–34, 40, 43; conflict 33; differences 32; discrimination 77; diversity 11, 24, 32; group 26–28, 34–35, 40–42, 43; identity 44; issues 38; majority 74; makeup 40; minorities 32–33, 44, 68, 73; origin 35; population changes 35; segregation 118
Rae, N.C. 112, 118–120, 123
redistricting 12, 66–69, 71, 73–78, 172, 176, 188; App 69; battles 159; commission 79; committees 72; congressional 73; contests 80; court-ordered 3; criteria 75; cycle 67, 69, 71; full-fledged 69; history 72; influence of 13; Majority Project (REDMAP) 71; partisan 77, 189; plans 72; process 69, 71–72, 176; questions 68; strategy 74; task 78
reform 66, 77–78, 80, 87, 94, 99–100, 103–104, 109–110, 116, 121–122, 156, 188–191; advocates 189; basic 94; comprehensive 33; efforts 94; electoral 79, 104, 116; finance 4, 92–94, 98; gerrymandering 65, 67, 77, 79; immigration 33; legislative 110; movement 170; objectives 115; organization 158; progressive 115–116; proposed 84, 95; radical 107; solutions 171; structural 110; voting rights 125
Reichelderfer, M. 73
representation: cross-partisan 170–171; Democratic 171; diverse 170, 178; frequent 56; heterogeneous 178; individual 68; proportionate 120; Republican 171; transformation of 67; urban under- 68; see also bipartisan
representatives 13, 65, 68, 129, 155, 171–173, 178; federal 1; House of 34, 64, 117, 153, 158, 165, 168; multiple 172
Republicans 1, 6–7, 17–18, 20, 24–25, 33–36, 38, 42, 44, 50, 66, 71–73, 75–76, 88, 102, 108, 115, 117, 120, 122, 133–135, 138, 140–141, 152,

154–156, 158–159, 161, 164–167, 188, 190; coalition of 116; College 73, 133; Congressional 36, 160; conservative 108; House 133, 156, 159; minority 120, 126; moderate 119, 153; national 72; primary-voting 107; progressive 119; Tea Party 153
Reynolds v. Sims 68
Roosevelt, F. D. **37**, 159, 190
Roosevelt, T. 90, 96
Rubio, M. 3, 33
Rucho v. Common Cause 66, 77
Rust Belt 31

scandal 120, 130–131, 139, 161; campaign 90; Enron 109; Presidential 1
Scott, R. 85
segregation 9–10, 12–18, 20–21, 117, 119; causes of 13; de facto 10; generational 38; geographical 7; political 7, 9–14, 16–18, 20–21; racial 118; rapid 10; regional 17; self- 39
Senate 2–3, 7, 33, 68, 72, 76, 78–79, 84–86, 89–90, 98–99, 108, 112, 114–119, 121–126, 131–132, 136–140, 142, 147, 151, 155, 157, 160, 163, 166, 171–172, 176, 189–190
Shor, B. 178
Sinclair, B. 121–125, 131, 139
Sink, A. 73
social media 7, 21, **37**, 51–54, 56–57, 60, 72, 131–132, 139–142, 147
Stop Act 88
Sullivan, D. 98
Supreme Court 2, 66–68, 73, 75–78, 80, 84, 86, 89, 91–94, 96, 99–100, 116, 123–125, 131, 189
swing: districts 64, 88, 108; states 9–10, 40, 189; voters 44, 77, 91

Tea Party movement 176
Terraferma, F. 72–73
The Center for Public Integrity 86
The People's Pledge 98
Thornburg v. Gingles 73–74
TIGER/Line program 69

Tillman Act 90
Troubled Assets Relief Program (TARP) 125
Trumbull, J. 2
Trump, D. 1, 3, 7, 34, 36–39, 43, 64–65, 94–96, 125, 154, 187, 190
Twitter 2, 56–58, 60, 87, 131–132, 140–143, 145–146

U.S. Bureau of Labor Statistics 31, 36
U.S. Census Bureau 27–29, *29–30*, 31–32, 35, **41**, 68–69
U.S. Congress 39

values 11, 19, 35, 168; political 10, 91
Vietnam War **37**, 118
voter: accountability to assessment 60; African American 74; black 75, 118–119, 176, 178; center–right 9; conservative 10; diverse 40; eligible 33; engagement 170; friendly 12; frustration 188; Hispanic 176, 178; hyper-partisan 50; ideology 14, 183; inactive 9; independent 7, 24; liberal 9; outreach 90–91; participation 43, 104, 106, 108; polarized 20; political identities 9; politically active 64; primary 65, 103; psychology 172; registration 25, 41–44, 69, 91, 97, 104, 106; Republican 14, 70; restoration restrictions 25; rural 7, 9; satisfaction 170; single-issue 7; targeting 7; turnout 13–14, 25, 50, 69, 188; ultra-partisan 64; unaffiliated 104; white 25, 42, 44; younger 42, 44; *see also* swing
Voting Rights Act 73–75, 77, 118, 120, 122

Warren, E. 67, 98
Washington, G. 2–4
Wesberry v. Sanders 68
White, W.S. 121–122
World War II 25, 28, **37**, 114–115, 168, 190
Wright, J. 120, 135

Young Turks 134–136

zero-sum game 35, 147, 165, 187

Made in the USA
Las Vegas, NV
21 January 2021